CRITICAL
INSIGHTS

War

CRITICAL
INSIGHTS

War

Editor
Alex Vernon
Hendrix College

SALEM PRESS
A Division of EBSCO Publishing

Ipswich, Massachusetts

Library of Congress Cataloging-in-Publication Data
War / editor, Alex Vernon.
    p. cm. -- (Critical insights)
 Includes bibliographical references and index.
 ISBN 978-1-4298-3740-8 (hardcover)
 1. War in literature. 2. War and literature. I. Vernon, Alex, 1967-
PN56.W3W325 2012
809'.93358--dc23
                        2012014117

Contents

Resources

About This Volume _____

Alex Vernon

From Homer's *Iliad* (c. 750 BCE; English translation, 1611) to William Shakespeare's *Henry V* (1600) and documentary films about the wars in Iraq in Afghanistan in the first decade of the twenty-first century, this book samples sparingly, but smartly, I'd like to think. It does suffer from a conspicuous, if understandable, bias toward English-language texts and, hence, armed struggles involving English-speaking nations, as well as toward the armed conflicts of the twentieth century (often considered the bloodiest). While it might be worthwhile to critique this book's innumerable omissions of texts, periods, and approaches, I would ask readers to attend to the book's primary goal of proposing why one should, and how one might, study the literature of war.

Tim Blackmore's essay on the shared concerns of military science fiction and realist war literature reminds readers of the deep connection between how war is imagined and how it is waged. As Doug Davis notes in his essay on the historical context of nuclear-age literature, the French philosopher Jacques Derrida once observed that the stand-off between superpowers meant that the Cold War was fought entirely in the imagination, in its public forms through (chiefly apocalyptic) literary and cinematic narratives. Nevertheless, this extreme example signifies something about stories of wars actually fought: Imagination and its verbal expression affect the world in very real ways. War stories not only reflect or express the past but also condition both the present and the future.

In his essay on the poetry of World War I, Tom McGuire fashions a different argument about the real effects of artistic expression. How the war dead are elegized, in poems or monuments, contributes to people's perceptions of those who died, the war in which they died, and the next war in which people will die. Readers might also consider the ways in which nonfictional accounts, either in writing or on film, use familiar or conventional techniques and strategies. On one hand, a well-known story helps familiarize an unfamiliar subject, allowing an essentially incommunicable experience to be more easily conveyed. On the other hand, trying to familiarize a war story might prove deceptive. A controversial war captured in a documentary film that is structured to feel like a fictional film about World War II, the "good war," risks being interpreted inaccurately and possibly being manipulated for political purposes—a suspicion that occurs to me as I read between the lines of Douglas A. Cunningham's essay comparing documentary films about the twenty-first-century US wars in Iraq and Afghanistan to Hollywood's version of World War II.

There are, of course, personal reasons to reflect on war literature. Some readers (or their friends or family members) have faced or will face war. It is something of a moral imperative to attempt to understand the war experience, such as the various struggles of those who fought in Vietnam in the 1960s and 1970s, as Philip Beidler's essay details, and, as Pat Hoy's essay beautifully describes, both the forces that work to draw countries and individuals into war and the postwar struggle to understand those currents and that experience (what Hoy calls "The Veterans' Tale"). No account (fictional or nonfictional) can perfectly or absolutely portray the war experience. Thus, if one reads war literature to learn about war, he or she must study how literature tries to relay the experience through language; story line and structure; and characterizations of participants, places, and events. Furthermore, texts must be placed in their proper contexts, as the essays in this book do. To understand the depicted war, one must understand the historical, political, social, cultural, and personal forces influencing the depiction.

Will Hacker's essay on the history of reading the *Iliad*, the oldest of European epic war poems, fittingly launches this book. As Hacker writes, "To describe the earliest critical responses to the *Iliad* is essentially to describe the beginnings of literary criticism." Tackling issues such as allegorical and moralistic readings, authorial intention, and the challenges of translation and adaptation, the essay addresses the fundamental problem of literary representation: The frustrating, albeit invigorating, gap permanently separating the represented subject from the narrative that tries to represent it, and the ensuing debates over the best ideas for narrowing that grand gap. The fact that commentators did not regard the *Iliad* as a war poem until relatively recently, historically speaking, reveals quite a bit about the uncertainty and dynamism of literary interpretation.

Appropriately, too, this book ends with Dorian Stuber's essay on the literature of the Holocaust. What Samuel Hynes, in his seminal *The Soldiers' Tale: Bearing Witness to Modern War* (1997), calls "The Literature of Atrocity, or perhaps the Sufferers' Tale" must also be told. Racist aggression has motivated many wars. Moreover, Stuber's analysis of Holocaust narratives poses war literature's primary questions: Who has the authority to speak authentically, and for whom? How does one express profoundly personal and collective traumas? Stuber reminds readers that the problem of mediation—of all those filters between readers and that which is covered with words—is hardly exclusive to war literature. As Tim O'Brien, an American veteran of the war in Vietnam, has said about his own novels, "The environment of war is the environment of life, magnified"—by which he means that life's stage is conveniently and dramatically compressed into the theater of war. One does not read war literature just to gain insight into war.

When perusing this volume, many readers will target a certain essay, even a portion of an essay, directly related to their interests. However, I strongly encourage readers to read the entire book, not necessarily in chapter order, or at least to explore a good portion of the essays. While this book aims to prompt ruminations on individual works, it also hopes to develop readers into commentators on war literature in general. In reading the entire book, or a fair portion of it, readers will discover where essays intersect thematically.

Hacker's essay, for example, will illuminate any translation of the *Iliad*, not to mention modern adaptations such as the film *Troy* (2004) and David Malouf's novel *Ransom* (2009) about the Trojan War's emotional toll on Achilles and Priam. Lindsey Claire Smith's essay on

Native Americans and American war literature might springboard into investigations of colonial peoples fighting for the very masters against whom they have struggled and continue to struggle (for example, black slaves fighting for the Confederacy, or Africans and Asians fighting for the European powers claiming them).

The ideas about *just war* theory in Mark Heberle's essay on Shakespeare's *Henry V* could be applied to any number of texts in terms of the war itself and the characters' behavior within it. The *beautiful death* and pastoral elegiac traditions invoked, according to McGuire's analysis, in British poetry's response to the unprecedented mass death of World War I, one might also discover in Walt Whitman's and Emily Dickinson's writings on the Civil War, which Ed Folsom's essay describes as "[America's] first confrontation with mass death and injury on a scale previously unimaginable." Though Robert Jordan's death at the end of Ernest Hemingway's *For Whom the Bell Tolls* (1940) appears to carry on these same traditions, the novel's preceding three hundred pages defy easy conclusions.

One of the fundamental tensions in war literature is between the impulse to particularize conflicts, insisting on the uniqueness of a war and a participant's experience, and the impulse to connect wars through intrinsic similarities, emphasizing the universal aspects of wartime life; studying nonfiction accounts of war might yield important insights in this regard. Robert C. Doyle's essay on POW narratives and John Nelson's coverage of soldiers' memoirs since World War II identify patterns of what Doyle calls the "natural contours" of the experiences—those elements or events that inevitably seek expression in the memoir. After all, as Hynes observes, "In most war narratives there is nothing to suggest that the author is aware of any previous example: no quotations or allusions or imitations of earlier models." (Admittedly, some "natural contours" might have indirect or unconscious literary and cultural contours shaping them.) However, Catherine Calloway's essay on women's nonfictional war writing and Elisabeth Piedmont-Marton's essay on contemporary nonfiction books by non-American writers seek those elements that distinguish these writers, their experiences, and their texts from one another.

The most evident disagreement between the contributors to this book is my own reading of the end of the film *The Hurt Locker* (2008) as hackneyed and trite and Pat C. Hoy's reading of it as powerfully, viscerally true. The fact that he and I so starkly disagree is an invitation for readers to enter this or any conversation about war literature.

Several of the book's essays touch on the relationship between war and gender. In addition to texts by female participants, such as the books in Calloway's essay and the two in Beidler's essay on the Vietnam War, one can think about how women outside war zones have written about war, in, for example, Dickinson's poetry, Sheri S. Tepper's and Lois McMaster Bujold's military science-fiction novels, or even nonwar stories by Flannery O'Connor reflecting the nuclear age. Hoy's discussion of Woolf's *Jacob's Room* (1922) and *Mrs Dalloway* (1925) is implicitly gendered. What, then, about the novel written by a male veteran—Kurt Vonnegut's *Slaughterhouse-Five* (1969)—that Hoy asks readers to juxtapose with them? Vonnegut's ridiculous male soldiers, primarily his protagonist Billy Pilgrim, are a mockery of military masculinity. More curious are the negative associations of women. For example, Billy Pilgrim has his first encounter with the alien Tralfamadorians, his first brush with a mental crack-up, on his daughter's wedding day. The orange and black stripes of her wedding tent correspond to the orange and black stripes of the German boxcars that cart him and his fellow prisoners of war to Dresden. For their engagement, he gives his future wife a diamond ring he brought back from Europe as war booty—this from a man whose Tralfamadorian guides scoff at the "female Earthling . . . associat(ing) sex and glamour with war."

One need not have personally participated in war to be able to join a conversation about it; a critical imagination is all nonveterans need. Dickinson and Woolf never saw battlefields, but their testimonies cannot be denied. A writer's depiction of war is based on historical, political, social, cultural, and personal forces. A reader's interpretation is also under these influences and may also be shaped by nationality, gender, generation, ethnicity, and family and educational experiences. The more readers are aware of the contours of the lenses through which they view war and war literature, the more balanced and informed their critical approaches to war literature will become.

On War

Alex Vernon

Can William Golding's *The Lord of the Flies* (1954) be considered war literature? It does not take place on a battlefield or a wartime home front. There are no soldiers, veterans, or their loved ones. There are not even any adults. Whether the novel is more informed by Golding's time living in cramped quarters as a British seaman during the World War II or by his years in a claustrophobic classroom teaching restless boys is unstated.

Golding's novel, about boys stranded on an island whose efforts at peaceful social organization collapse, is a popular classroom text because of, among other reasons, its provocative Hobbesian argument about humans as base, warring creatures. At its wonderfully teachable and devastating finale, when the boys are saved from their natural savagery by mature adults (representative of nurturing civilization), in the form of a warship, no less, a teacher might write and underline "irony" on the board. Thus, Golding seems to weigh in on the topic Azar Gat calls "the first and most commonly asked question when people ponder the enigma of war," the question of the connection between war and human nature. Throughout the ages, historians, philosophers, anthropologists, scientists, psychologists, politicians, theologians, public intellectuals, and military leaders have wrestled with the connection between war and human nature, as have poets, memoirists, diarists, dramatists, letter writers, fiction writers, journalists, filmmakers, bloggers, and video-game makers.

Whether or not video games, with their open-ended story lines, will one day be recognized alongside such texts as the *Iliad* (c. 750 BCE; English translation, 1611) and *Im Westen nichts Neues* (1928; *All Quiet on the Western Front*, 1929) as formative war narratives remains to be seen. The standards by which a text can be considered a war narrative are not irrevocably defined. While a story written by a veteran of ground combat is about as hands-on as a war narrative can be, it is by no means the only type of story that qualifies as part of the genre. Stepping out of the trenches, for example, takes readers to stories of pilots and sailors. Leaving the battle offers writings by and about intelligence officers, medical personnel, prisoners and prison guards, and support soldiers sometimes an ocean away from the fighting. The veteran's tale, which does not necessarily require any recounting of the particular war in which the soldier participated, decidedly counts as war literature. War correspondents (journalists) have used their talents and their proximity to soldiers and the action to write powerful testimonials. Civilians caught in an area of military operations also have essential stories to tell (and the line between combatant and noncombatant is not always clear). Narratives of civilians away from the fighting (soldiers' loved ones on the home front, for example) also should be considered in a discussion of what makes a war narrative, as should antiwar stories, including, for example, the tribulations of draft dodgers and the lyrics of protest songs.

One must not forget literature written by nonparticipants. Some classics of the field, such as Stephen Crane's *The Red Badge of Courage* (1895), Dalton Trumbo's *Johnny Got His Gun* (1939), and even Margaret Mitchell's *Gone with the Wind* (1936) can be categorized as historical war fiction written by people who never experienced war firsthand. Crane was not even alive during the Civil War, yet few readers would exclude *The Red Badge of Courage* from the canon of war literature.

Books and screenplays written during wartime, but not necessarily about war, constitute their own brand of war literature. Sam Peckinpah loaded his 1969 film *The Wild Bunch* with a level of violence shockingly new to the western genre in order to speak to the war the United States was fighting in Vietnam. The SyFy Channel's *Battlestar Galactica* series (2004–2009) deliberately challenged its viewers to reflect on their ideas about the US war in Iraq; the show's "good guys" resorted to torture during interrogation; terrorist-style insurgent tactics, such as suicide bombings; secret military tribunals resulting in capital punishment; and genocide through biological weapons of mass destruction.

Given that the Cold War between the United States and the Soviet Union did not include any actual combat, even peacetime texts, with peacetime settings, can, in a certain light, be regarded as war literature. Susan Griffin's *A Chorus of Stones: The Private Life of War* (1992), a first-person nonfiction account of being an American civilian in the second half of the twentieth century, proceeds exactly on the claim that simply being a citizen qualifies her as a Cold War veteran.

> I was born and brought up in a nation that participated in the bombing of Dresden, and in the civilization that planned the extermination of a whole people. We are not used to associating our private lives with public events. Yet the histories of families cannot be separated from the histories of nations. To divide them is part of our denial. (11)

Changez, the Pakistani protagonist of Mohsin Hamid's post–9/11 novel *The Reluctant Fundamentalist*, eventually comes to the realization that his job at an American financial company, for all intents and purposes, turns him into weapon, a soldier in pinstripes, because "finance was a primary means by which the American empire exercised its power" (156).

Author Joshua Goldstein would contend that any narrative featuring peacetime (or otherwise) domestic gender roles could justifiably be taught in the war literature classroom. In organizing themselves for self-preservation, societies tend to define manhood in terms of the potential for soldiering and womanhood in terms of the support for and production of soldiers: "War is a pervasive potential in the human experience that casts a shadow on everyday life—especially on gender roles—in profound ways" (403).[1] Changez's relationship with his American "dream girl" could easily be read through Goldstein's idea. Just as the financial company that employs him, Underwood Sampson, bears the significant initials "U.S.," his girlfriend Erica bears a correspondingly significant name, as you cannot spell "America" without "Erica."

Also tricky in categorizing war literature are those war books written by authors who do not consider themselves war writers. Joseph Heller has said that *Catch-22* (1961), his darkly comic novel of airforce life during World War II, is not about the war at all, but uses the military bureaucracy to comment on the corporate and government bureaucracies he found so absurd and stifling in the 1950s. E. E. Cummings's semiautobiographical, but also surreally allegorical, World War I novel *The Enormous Room* (1922) has more in common with Franz Kafka than with most war writers. Tim O'Brien, one of the most celebrated American authors to fight in and write about the war in Vietnam, resists the limiting label of "war" as his subject. Life is his subject; people are his subjects. The Vietnam War happens to be the compact dramatic situation with which he is deeply familiar, the most convenient setting at his disposal. Readers do not engage war literature only to gain insight into war. As O'Brien maintains: "The environment of war it the environment of life, magnified" (23).

Catch-22 is a reminder of the importance of the context. Ernest Hemingway wrote *A Farewell to Arms* (1929) ten years after his World War II involvement, and the novel can be understood as a first-person retelling of Hemingway's war experience. Hemingway's Frederic Henry, then, is not only a veteran telling his war story but also a veteran informed by how he and his society have come to view the war after a decade's worth of reflection, personal and historical consequences, and war memoir models. One might validly ask how many years must pass before a veteran's novel about his or her war experiences loses something of its authentic authority and becomes a work of historical fiction. Another question can be raised about how to receive a novel written by a veteran set in a war in which he or she did not participate.

The literature of war resembles the literature of any other subject in that it is only a representation and not the thing itself. A war story includes a specific perspective, interpretation, and imposition of meaning. Even in memoir and autobiographical fiction, poetry, and drama, a gap always separates the tale—what it wants to tell—and the events it actually describes. Nonfiction accounts are invariably partial in both senses of the word. Moreover, war narratives function in the context of other war narratives (the tradition of expressing war through stories). Readers learn a great deal from analyzing a single text in any genre about war. In addition, a great deal can be learned by regarding a text as it exists in conversation with other texts; to study this conversation is to study the intertextual connections between works.

Allusion is one form of intertextuality, an example of which can found in Virginia Woolf's novel *To the Lighthouse* (1927), a domestic drama taking place around World War I, when a character storms about quoting Alfred, Lord Tennyson's poem "Charge of the Light Brigade" (1854). Readers must ask why Woolf uses that particular allusion and what it is about Tennyson's poem and the battle it depicts that matters to Woolf's novel. Certain texts and writers receive sustained discussion—writers dealing with the subject of war who have followed Hemingway, for example, often feel obliged to deal with him in some way, given his prominence in twentieth-century American war literature. Intertextuality can also manifest structurally. As Paul Fussell observes in his indispensible *The Great War and Modern Memory* (1975), Robert Graves's *Good-bye to All That* (1957) is best understood with the knowledge that Graves deliberately and wryly loaded it with the elements of popular memoirs, at the expense of documentary duty, in order to make money (203–20).

Michael Herr's *Dispatches* (1977), a work of nonfiction emerging from Herr's war reporting from Vietnam for *Rolling Stone* and *Esquire* magazines, has become something of a touchstone of contemporary American war literature. If book reviewers want to claim that a new nonfiction work about war is a masterpiece, they inevitably rank it alongside *Dispatches*, as reviewers did with both Anthony Swofford's *Jarhead* (a memoir of the Persian Gulf War published in 2003) and Dexter Filkins's *The Forever War* (2008), a journalist's account of the Iraq War. To further explore the idea of intertextuality, *Dispatches* can be examined as one node in a web of connections among several works, including films. (Indeed, film has come to so dominate representations of war that it is impractical to speak of intertextuality in late-twentieth-century and early-twentieth-first-century war stories without mentioning examples from the genre.)

Dispatches deliberately includes war movies in its narrative. On occasion, Herr compares the war-in-the-head "fantasies" that soldiers and journalists bring with them (194), mostly garnered from films, with what they actually experience. However, he pushes this idea further, observing—as he perceives it—people in the war comporting themselves cinematically. Sometimes this happens in the presence of a television crew, with soldiers "actually making war movies in their heads" as they "run around during a fight" for the sake of the camera (209). The first fighting and carnage Herr witnessed struck him as quite "familiar . . . only moved to another medium," from celluloid to the battlefield. However, even after he understood the differences between how war is portrayed in film and the real thing, even after he had "unlearned" the preconceptions, "you couldn't avoid the ways in which things got mixed, the war itself with those parts of the war that were just like the movies" (209–10). His entire experience came to be viewed cinematically: "Life-as-movie, war-as (war) movie, war-as-life" (65). Tellingly, the films to which he refers in the passage about everything getting mixed up are adaptations of war novels: Graham Greene's *The Quiet American* (1955) and Heller's *Catch-22*. Herr further mixes films with literature in the very way he conceives his own book:

> In any other war, they would have made movies about us [journalists] too. . . . But Vietnam is awkward, everybody knows how awkward, and if people don't even want to hear about it, you know they're not going to pay money to sit in the dark and have it brought up. . . . So we have all been compelled to make our own movies, as many movies as there are correspondents, and this one is mine. (188)

Elsewhere in the same section of *Dispatches*, references to "this movie" blur the distinction between his film-informed experiences and his cinematic vision of the book (206).

In addition to referencing war films, *Dispatches* looks at the western, through films such as *Fort Apache* (1948) and *Nevada Smith* (1966). Herr further invokes the American West when he labels as "frontier" (45) the military area of operation near the border between North and South Vietnam, and he quotes a military commander who refers to the war as a game of "Cowboys and Indians" (61). The soldiers with whom he partied in Saigon and Da Nang were "classic essential American types" (35), men who inherited the spirit of the American frontiersman and the Wild West maverick, men of action, violence, and isolation. In terms of intertextuality, this rhetorical move by Herr is significant both because he applies the argument from an earlier book and because the argument reappears in later narratives, such as *The Hurt Locker* (2008).

That earlier book to which Herr makes reference, Richard Slotkin's *Regeneration through Violence: The Mythology of the American Frontier, 1600–1860*, appeared in 1973, four years before *Dispatches*. Though Herr derived much of his book from his wartime correspondence (1968–70), he substantially reworked the material for its publication in book form. Herr references Slotkin's book when he mentions being in Saigon and seeing *Nevada Smith*, with the actor "Steve McQueen working through a hard-revenge scenario, riding away at the end burned clean but somehow empty and old too, like he'd lost his margin for regeneration through violence" (60). Slotkin's book offers a cultural interpretation for the violence of American westward expansion, arguing that the national identity was continuously revitalized through that violence. Herr borrows from Slotkin's ideas and extends them, implying that their end result is the Vietnam War: "Vietnam was where the Trail of Tears was headed all along" (49). Understanding Herr's conclusion equips readers formidably in efforts to understand *Dispatches*. A reader who accepts Slotkin's theory about the Wild West might be inclined to accept Herr's corollary about Vietnam; a reader who does not accept Slotkin's theory will have little patience for Herr.

Regarding *The Hurt Locker*, one reason for its resonance has to do with its focus on improvised explosive devices (IEDs), the roadside bombs that, for many, symbolize the US soldiers' war experience in Iraq. Another reason the film has been hailed is because of its characterization of the main character, the wildly successful IED disposer Sergeant First Class William James, as the "classic essential American type," with which Herr populates his Vietnam memoir, and that is derived, ultimately, from western films; he is a lonely maverick who rides in to save the day, who cannot abide the domesticity of wife and child and a regular job, and who is last seen strutting alone, pistol on his hip, down an empty street in a small desert town toward his next potentially fatal encounter. At best, this final image of James is as forlorn as Herr's description of Steve McQueen's character in *Nevada Smith*. The movie even gives us a veritable circle-the-wagons ambush, when James and his team (and several British intelligence agents), surrounded by Iraqi insurgent snipers, take cover in an Arabian wadi (supplanting the Arizona gulches of a western film).

Herr's classic American types are crazy for the war (35), a proclivity that flirts with a more general craziness and that also applies to James. Such portrayals are also informed by the intertextual literary tradition of the war lover, a man absolutely necessary for military success but barely (if at all) suited for civilian life, who appears in narratives such as Oliver Stone's Vietnam War film *Platoon* (1986) and John Hersey's World War II novel *The War Lover* (1959). Such tales present a reincarnation of sorts of William Shakespeare's Hotspur, from *Henry IV, Part 1*, and Homer's Achilles. Such a character often has a foil, a man who is both duty-bound to join the fight and plenty competent despite his milder personality; the dramatic opposition between these split heroes plays out as a war waged for the soul of another character, an innocent, either a younger soldier or a beautiful woman.

Platoon pits the brutally effective, conscience-challenged, war-loving SSG Robert Barnes against the equally effective but moral Sgt. Elias Grodin; the new soldier Chris Taylor is the prize. The film opens with Taylor walking out of the plane and down the ramp on his first day in Vietnam, the fate of his soul very much in question. *The Hurt Locker* answers *Platoon* by having its war-loving protagonist walk off the helicopter and down a ramp on the first day of his next tour, but at the end of the film. The Elias Grodin and Chris Taylor characters (J. T. Sandborn and Owen Eldridge are their counterparts in *Hurt Locker*), are all but forgotten. (Though the professionalization of the US armed forces during the thirty years between the wars—including the move to an all-volunteer military—explains the transformation and promotion of *Platoon*'s SSG Barnes into *The Hurt Locker*'s Sergeant First Class James at least as much as some proposed commentary on human nature.)[2]

Regeneration through Violence is not the only attitudinal source text for *Dispatches*. The other major literary work whose spirit Herr embeds in his story is Joseph Conrad's *Heart of Darkness* (1902). As he does with Slotkin's text, Herr alludes to Conrad's book obliquely, in describing his journalist colleague Sean Flynn who "sometimes . . . looked more like Artaud coming out of some heavy heart-of-darkness trip, overloaded on the information, the input! The input!" (echoing Conrad's "The horror! The horror!," uttered by Kurtz), as Flynn will go missing in action on one of his free-spirited outings to cover the war. For Herr, the intelligence operatives and special-forces soldiers who pioneered the US entry into the war—the "spooks"—bore the spirit of "older adventurers who'd burst from their tents and bungalows to rub up hard against the natives, hot on the sex-and-death trail, 'lost to headquarters'" (50)—men exactly like Conrad's Kurtz. The spooks' "adventure became our war" (51) in both spiritual and realistic senses.

The American combatants Herr chooses to depict in his book lustfully embrace violence and killing in a manner deeply disquieting to readers who prefer to imagine their fellow citizens-turned-soldiers as reluctant heroes. *The Hurt Locker* carries on the tradition of previous ruminations of war. By replacing human enemies with IEDs, the film converts Herr's bloodlust to adrenaline-charged wire-snipping. Reembodied as James, the Kurtz archetype has been tamed, contained in the body armor that protects him, as a mere technician. James's rejection of a robot's help insufficiently disguises the geekier aspect of this warrior's trade, and the racism that many critics see as endemic to US military operations (in this case, toward an Arab population) has similarly been smoothed over (though the diminished racism might reflect an increased professionalism of the US military). Herr fluctuates between romanticizing and judging what he sees as the bloodlust of the American military; *The Hurt Locker*'s judgment of its characters is less obvious.

Though *Dispatches* bemoans the absence of films about the war in Vietnam and undertakes to write itself as the movie of the war in book form, Herr, in fact, famously contributed to a film about the war in Vietnam, collaborating with Francis Ford Coppola on *Apocalypse Now* (1979), with characters and general plotline taken directly from Conrad. The passage about adventurers gone "native" and "lost to headquarters" is the film's premise, and the Kurtz character is based on "one man who 'owned' Long An Province, a Duke of Nha Trang, [and] hundreds of others whose authority was absolute in hamlets or hamlet complexes where they ran their ops until the wind changed and their ops got ran back on them" (50). The film's version of Kurtz (played by Marlon Brando), however, is an exaggeration, an imaginative amalgamation of the men Herr came across and Conrad's Kurtz. This piece of intertextuality, between Herr's book and the film, should further equip the reader in an analysis of *Dispatches*.

In addition to *Regeneration through Violence* and *Heart of Darkness*, *Apocalypse Now* turns to Sir James George Frazer's work of comparative mythology, *The Golden Bough* (1890), to construct its mythic story. A ritual described in the book is used in the film, in a scene depicting the sacrifice of a water buffalo; also, Willard (Marlow) goes "savage" to complete his mission of decommissioning Kurtz, thereby evoking Fraser's discussion of symbolic ritualistic killing used in ancient societies to replace the old king with the new. Thus, if *Apocalypse Now* has achieved status as one of the great films depicting the US war in Vietnam, one could make the argument that the intertextuality driving the film overwhelms the war setting, meaning the film is no longer a war film but a metaphor for something else, a statement on the human condition. However, the film's deliberate dependence on Slotkin's thesis, for example, does not prove that thesis; it only gives it dramatic, hypothetical form. Had the film unintentionally rewritten Slotkin, Conrad, or Frazer, one might be more tempted to ascribe a truth in this coincidental expression.

Naturally, given its status, *Apocalypse Now* has entered the intertextual lexicon of war narratives. *Jarhead* (2003), Anthony Swofford's memoir of the first US–Iraq war, the Persian Gulf War of 1990–91, famously draws a scene of the author's Marine unit, before deploying to war, watching *Apocalypse Now* and other Vietnam War films. Enthused by the violence, they whoop it up:

> [W]e yell *Semper fi* and we head-butt and beat the crap out of each other and we get off on the various visions of carnage and violence and deceit, the raping and killing and pillaging. . . . There is talk that many Vietnam movies are antiwar. . . . But actually, Vietnam war films are all pro-war, no matter what the supposed message. . . . Filmic images of death and carnage are pornography for the military man. (5–7)

Swofford is not the first to propose the inherent impossibility of an antiwar film; literary narratives may suffer the same fate. However, if, because of their absence of the visual and their capacity to describe smells and express repugnance through language, they can accomplish what films cannot. Indeed as Susan Sontag has offered, reading is not watching; it requires more time, and more conspicuously invites contemplation—and "To paraphrase several sages, 'Nobody can think and hit someone at the same time'" (118). On the other hand, because of its visual medium, the cinematic adaptation of *Jarhead* delivers irony in ways the book cannot. Instead of showing the Marines in their unit recreation room watching rented movies on a small television screen, the adaptation places them in a theater, so that audience members become part of the Marine audience as its watches the early battle scene in *Apocalypse Now*, during which US helicopters gun down Vietnamese in a riverside village. At the end of *Jarhead*, the Swofford character wanders desolately among the charred Iraqi vehicles and corpses; later, he regrets not having fired a single shot during the ground war, as the war turned out to be exactly what he and his Marine buddies had so roundly cheered while watching *Apocalypse Now*: destruction from the air.

Three Kings, a Persian Gulf War film that came before *Jarhead*, converses with *Apocalypse Now* in a scene in which a buffalo explodes as the result of the playful antics of the three soldiers chasing rumors of gold hidden in the Iraqi desert. If *Apocalypse Now*'s ritual slaughter of the water buffalo bespeaks that war's epic dimensions, the comical twist in *Three Kings* (1999) exposes its war as something of a joke (though this claim can be mitigated by noting the film's main intertextual reference, the World War II caper *Kelly's Heroes*, 1970). The animated film memoir (and later graphic novel) *Waltz with Bashir* (2008), redraws the postbattle surfing scene from *Apocalypse Now* with its own postbattle surfing scene on a beach outside Beirut. The blatant quotation, in its effort to communicate the spirit of the moment, is a bit distracting to those who recognize it. Nonetheless, one gains from the recognition. First, its apparent fictionality calls attention to the creative means by which the film expresses its nonfiction account. It reminds the audience, in other words, of the narrative's constructed perspective. Second, the surfing quotation, by incorporating a famous war film known for depicting the potentially intoxicating nature of barbarous violence, infuses the message of *Apocalypse Now*, attaching it to *Waltz with Bashir*'s equally horrific depiction of war (the film ends with the revelation of a genocide-inflected massacre of civilians). Throughout, *Heart of Darkness* is the intertextual reference binding all of these depictions of war.

This introduction to war literature has focused primarily of films because many readers are likely more familiar with the films than with some of the literature and because the two mediums have become nearly inextricable. The inextricability demands that Herr's "war-movies-in-the-head" be rewritten as "war-stories-in-the-head." The fantasy, nightmare, and even mundane visions each individual has of war come from centuries of war narratives. Impressions come from the Bible, the Mahabharata, the *Chanson de Roland* (twelfth century; *Song of Roland*, 1880), *Beowulf* (c. 1000), Leo Tolstoy's *Voyna i mir* (1865–1869; *War and Peace*, 1886), and Ambrose Bierce's *Tales of Soldiers and Civilians* (1891). Readers have impressions from Wilfred Owen's war poem "Dulce et Decorum Est" and Randall Jarrell's war poem "The Death of the Ball Turret Gunner," among numerous novels, stories, poems, memoirs, plays, films, and other forms of media. New texts inherit the old and join the legacy to be referenced in future texts.

Literature has shaped the ways readers think about war, influencing the decisions people and governments make when confronting war, motivating actions during the war, and coloring the way one reflects on the war experience. The military truism that each new generation of war makers will initially repeat the strategy and tactics of the last war before it learns the nature of the new conflict finds a parallel in war literature, as each new text struggles to reconcile known methods of expression with the reality of new experiences.

The primary reason to read and write about war literature is to make sense of it: Talking and writing about war literature is an ongoing effort to create understanding such that anyone's contribution becomes another piece of dialogue in the rich and crucial intertextual conversation. These fifteen essays might seem inadequate to the vast body of war literature. Nevertheless, they put texts in conversation, and they are often in conversation with one another, in sometimes obvious, sometimes subtle ways. The kind of questions the essays ask of their texts and the kind of thinking they propose about their texts model how scholars might approach pieces of war literature in order to make sense of them as well as enter in the conversation war literature in general.

Notes

1. Barbara Ehrenreich, in *Blood Rites*, locates the war passion in "the anxiety and ultimate thrill of the prey-to-predator transition" humanity made long ago (22), a transition that necessitated a clear assignment of gender roles.
2. James is first seen smoking in his darkened quarters, with music blaring, in a scene that perhaps intentionally echoes the introduction to Captain Marlow (named Willard in the film) in *Apocalypse Now*. The introduction of James, however, is an extremely mild, sanitized revisiting. He is comfortable in his skin, his war, and his job.

Works Cited

Ehrenreich, Barbara. *Blood Rites: Origins and History of the Passions of War*. New York: Metropolitan Books, 1997.

Fussell, Paul. *The Great War and Modern Memory*. New York: Oxford UP, 1975.

Gat, Azar. *War in Human Civilization*. New York: Oxford UP, 2006.

Goldstein, Joshua S. *War and Gender: How Gender Shapes the War System and Vice Versa*. Cambridge: Cambridge UP, 2001.

Griffin, Susan. *A Chorus of Stones: The Private Life of War*. New York: Doubleday, 1992.

Hamid, Mohsin. *The Reluctant Fundamentalist*. Orlando: Harcourt, 2007.

Herr, Michael. *Dispatches*. New York: Knopf, 1977.

O'Brien, Tim. Interview by Brian C. McNerney. "Responsibly Inventing History: An Interview with Tim O'Brien." *WLA: War, Literature and the Arts* 6 (Fall–Winter 1994).

Sontag, Susan. *Regarding the Pain of Others*. New York: Farrar, Straus and Giroux, 2003.

Swofford, Anthony. *Jarhead: A Marine's Chronicle of the Gulf War and Other Battles*.

New York: Scribner, 2003.

CRITICAL
CONTEXTS

Reading the *Iliad*: A History _____

Will Hacker

Perhaps the best way to understand the reception of the *Iliad* (c. 750 BCE; English translation, 1611) is in the terms that the poem itself gives: Its imitators have been happy to wear the borrowed armor of Homer's authority; its commentators outnumber the ships Homer catalogs; and its translators have at times treated the body of its text with a rudeness associated with Achilles. Following some of these imitators, translators, and commentators, this essay presents some of the ideas that have organized themselves around the poem at various moments in the history of its reception. The opening section discusses the *Iliad* in antiquity; the second section, treating translation as a form of interpretation, focuses on versions of the poem in English from the Renaissance to the nineteenth century; and a brief concluding section outlines twentieth-century treatments of the *Iliad* as a war poem.

Reception of the *Iliad* in Antiquity

To describe the earliest critical responses to the *Iliad* is essentially to describe the beginnings of literary criticism. Though many of those who responded to Homer in this earliest period are more often treated as philosophers or are better known as poets, a reasonably clear line can be traced from Homer's interpreters of the sixth century BCE, through Plato and Aristotle, to the more recognizably literary-critical work of Alexandrian scholars. Though these responses have been handed down in fragments, many of the problems that occupy early critics are familiar: They are interested in what Homer means (and, as a result, how he conveys it). Determining what Homer meant was particularly important in a period in which the ethical responsibility of a poet could be taken for granted, and it is hardly surprising that some of the first extant responses to the poetry tax him with not having lived up to that responsibility. While later critics have been compelled to apologize for the *Iliad*'s luxurious violence, writers in the sixth century were scandalized by the poem's treatment of the gods, the figures notoriously both more and less than human who shape its action.

Particularly embarrassing was the "theomachy," or battle of the gods, in book 21, in which Athena gleefully attacks Ares and Aphrodite; problematic as well was Hera's seduction of Zeus in book 14. These scenes, among others, led the sixth-century philosopher Xenophanes to condemn the *Iliad*. According to Sextus Empiricus, writing in the last third of the second century CE, Xenophanes objected that Homer had "attributed to the gods all things which among men are shameful and blameworthy—theft and adultery and mutual deception" (qtd. in Barnes 95). That Xenophanes, who denied the existence of anthropomorphic gods, should react strongly is to be expected; his fellow pre-Socratic Heraclitus argued that Homer "should be turned out of the lists and whipped" (Burnet 112, 141; Jaeger 170–72). Heraclitus also apparently rebuked Homer for some his characters' inadequately bellicose sentiments, holding that the end of strife was tantamount to the destruction of the universe. The earliest critics of Homer, then, responded to what they perceived as moral and didactic failures.

No sooner did some early commentators censure Homer, however, than others rose in his defense; the *Iliad* was in need of moral rehabilitation. Theagenes of Rhegium, a rhapsodist trained in the art of Homeric recitation who flourished around 525 BCE, seems to have been the first to respond to Xenophanes, arguing that the gods in Homer represented mental states or physical elements. Anaxagoras and his followers, too, held that Homer was ultimately an apostle of "virtue and justice" (qtd. in Sikes 13).

The search for *hyponoia*, or "undermeaning," (a clear predecessor of allegorical interpretation) in Homeric verse could take place within an ethical or a physical framework. While in the fifth century, the Anaxagorean philosopher Diogenes of Apollonia praises Homer for speaking "not mythically, but truly about the gods: by 'Zeus' he meant the air" (qtd. in Burkert 320), reducing the poem's gods to personifications of natural phenomena, the later *Homeric Allegories* would argue that "Athena preventing Achilles from killing Agamemnon [in book 1] represents wisdom" (Kearns 71), suggesting that the gods should be seen as ethical values incarnate. Though the attempts to save the *Iliad* with physical allegory have in general worn less well than ethical rescue attempts,[1] there are moments in the poem when they remain relevant. As E. E. Sikes points out, in the battle between Hephaestus and the river Scamander in book 21, it is hard not to see a battle between Anaxagorean Fire and Water (14).

Allegorical interpretations had to weather objections from the Epicureans, for example, who argued that in its strong form the method reduced Homer—anachronistically—to a Stoic philosopher. Changes in philosophical fashion no doubt quickly outmoded some of these interpretations as well, but on the whole, they have proved durable. When in the first century CE, Plutarch rejects the claim that Hera's seduction of Zeus represents "the purification of the air in the neighborhood of fire," concluding instead that the episode teaches "that favours obtained by means of cunning are but fickle and short-lived" (Atkins 322), he is squarely within the allegorical tradition. So too is Horace's treatment of the *Iliad* in his epistle to Lollius. The allegorical method inflects much later interpretation as well; when E. R. Dodds, for example, shows that the gods' physical intervention reproduces a psychic intervention (a prompting of Homer's characters that feels to them as if it comes from the outside), the kind of "overdetermination" he proposes is a response to a reading that sees that divine machinery as straightforwardly allegorical and, hence, redundant (Dodds 14–18).

If many of these earliest respondents have faded into relative obscurity, the *Iliad* later received attention from some of the most important writers in antiquity. Even if one wants to question the centrality Werner Jaeger assigns to Homer in Greek education, the engagement of Athenian thinkers was inevitable: Socrates's contemporary Xenophon suggests in his *Symposion* (n.d.; *Symposium*, 1710) that Athenian youth were referred to the Homeric heroes for lessons in practical life; Isocrates, an Athenian orator contemporary with Plato, contends that a model of *aretē* (valor, strength, excellence) is to be found in Achilles's fighting with the Trojans, now styled "barbarians" (King 104). Achilles was felt to be the finest exemplar of those virtues the Greeks prized most: "youth, nobility, high intellect, and (that nothing should be wanting) he was both musical and swift of foot" (Sikes 65). The ubiquity of references to the *Iliad* in Plato's dialogues, then, is natural, and readers should not reflexively assume that the enthusiasm with which Socrates imagines meeting Homer in Hades is disingenuous.

Best known in Plato's engagement with Homer is his rough handling of epic poetry in the utopian exercise of the *Politeia* (388–68 BCE; *Republic*, 1701). Even before the notorious "banishment" of Homer, Plato is clearly uncomfortable with the allegorical contortions of Homeric interpreters. He sidesteps an argument about the character of Odysseus in the *Hippias Minor* (English translation, 1761), objecting to claims that presume knowledge of Homer's intentions (Hunter 246–47), and in the *Phaedrus* (English translation, 1792) he describes "scientific" allegorical explanations as "the invention of clever, industrious people who are not exactly to be envied" (478; sec. 229d). In the *Ion* (English translation, 1804), Socrates's foolish interlocutor is linked with one of the famous allegorists, Metrodorus (216; sec. 530 c–d), and the *Iliad* is exposed as free of practical knowledge, which instead devolves to the experts who can judge it as adepts of their own crafts—the dialogue isolates the connection between rhapsodic recitation and useful military knowledge as one particularly tenuous (226–27; sec. 540e–542b). Though the condemnation of Homeric poetry in the *Republic* has enjoyed its most vigorous afterlife as a more general argument about representation, it is worth remembering in a treatment of the *Iliad*'s reception that Plato is especially interested in the way Homer presents the warrior. He objects to Achilles's immoderate anger, to his mistreatment of Hector's corpse, and to the poem's less-than-consoling picture of the afterlife, a picture hardly motivational for those about to enter combat. Across the dialogues, Plato is trying to recuperate heroism, but heroism of a different kind: As Katherine King puts it, he is trying to "ethicize Achilles," "to transfer the concept of heroism from the wreaking of vengeance to the avoidance of wrongdoing" (106).

The example on which King draws in making her claim is not from the *Republic*, but from the *Apology* (English translation, 1675), in which Socrates compares his acceptance of his fate to Achilles's accepting the knowledge, relayed by his immortal mother Thetis, that if he avenges the fallen Patroclus he cannot escape death. The passage is an intriguing example of Plato's (or perhaps here, Socrates's) ambivalence about the *Iliad*: The precedent that he cites in rejecting vengeance turns on Achilles's need for vengeance. On one hand, it is a powerful example of the reappropriation of Homer's accounts of martial prowess but, on the other hand, is a remarkable instance of the persistence of these accounts, of the inability of a writer to escape fully (to write himself out of) the Homeric celebration of incontinent violence. Even as he tries to establish the virtue of ethical surrender, Plato can only communicate the force of his conviction by invoking a warrior. Alberto Manguel interestingly suggests that in his relationship to Homer, Plato is both the curate, who burns Don Quixote's books to protect him, and Don Quixote himself, whose life is a testament to his conviction of their worth (41–42).

After Plato, Aristotle continued to explore the theory of mimesis in his *Peri poētikēs* (334–23 BCE; *Poetics*, 1705), but in his *Technē rhētorikē* (n.d.; *Rhetoric*, 1686) is an appreciation of the seductiveness of the *Iliad*'s call to battle. In an example of the power of statements not "universally true," but "taken for truth," because they are "commonplace," he gives Hector's pronouncement in book 12: "One omen of all is best, that we fight for our fatherland" (1415–16; II.2,1395a). Perhaps more interesting than Aristotle's engagement with Homer is that of his pupil, Alexander the Great. According to Plutarch, Alexander read the *Iliad* as a "vade-mecum of warfare," and the stories of his conquests are punctuated by episodes of heroism and rancor as colorful as those found in his source—where Achilles abused the dead body of

Hector, Alexander ordered a living man to be dragged to death (Sikes 165). It is unsurprising, then, that scholars in the city he founded were particularly interested in Homeric texts. The Alexandrian critics of the third century BCE were adept textual scholars and preparers of scholia (collections of notes on canonical texts, explaining language or subject matter). During this period, an obsession with *prepon* (fit or propriety) imposed a limit on the variety of interpretations they could offer: The *Iliad* was less a poem through which one might think about war than a classic to be authenticated and preserved. Nonetheless, if their critical judgments were straitjacketed, the Alexandrians' work was essential in fixing the texts on which later generations would set to work.

Roman interpretation in the first century BCE was not particularly innovative either. Educated Romans learned Greek and read the *Iliad* in its original language, and the letters of Cicero exhibit an offhand familiarity with the poem. Horace's interpretation in his epistle to Lollius seems to be paradigmatic: In describing briefly the plot of the *Iliad* and the *Odyssey* (725 BCE; English translation, 1614), Horace writes, "As much as the kings go mad, the Argives suffer" (1.2.14; Quidquid delirant reges, plectuntur Achivi).[2] In associating the madness of the rulers with the role of the gods in the fate of the poem's characters, Horace turns the *Iliad* into a primer on moral conduct and renews the tradition of allegorical interpretation. Joseph Farrell encourages readers to consider that the reception of Homer in Rome not only is to be understood as a system of literary influence but also registers outside of literature: He points to Roman general Scipio Aemilianus's allusion to the inevitable fall of Troy on his destruction of Carthage and the mapping of Roman encounters with Etruscans, Rome's rivals for control of Italy, onto Greek encounters with Trojans in urns and wall paintings (263, 257). Though there was not yet a reliable Latin translation of Homer's poem, the Greek *Iliad* was essential to the Roman sense of self.

It is perhaps inevitable, then, that the Roman national epic is so consistently responsive to Homer. One need not invoke elaborate theories of authorial influence to see that a Roman exploration of civic and martial identity would take place in Homeric terms. Much of the work left undone in treatments of the *Iliad* as a catalog of moral examples was taken up not in criticism but in Virgil's epic itself.

The link between the *Iliad* and the *Aeneid* (29–19 BCE; English translation, 1553) consists of more than thematic similarity: In assigning the role of founding Rome to a refugee from the ruins of Troy, Virgil actually deploys a character from Homer's poem. Virgil's hero, Aeneas, is not perhaps the cynosure of martial glory in the *Iliad*, spending his time—in book 20, for example—in battles of genealogical one-upsmanship with Achilles and being miraculously saved by the gods. However, he is nevertheless an important Trojan, one well worth renovating.

Virgil takes the character with whom Achilles stands face-to-face and reconstructs him, creating a much fuller (if not rounder) character than how Homer has left him. Where Aeneas's opponent in the confrontation is associated from the opening of the *Iliad* with his *mēnis*, or ungovernable wrath, Aeneas, though he too is capable of error, models discipline and restraint. Aeneas is clearly a national character, one who, the poem repeatedly affirms, will found Rome. If Achilles's destiny is defined as insistently as Aeneas's is, it is nevertheless a private destiny, a fact underlined by his withdrawal to his own quarters for the bulk of the poem as well as the slights, grief, and anger he feels so acutely are his alone. The stitched-together quality of the Achaean forces assembled before Troy is the precondition of the *Iliad*'s crisis; the provisional quality of the alliance becomes the counterpoint for the lasting bonds that Aeneas will forge. Virgil is consistent with the tradition of the *Iliad* in concentrating attention on the exploits of individual warriors, each of whom in Homer's poem must complete his *aristeia*, or demonstration of martial excellence. However, the context in which these deeds are transacted is radically changed. What King describes as "primitive" heroism is replaced by an expansive concept of *pietas* in the *Aeneid*: "loving devotion to the state, the gods, and the family" (122). The impious furor that motivates the *Iliad*'s warriors is transferred to, among others, the impetuous Juno, a figure who, in her resistance to the coming Rome, seems almost a vestigial reminder of an era long past.

The contrast between the *Iliad* and the *Aeneid* is in part a contrast between a poem that emerged from an oral tradition and a poem that is self-consciously literary. In a judgment that dovetails with Matthew Arnold's, C. M. Bowra suggests that the oral epic "triumphs through its simplicity and strength and straightforwardness, through the unhesitating sweep of its narrative and a brilliant clarity in its main effects," but in the literary epic what matters is "the richness of half-lines," the "precision or potency" of the single word (5). While this is perhaps to undersell the finesse the former and the momentum the latter sometimes achieve, the assessment is not particularly controversial. What may be most interesting, however, is the way that the literariness of the *Aeneid* conspires with its subject in a reappraisal of the Homeric understanding of war. Gone in Virgil's epic is much of Homer's sanguinary inventiveness—the horses stepping on the dead in book 10, accounts of how a spear "push[ing] the eyeball out . . . went clean through / the eye-socket and tendon of the neck" (15.493–94). Gone also is the energy that drives the hero from victim to victim. Instead there are passages such as the one Bowra cites as characteristic:

> Caedicus kills Acathous, Sacrator
> Hydaspes, Rapo kills Parthenius
> And mighty Orses, and Messapus kills
> Clonius and Erichaetes, Lycaon's son. (39)

Though "hacks down" or "cuts to pieces" would probably be a fairer translation of the passage's *obtruncat*, which Bowra renders merely as "kills," his claim that the passage is "purely literary," the discharging of Virgil's duty to his epic predecessors, is convincing. Bowra contends that the deferral of some obligatory battle scenes to the tenth book of the *Aeneid* reflects Virgil's failure to understand the frenzy of war; Napoleon condemned Virgil as "nothing but the regent of a college, who has never gone outside his doors and did not know what an army was" (qtd. in Bowra 41).

In the revision of heroism, however, and in particular his revisionist account of the Greek victory, Virgil achieves a kind of vividness. After the aged Priam feebly throws his sword, the boastful Greek Pyrrhus seizes him: "altaria ad ipsa trementem / traxit et in multo lapsantem sanguine nati" (2.550–51).[3] The pathos of the scene is more acute because readers know the warrior that Priam has been. In light of a scene like this, Peter Levi's judgment, quoted by Manguel, that Virgil "did not understand the fundamental principle in Homer's world, that poetry belongs to the defeated and the dead" (54), needs to be softened. If the nationalization of the struggle to found Rome at the close of the *Aeneid* blurs the sharp outlines of Homeric battle, the awareness of what is lost in the fall of Troy, the one social whole offered in the *Iliad*, animates these earlier scenes. Though it is not actually narrated in the poem, the inevitability of Achilles's death gives the *Iliad* much of its poignancy; Virgil's poem draws on a similar sense of loss. If Achilles's death is the condition of his victory over Hector, the destruction of another state is the price that Rome must pay for its birth.

Translation and Reception

Though it is certainly overstatement to suggest that the critics in the West after Virgil were uninterested in Homer (after all, interest in the *Iliad* was sufficient for the production of the *Ilias Latina*, a 1077-line rendering of the poem in Latin in the first century CE), in the centuries that followed, poets and critics without Greek increasingly came to the poem through Virgil. The texts from which artists and scholars drew their understanding of the Trojan War were less often the Homeric poems themselves than an expanded body of literature, some of it directly challenging the *Iliad*'s version of events. Studies of the influence of Dares the Phrygian's and Dictys the Cretan's retellings of the war (the former replacing Achilles's wrath with clemency, the latter diminishing Achilles's accomplishment and making his mother mortal) can be found in King and Georg Danek. Their recasting of the events at Troy culminates in a series of intriguing medieval romances, among them Geoffrey Chaucer's *Troilus and Criseyde* (c. 1382).

When translations of the *Iliad* into English, at least putatively from the Greek, appeared at the end of the sixteenth century, writers were returning to an interpretive tradition that had been dormant for some time, and their renderings are a critical part of the period's reception of Homer. Translations from the Greek on any significant scale were, as Simeon Underwood points out, rare. Though Arthur Hall had translated ten books of the *Iliad* in 1581, the only "major act of translation from the Greek" before George Chapman's *Iliad* (1611) was the Elizabethan version of the Bible (18). Chapman's renderings are best known as the inspiration for Keats's sonnet "On First Looking into Chapman's Homer," and his *Odyssey*, in particular, enjoyed a vogue among the romantics.

At its best, Chapman's *Iliad* demonstrates a powerful responsiveness to Homeric language. Underwood suggests that Chapman felt that he had a special "affinity" with and a responsibility to Homer, and the fourteen-syllable lines can at times move briskly in parallel with the original. Perhaps on the basis of his presumed affinity, Chapman is often free with his source. When, for example, Hector, in a respite from battle, removes the helmet that has frightened his son Astyanax, Chapman writes that he "tooke and kist his loving sonne and (ballancing his weight / In dancing him)" (150–51; 6.512-513); the parenthetical phrase replaces the less colorful but more typical "tossed" or "swayed" for *pēle* (the dancing is his invention). Chapman's development here seems a virtue: Where in a conventional translation the point of view remains that of an observer of Hector, the richness of the additional detail forces readers into Hector's perspective, sharpening the contrast between the pleasant domestic scene and the battle to which Hector will return. The example seems a case of Chapman's realizing Johann Wolfgang van Goethe's advice, writing "not according to Homer, but like Homer" (qtd. in Winkler 14; nicht nach dem Homer, sondern wie Homer).

If the effect of this passage is to point up the consequences of war, most of Chapman's changes to the original tend to diminish them. Though he is faithful in the repetition of the *Iliad*'s violent acts, Chapman's presentation often redirects the reader's attention. In his version of the slaying of Ilioneus

> The dart did undergore
> His eye-lid, by his eye's deare rootes, and out the apple fell
> The eye pierc't through (292; 14.408–10)

The bizarre botanical metaphor undercuts the passage's terrifying anatomical accuracy. In another harrowing scene, Menelaus is about to ransom the captive Adrestos but, exhorted by Agamemnon, kills him; in Richmond Lattimore's 1951 translation, Agamemnon urges his brother to spare no one, "not the young man child that the mother carries / still in her body, not even he, but let all of Ilion's people perish, utterly blotted out and unmourned for" (6.58–60). Chapman's Agamemnon is similarly unmerciful, but he renders the conclusion as "nor [shall] their race have more fruite than the dust" (138; 6.61); the phrase has a quasi-biblical power, but the substitution of the metaphor betrays Agamemnon's severity. Finally, in a crucial episode in which Achilles, renouncing his earlier mercy ("it was the way of my heart's choice to be sparing," according to Lattimore), refuses to spare the suppliant Lycaon, Chapman adopts very different language. When Achilles was merciful he "did grace to Troy, and many lives did rate / At price of ransome" (424; 21.100–101). The episode reflects not the blackness of a heart scorched by loss but by an adjustment in calculation.

The motivation for Chapman's shifts in emphasis become clearer when considering the dedicatee of seven books of his translation published in 1598, "the most honoured now living Instance of the Achilleian vertues eternized by divine HOMERE, the Earle of ESSEXE" (503). Essex had early distinguished himself in the court of Elizabeth and as an officer on the field of battle, but he suffered the vicissitudes of royal favor and military success in a number of well-publicized political and military campaigns. Essex's notorious impetuosity finds a fit counterpart in Achilles, and Chapman is clearly interested in preserving his dedicatee and his central character from those "that count all things servile and simple that pamper not their own private sensualities" (504). Chapman's position is delicate: If Achilles is a model warrior, he is also impulsive and violent; hence, the need to formalize the language in which he speaks at problematic moments. In general, Chapman wants to rescue the *Iliad*'s heroes for contemporary use. The troublesome "primitiveness" of Homeric war can be salvaged by a connection to the Elizabethan rationalization of violence: If Hector fights in Homer for his father's glory and his own, in Chapman he gives,

> No danger pass
> Without improvement. In this fire must Hector's trial shine:
> Here must his country, father, friends, be in him made
> divine. (qtd. in Arnold 116)

Though Chapman's translations were popular immediately after their publication, poets of the sixteenth century were in no hurry to put their stamp on Homer; translations of the more decorous *Aeneid* significantly outnumbered translations of the Greek epics (Underwood 31). So, the completion of Alexander Pope's version of the *Iliad* in 1720 and the warm reception it received in a Virgil-friendly climate is all the more impressive. In translating Homer, Pope makes a case for "Invention" as "the very Foundation of Poetry," resisting arguments that "Judgment" is by itself adequate to our artistic and moral demands (3). The preference for invention is partly a reply to those who preferred the sober good judgment of Virgil to the unchecked energy of Homer, but it is also an attempt to make a place for what Pope describes as the "Fire" and "Rapture" of the imagination in eighteenth-century social life. Pope had inherited a debate in which the relative merits of the ancient and modern authors were contested,[4] and he was willing to rehabilitate even the most challenging moments of Homeric violence in order to ensure that the lessons of *Iliad* were retained.

Among the most interesting aspects of Pope's translation is its inclusion of copious commentary. As an author not entirely confident in his Greek in an age in which classical scholarship was gaining confidence, Pope drew heavily on available commentaries and the knowledge of his friends and left a record beneath the text of his engagement with them. One might assume that the responsibility to the scholarship would be debilitating, but as James Tatum, a surprising modern champion of Pope, suggests, the luxury of running commentary often usefully frees Pope from the obligation to be totally faithful to his source (70–71). The commentary also makes visible what often remains latent in translation: what George Steiner calls the "triangular" interaction, where added to the relationship between source and target texts is the third term of earlier translations or imitations (xvi). When Pope describes Hera's seduction of Zeus (that episode that so troubled earlier commentators) he is able to redeem the passage, as Penelope Wilson points out, by reference to "a moral lesson in [John] Milton" (280) appearing in *Paradise Lost* (1667). The tendency to indulge in exaggerative excess, particularly in representations of violence—the conversion of Homer's "many shall fall" into "Mountains of the Dead," for instance (qtd. in Mack lii)—is offset by the commentary's moralizing judgment.

The exchange between Pope's text and commentary is characteristic of his search for a third way in the battle of the ancients and the moderns. In his preface he warns against "magnify[ing] the Felicity of those Ages when a Spirit of Revenge and Cruelty . . . reign'd thro' the world," but suggests that the reader who can bear in mind that Homer is "the most ancient Author in the Heathen World" will nevertheless be morally educated (14). In practice, Pope's drawing out these moral lessons involves generalization and the treatment of the *Iliad*'s episodes as types. The tendency is so strong that, as Maynard Mack suggests, even the horror of Achilles's refusal to spare Lycaon can be turned into a lesson. When Achilles asks of Lycaon:

> What boots it to deplore?
> The great, the good Patroclus is no more!
> He, far thy better, was foredoom'd to die,
> "And thou, dost thou, bewail Mortality?" (21.115–18)

The suppliant is not hidden in the shadow of the killer who stands above but as a radiant example of natural law. Readers can perhaps take this cynically as an example of Pope's need for moral hygiene,[5] but with Mack, one might also take Pope's fondness for generalization on its own terms as an attempt to use Homer "to [give] non-Christian sanction to certain crucial insights about man as a suffering, struggling but creative and significant being" (clxxxiv). In this sense, Pope's efforts to generalize are not so far from those later readings that will consider the *Iliad* as a war poem.

An account of translations of the *Iliad* is incomplete without reference to Arnold's lectures "On Translating Homer," delivered in 1861 and published in 1861–62. Arnold's lectures appeared in a period strikingly different in its vision of Homer from Pope's. In 1795, in his *Prolegomena ad Homerum*, the German philologist Friedrich August Wolf had argued that the Homeric poems were composites of separate lays passed down orally and had been assembled more recently than scholars had previously believed. As James Porter suggests, Arnold's discussion of translation assumes the feeling of loss that such a theory engenders: In an important sense, Arnold concedes, "the Greeks are dead," and the effect Homer would have had on his original audience is irrecoverable (qtd. in Porter 339).

The scramble had begun to determine what translation should do next. The four qualities in Homer that Arnold argues the translator should strive to re-create—his rapidity, his plainness and directness in syntax and diction, his plainness and directness in development of ideas, and his nobility (102)—are well-known and continue to inform much contemporary translation, but perhaps most interesting and most modern is his attempt to balance philological responsibility and poetic license. While scholars are "the only competent tribunal," the only readers equipped to judge whether or not a translation reproduces their experience in reading the original, these scholars must also possess "adequate poetical taste and feeling" (99). Arnold damns the translation of his contemporary Francis Newman for its author's poetic insensibility, but he reserved for the scholar (and as Arnold concedes in a follow-up lecture, Newman is no mean scholar) the ultimately important assessment of a translation's fidelity to experience. Though it perhaps carries hidden political cargo and essentially ignores the content of the poems, Arnold's discussion remains resonant: even critics least likely to find his cultural project sympathetic reproduce the comparative work he performs (for example, Frow 175–78).

A War Poem: The *Iliad* in the Twentieth Century

Tatum comments that "only recently have classicists begun to read the *Iliad* as a war poem," noting that the 1962 edition of the Macmillan *Companion to Homer* lacked entries for "war" and "battle" (49–50). While it is clear that earlier interpreters of the poem have been perennially interested in war and the acts perpetrated under its name, the exploration of war has typically taken place in the context of more conventional philological work. Adam Parry, for example, has demonstrated that a reading attentive to Achilles's misuse of language brings out his disillusionment with war. Recent studies, however, have made increasingly vivid the fact that, as Frederick Ahl puts it, "The myth of Troy has come to define, and to be defined by, all subsequent wars" (171).

Of particular interest in the criticism of the *Iliad* as a war poem are essays by Simone Weil and Rachel Besploff published in 1940 and 1942. Weil's "The *Iliad*, or the Poem of Force" argues that "the true hero, the true subject, the center of the *Iliad* is force" (3), force that becomes visible once individuals are removed from domestic comfort, represented in Weil by the "hot baths" the women of Troy have prepared in vain for Hector's return. Force (the power to kill) transforms those subjected to it into objects: "In whatever aspect, its effect is the same: it turns a man into a stone," an inert object no better than a corpse.

In a reading of Lycaon's plea for mercy perhaps as far removed from Pope's as can be imagined, Weil emphasizes the fragility of the suppliant's existence, which a "moment of impatience" will suffice to destroy (6). In an interpretation consonant with Dodds's stress on Homeric heroes' receiving their *menos* (might, power) from without (9), Weil argues that he who wields force in the *Iliad* cannot ultimately control it: Characters are alternately intoxicated or crushed by force and no one escapes its effects. The *kleos* or fame to which Homeric warriors lay claim is merely the result of "blind destiny" (13); Weil's reading is a sobering reminder of what most tend to forget in tracking warriors' progress—that their triumphs and losses have been preordained and that the gods sit at an alien distance from human concerns.

War consists in these shifting patterns of force, the inexorable work of which is to enclose the soldier in the "hand of necessity" (22). Generalizing from Achilles's despair (a move that is perhaps questionable, given that other characters do not share his divine channel of communication and have not had their deaths foretold), Weil contends that for the soldier death is the future, not a limit set on the future; because such a future cannot be faced, any movement beyond the present is foreclosed, any contemplation of purpose or goal, including "war aims" (23) impossible, a situation in which the end of war cannot be achieved. Intolerable sufferings "continue because they have deprived the sufferer of the resources which might serve to extricate him." As critics have frequently observed, the scenes from the world of "hot baths" bring the losses soldiers suffer into sharper relief. For Weil, the result of the contrast is a bitterness, ultimately founded in an impartial tenderness for all of the war's victims.

Bespaloff also detects the operation of force in the Lycaon episode, force that once again is ultimately ungovernable. However, at the end of her reading of this episode, she reaches a conclusion unthinkable in Weil: "Without Achilles, men would have peace; without Achilles, they would sleep on, frozen with boredom, till the planet itself grew cold" (54). Though she ultimately prefers Hector as "resistance-hero," defender of civic values and domestic comforts, Bespaloff concedes a good deal to Achilles, the "force-hero." The threat of war is essential in her view to the readers' appreciation of what might be lost—"Anything destined for destruction and ignorant of its danger, or hoping to escape . . . is lit up with tenderness" (72).

In Hector, readers find realized the understanding that the desire to protect civilization is "no pious and comfortable feeling, but a grim demand imposed on his whole being" (73). Bespaloff seems to confirm Freud's suspicion that life is impoverished without risking "the highest stake in the game of living, life itself" (290). Her reading of the encounter of Priam, who is seeking the return of his son's body, and Achilles, near the close of the *Iliad*, is an attempt to restrain the violent potential of her interpretation; in Priam's appearance "the prestige of weakness triumphs momentarily over the prestige of force" (84). Bespaloff's essay is perhaps an object lesson in the unmanageability of intoxicating force, mobilized here to protect the Trojans but not easily put back to bed at the argument's close.

Other recent critics have offered intriguing interpretations of the *Iliad* as a war poem. Caroline Alexander, in presenting Achilles as a hero of folktale unnaturally conscripted for service in an epic, gives us a context in which many of his remarks might be read as pacifist. In discussing connections of the poem to the rest of the Epic Cycle (the collection of non-Homeric poems that fill out the story of the Trojan War) she suggests as well that it is haunted by the tragic futures of many of its characters.

A final example of the focus that an interpretation of the *Iliad* can achieve is Jonathan Shay's *Achilles in Vietnam*. Shay's emphasis on an army as a fragile "moral construction" allows him to explore the consequences of Agamemnon's failure of leadership on Achilles and to draw connections between the tragedy of his "moral ruin" (32), particularly visible in the Lycaon episode, and the post-traumatic stress disorder he treats in his clinical practice. Shay is particularly powerful in detailing the comradeship of Patroclus and Achilles and in describing the impact of the denial of war comrades on soldiers who lost them in Vietnam. His celebration of the virtues of Patroclus (his gentleness and valor) almost amounts to an act of therapy for those whose comrades were treated as interchangeable parts in a war Shay presents as industrially managed.

In the strongest moments of *Achilles in Vietnam*, the *Iliad* once again becomes vibrantly alive. In its evenhandedness and in its stubborn refusal to vilify the Trojans, it offers lessons about how the enemy in combat is imagined; in its honest presentation of grief and in the dedication of its final lines to the obsequies for Hector, it insists on the importance of making time to mourn. In the end, Shay argues that the poem is less about the *kleos* of its heroes than the world of domestic peace they leave behind (206–207). With this work readers come to the concerns of the earliest respondents to the poem: Like Xenophanes, Shay is interested not only in what can be learned about the *Iliad* but also in what can be learned from it.

Notes

1. Because "physical allegorical" readings in their search for Homer's secret or "other" meaning treat him as a cryptic scientist or natural philosopher, this is to be expected. While ethical interpretations can be almost infinitely renovated, Homer's alleged natural philosophy struggled to remain relevant.
2. Epistle also quoted by King (139).
3. Translated by Allen Mandelbaum as "he dragged him to the very altar stone, with Priam shuddering and slipping in / the blood that streamed from his own son" (47; 2.738–40).
4. Though the battle was originally French, involving on one side Louis Racine and company, defending the standard of the ancients, and on the other Charles Perrault and his allies, championing the moderns, Pope was certainly alive to the controversy, particularly because his translations were an international affair and drew on a wealth of Continental knowledge about the classics.
5. To do so would be to suggest that Pope has found in Achilles what Horkheimer and Adorno find in Odysseus: an early victim of Enlightenment (45).

Works Cited

Ahl, Frederick. "Troy and the Memorials of War." *Troy: From Homer's* Iliad *to Hollywood*. Ed. Martin Winkler. Malden, MA: Blackwell, 2007. 163–85.

Alexander, Caroline. *The War That Killed Achilles*. New York: Viking, 2009.

Aristotle. *The Basic Works of Aristotle*. Ed. Richard McKeon. New York: Random House, 1941.

Arnold, Matthew. "On Translating Homer." *The Complete Prose Works of Matthew Arnold*. Ed. R. H. Super. Vol. 1. Ann Arbor: U of Michigan P, 1960.

Atkins, J. H. W. *Literary Criticism in Antiquity*. Vol. 2. Cambridge: Cambridge UP, 1934.

Barnes, Jonathan, ed. *Early Greek Philosophy*. Harmondsworth, Eng.: Penguin, 1987.

Bespaloff, Rachel. "On the Iliad." *War and the* Iliad. Trans. Mary McCarthy. New York: New York Review Books, 2005.

Bowra, C. M. *From Virgil to Milton*. London: Macmillan, 1948.

Burkert, Walter. *Greek Religion*. Trans. John Raffan. Cambridge, MA: Harvard UP, 1985.

Burnet, John. *Early Greek Philosophy*. New York: Meridian, 1957.

Cary, M., et al., eds. *Oxford Classical Dictionary*. Oxford: Clarendon, 1961.

Chapman, George. *Chapman's Homer*. Ed. Allardyce Nicoll. Princeton, NJ: Princeton UP, 1967.

Danek, Georg. "The Story of Troy through the Centuries." *Troy: From Homer's* Iliad *to Hollywood*. Ed. Martin Winkler. Malden, MA: Blackwell, 2007. 68–84.

Dodds, E. R. *The Greeks and the Irrational*. Berkeley: U of California P, 1951.

Farrell, Joseph. "Roman Homer." *The Cambridge Companion to Homer*. Ed. Robert Fowler. Cambridge: Cambridge UP, 2004. 254–70.

Fowler, Robert, ed. *The Cambridge Companion to Homer*. Cambridge: Cambridge UP, 2004.

Freud, Sigmund, "Thoughts for the Times on War and Death." *Standard Edition of the Complete Psychological Works of Sigmund Freud*. Ed. James Strachey. Vol. 14. London: Hogarth, 1977.

Frow, John. *Marxism and Literary History*. Cambridge: Cambridge UP, 1986.

Homer. *Homeri Opera*. Eds. D. B. Monro and T. W. Allen. 4 vols. Oxford: Oxford UP, 1920.

_____. *The* Iliad *of Homer*. Trans. Richmond Lattimore. Chicago: U of Chicago P, 1951.

Horace. *The Works of Horace*. Ed. J. L. Lincoln. New York: Appleton, 1882.

Horkheimer, Max, and Theodor Adorno. *Dialectic of Enlightenment*. Trans. John Cumming. New York: Herder, 1972.

Hunter, Richard. "Homer and Greek Literature." *The Cambridge Companion to Homer*. Ed. Robert Fowler. Cambridge: Cambridge UP, 2004. 235–51.

Jaeger, Werner. *Paideia: The Ideals of Greek Culture*. Trans. Gilbert Highet. Vol. 1. New York: Oxford, 1965.

Kearns, Emily. "The Gods in the Homeric Epics." *The Cambridge Companion to Homer*. Ed. Robert Fowler. Cambridge: Cambridge UP, 2004. 59–73.

King, Katherine Callen. *Achilles: Paradigms of the War Hero from Homer to the Middle Ages*. Berkeley: U of California P, 1987.

Lamberton, Robert. *Homer the Theologian*. Berkeley: U of California P, 1989.

Mack, Maynard. "Introduction." *The* Iliad *of Homer: Poems of Alexander Pope*. Ed. Maynard Mack. Vols. VII-VIII. New Haven: Yale UP, 1967. xl–ccxx.

Manguel, Alberto. *Homer's* The Iliad *and* The Odyssey*: A Biography*. New York: Grove, 2007.

Parry, Adam. "The Language of Achilles." *Transactions of the American Philological Association* 87 (1956): 1–7.

Plato. *Collected Dialogues of Plato*. Eds. Edith Hamilton and Huntington Cairns. New York: Bollingen, 1963.

Pope, Alexander. *The* Iliad *of Homer: Poems of Alexander Pope*. Ed. Maynard Mack. Vols. VII–VIII. New Haven: Yale UP, 1967.

Porter, James I. "Homer: The History of an Idea." *The Cambridge Companion to Homer*. Ed. Robert Fowler. Cambridge: Cambridge UP, 2004. 324–43.

Shay, Jonathan. *Achilles in Vietnam: Combat Trauma and the Undoing of Character*. New York: Atheneum, 1994.

Sikes, E. E. *The Greek View of Poetry.* New York: Barnes and Noble, 1931.

Steiner, George, ed. *Homer in Translation*. New York: Penguin, 1996.

Tatum, James. *The Mourner's Song: War and Remembrance from the* Iliad *to Vietnam*. Chicago: U of Chicago P, 2003.

Underwood, Simeon. *English Translators of Homer*. Plymouth, Eng.: Northcote House, 1998.

Virgil. *The Aeneid of Virgil*. Trans. Allen Mandelbaum. New York: Bantam, 1991.

_____. *P. Vergili Maronis Opera*. Ed. R. A. B. Mynors. Oxford: Oxford UP, 1969.

Weil, Simone. "The Iliad, or the Poem of Force." *War and the* Iliad. Trans. Mary Mc-Carthy. New York: New York Review Books, 2005.

Wilson, Penelope. "Homer and English Epic." *The Cambridge Companion to Homer*. Ed. Robert Fowler. Cambridge: Cambridge UP, 2004. 272–86.

Winkler, Martin, ed. *Troy: From Homer's* Iliad *to Hollywood Epic*. Malden, MA: Blackwell, 2007.

Xenophon. *Symposium*. Trans. O. J. Todd. New York: Putnam, 1923.

Shakespeare's *Henry V* and Just War Theory _____

Mark A. Heberle

Between September and November 2001, HBO broadcast a World War II miniseries, *Band of Brothers*, about a company of GIs that fights its way from Normandy to Berchtesgaden, Hitler's Bavarian retreat. There, the men learn that the war in Europe has been won and that, consequently, the sacrifices they have made and the trauma that they have endured for four years (and ten episodes) have been vindicated. The series, which won numerous film and television awards, was based on a 1992 book of the same name by historian Stephen E. Ambrose.

The phrase "band of brothers," however, was first uttered at the first performance of William Shakespeare's *Henry V* in 1599 in a splendid speech by the actor playing the king. The phrase has become one that calls attention to the heroism, shared suffering, and mutual affection of men at war. The king's speech occurs in act 4, scene 3 and culminates with King Henry's attempt to rally his soldiers as he addresses them directly:

> We few, we happy few, we band of brothers.
> For he today that sheds his blood with me
> Shall be my brother; be he ne'er so vile,
> This day shall gentle his condition.
> And gentlemen in England now abed
> Shall think themselves accurst they were not here,
> And hold their manhoods cheap whiles any speaks
> That fought with us upon Saint Crispin's Day. (4.3.59–67)

Although Shakespeare made up the speech and the scene, the circumstances presented in the play are authentically historical: The English are about to encounter the French army at the Battle of Agincourt on October 25, 1415, the feast day of Saint Crispin in the church calendar. They were outnumbered by about five to one on the battlefield that day, so that the "happy few" to whom Henry appeals would have little reason to be hopeful on the morning of St. Crispin's Day, 1415. In the event, both in the play and on the actual battlefield, the undermanned English army achieved an astonishing victory, one of the greatest military triumphs in European history, which Shakespeare's play has immortalized for more than five hundred years. The actual details of the battle, which are scarcely represented in the play as written, have been reconstructed by the military historian John Keegan in *The Face of Battle* (1976). Henry's speech makes extraordinary claims within the closed class structure of early modern England, where to be "gentle" was not so much an individual virtue as it was a class marker (coming from aristocratic bloodlines): Those who fight with the king will become his kinsmen and will be more truly "gentlemen" than any man left in England. Judging from its effects upon his comrades, the speech can be considered the most rousing and most rhetorically successful to be written, at least for the stage. By the end of the play, Henry V has not only won a great battle, but also he has won the hand of Princess Katherine of France and forced the French king to guarantee that Henry's first son will rule both kingdoms.

Henry V is the culmination of a series of four plays that Shakespeare composed between 1595 and 1599: *Richard II*; *Henry IV, Part 1*; *Henry IV, Part 2*; and *Henry V*. In these works, Shakespeare deals with political events between 1397 and 1422 that derived from the deposition and indirect murder of King Richard II by Henry Bolingbroke, Duke of Lancaster, who replaced Richard on the English throne as Henry IV. Besides consulting the historical record of those years in his major source—Raphael Holinshed's *Chronicles of England, Scotland, and Ireland* (1587)—Shakespeare drew on popular legends that had grown about Henry's son, "Prince Hal," which had also been dramatized in a popular play from the 1580s, *The Famous Victories of Henry the Fifth*.

The life of the prince, who was to become Henry V, was assimilated to the folkloric motif of the prodigal son: Alienated from his royal father, the young man spent his early years consorting with a crowd of hedonistic and socially and legally disreputable companions until he underwent a self-transformation that included dismissing his former companions upon his father's death, assuming the throne, and winning the battle of Agincourt as part of a successful military campaign in France. In Shakespeare's dramatization of this process, Prince Hal helps his father put down a civil rebellion in the first *Henry IV* play and then publicly repudiates his former companion Sir John Falstaff, the greatest comic character ever created by Shakespeare, at the end of the second part, when he assumes the throne as Henry V. The last of these four plays is largely a celebration of the new king's political, military, and romantic triumphs as he becomes "the mirror of all Christian kings," in the words of the play's chorus in act 2.

Henry's accomplishments thus bring to a climax Shakespeare's massive four-part re-creation of medieval English politics and warfare and do so in a play that seems to be simpler in plot and purpose than any of its predecessors. In act 1, the king determines that his claim to the French crown is legitimate and, after his demands have been shabbily mocked by ambassadors from France, he determines to enforce his claim by right of conquest. In act 2, he uncovers a plot to assassinate him by traitorous English nobles, bribed by the French. After sentencing his almost slavishly penitent former friends to death as traitors, he encourages the rest of his men to follow him to glory: "Cheerly to sea! The signs of war advance! / No king of England, if not king of France!" (2.2.191–2).

Act 3 begins with the king besieging Harfleur, which yields after a bloodthirsty threat from Henry to sack and plunder without mercy. The defenders, who have already given up hope, yield without further fighting, and the king orders the Duke of Exeter, his garrison commander, to "use mercy to them all" (54). By now it is October, however, the end of the campaign season. With his army suffering from fatigue and illness after this victory, Henry hopes to reembark for England but finds his way barred by an enormous French force of armored knights. In act 4, he visits his men in disguise the night before the decisive battle, rallying their spirits, and on the morrow, after effectively heartening his "band of brothers," Henry wins a miraculous victory.

The fifth act dramatizes the political and romantic dividends of Agincourt: The French yield to all of Henry's demands while he is successfully courting Princess Katherine. Alongside Henry's achievements, other scenes follow the degradation and eventual dispersal of his former rowdy companions on the battlefields of France; the successful exploits of a new group of subplot characters, led by the Welshman Fluellen, who not only admire the king but fight for him courageously and patriotically; and a series of scenes among the French knights that advertise comically their fatuous arrogance and overconfidence. Princess Katherine is already learning English in act 3, scene 4, presumably preparing herself for her, and her country's, new lord and master. The play ends with England and France at peace and Henry anticipating his marriage to the French princess and the birth of a son who will be acknowledged by both kingdoms as its legitimate monarch. A brief epilogue reminds the audience of the less glorious history that followed: Henry, "this star of England" (epilogue 6), died when his son was nine months old, and later in the fifteenth century, the English lost France and then fell into civil war, events covered in an earlier series of *Henry VI* plays by Shakespeare (1591–93).

Despite his fairytale-like historical successes, Shakespeare's Henry and his play have been widely attacked by critics and scholars ever since the English romantic man of letters William Hazlitt condemned Shakespeare's hero, in 1817, for being "careless, dissolute, and ambitious." According to Hazlitt, a political liberal and critic of the post–Waterloo conservative English government, Henry "seemed to have no idea of any rule of right or wrong, but brute force, glossed over with a little religious hypocrisy and archepiscopal advice" (*Shakespeare Henry V: A Casebook* 36). Hazlitt's objections to Henry's character are typical of later critics, readers, and audiences, who are disturbed by his using and then discarding his former friends in order to burnish his own reputation. Indeed, Falstaff, who dies offstage near the beginning of *Henry V*, never comes into contact with the former prince in this play, and his death is at least indirectly charged to Henry by the tavern hostess who is with Sir John when he dies: "The King has killed his heart" (2.1.88).

Hazlitt's other charges are political, and they anticipate subsequent criticism of both the theatrical and the historical Henry V—and sometimes of Shakespeare—as a moral hypocrite and martial bully. One valuable method of analyzing the play as it relate to these issues is through just war theory and conventions. Just war principles are probably as old as war itself, but they were articulated as early as Saint Augustine in the fourth century BCE (Mattox); were implemented in first Muslim and then Christian war doctrine and practiced in the early Middle Ages; and, in the Christian tradition, were most fully formulated by Thomas Aquinas in the thirteenth century. Indeed, the two principal categories of moral considerations retain their medieval Latin formulations: *jus ad bellum* (determining whether or not a war is just) and *jus in bello* (determining whether or not combatants fight justly in a war).

These moral and quasi-legal principles of war were codified relatively recently, beginning with the Hague Conventions of the second half of the nineteenth century, and have largely retained that century's assumption that wars are transnational military conflicts that involve the hostile crossing of well-defined borders into well-defined national political entities. Applying such concepts to Shakespeare's play is far from an anachronistic exercise, however. The most widely accepted exposition of such principles, Michael Walzer's *Just and Unjust Wars* (first published in 1977 and nearly unchanged in subsequent editions through 2000), includes an analysis of Henry's order to kill French prisoners at Agincourt (16–20). After discussing what he calls "the moral reality of war" in part 1 of his treatise, Walzer covers *jus ad bellum* (which he titles "The Theory of Aggression") and *jus in bello* ("The War Convention") in parts 2 and 3, respectively, and then handles moral problems in which fighting a just war and fighting justly might seem to be in conflict (parts 4 and 5). Historical examples, which include Agincourt, illustrate but also complicate the theory.

Although principles and practices of just warfare may become complex and may seem to be armchair moralizing, when considering the realities of the "hell" that combatants endure on various battlefields, the fundamental precepts of *jus ad bellum* and *jus in bello* are almost self-evidently righteous to all people. The only just war is a war fought against aggressors; and any party that begins a war for any other purpose is engaging in aggression, or, to use Walzer's expression, "the crime of war" (21). With regard to fighting well, combatants on one side have a right to kill those on the other side but do not have the right to harm or endanger noncombatants, including both civilians not involved in the fighting and prisoners of war. Although a just war and just actions in warfare might seem to be logically compatible, Walzer points out that they have seemed to be in moral conflict in many cases, such as General William Tecumseh Sherman's march across Georgia (an attempt to bring a just war to a close by terrorizing the civilian population of the South) or the rules of engagement mandated by German generals like Erwin Rommel (whose armies followed the war convention justly, but did so in obedience to an aggressive, morally criminal regime that had started the war).

Not only can issues of just war be applied analytically to Shakespeare's celebration of the famous victories of Henry V, but also Shakespeare has written a play in which such issues are explicitly (and perhaps deliberately) addressed. As recent critics of the play and Shakespeare's treatment of war have made clear (such as Simon Barker, Ros King and Paul Franssen, Theodor Meron, Paola Pugliatti, Nina Taunton), *Henry V* is almost unique in the canon for not only representing war on stage but also directly and continually engaging its cast, its audience, and its readers in considering the moral problematics of warfare. One of Henry's most die-hard supporters, Fluellen, is concerned, somewhat comically, with the difference between "modern" warfare (referencing the late sixteenth century, since here, as in other plays, Shakespeare updates his medieval setting with contemporary references like the employment of cannons) and the "true and ancient [i.e., Roman] prerogatifs and laws of the wars" (4.1.68–69). He even decries the underhanded (and medieval) tactics of using mines and countermines in the siege of Harfleur.

More seriously, however, most of act 1 is dedicated to assuring Henry that his war in France is legal, moral, and winnable, conditions that ought to be met to justify going to war. Shakespeare draws on Holinshed's not entirely accurate record at the beginning of the play (a brief account of the actual historical situation can be found in Peter Saccio's *Shakespeare's English Kings*), but he arranges the scenes and episodes to raise, and not entirely allay, readers' uneasiness with his hero's campaign in France. In the first scene, the archbishop of Canterbury reveals to the bishop of Ely (figures who represent the sanction of the church) that he has promised Henry lavish financial support for "causes now in hand . . . touching France" (1.1.77, 79) at a time when Parliament has raised a bill to confiscate church lands and transfer them to the king. The obscure "causes in hand" become clear in the subsequent scene, in which the archbishop is called upon to justify Henry's project to enforce his claim to the French crown through military action if necessary. The advice that he gives, however, like the subsidy he has promised the king, seems compromised by institutional self-interest: A king who has been provided the church's financial and legal support for war would be likely to support the church's interests against those of Parliament.

Henry needs the archbishop's doctrinal support, because he is planning a war that seems to be unjust by both twentieth-century and sixteenth-century conventions of *jus ad bellum*. Although his invasion of France might seem a clear-cut case of aggression, the second scene of the play aggressively provides justification in four episodes that appear sequentially: The archbishop uses archaic and contemporary historical and legal documents to validate the king's rightful claim to the crown of France; members of his council of state (who symbolize the English nobility, just as the two bishops stand for the church as a whole) urge him to renew England's former claims to France and therefore England's national glory; they then assure him that the country will be remain safe from Scottish or French aggression if he takes an expeditionary force to France; and, finally, the ambassadors of France appear before Henry—in response to his earlier arguments to be recognized as heir to France—with a present (tennis balls) from the dauphin (the French heir to the throne).

The fundamental legal justification for the war is presented at great length at the beginning of the scene by the archbishop as he expounds the circumstances of a hoary statute, the Salic law, that the French have used, dubiously, to bar Henry's claim to the crown, a claim based on genealogical succession through the female line. Even summarizing the argument is tedious, and most of Shakespeare's audience would have been as bewildered as modern readers are by its references to eight hundred years of French royal history. Nonetheless, the thoroughness of exposition convinces the king that his right is valid, and he doubles down on its validity by ceding moral responsibility for the consequences of twisting the truth to the church:

KING: May I with right and conscience make this claim?
CANTERBURY: The sin upon my head, dread sovereign. (1.2.96–97)

Similarly, the king seems nearly a bystander when his councillors, one by one, reinforce the archbishop's initial call to action ("Stand for your own, unwind your bloody flag, / Look back into your mighty ancestors" 101–102) and urge him to resume the Hundred Years' War (1337–1453) to win France that was initiated by his great-grandfather, Edward III. Finally breaking his silence, the king worries about leaving England unprotected from its enemies if he crosses the English Channel, but the nobles outline an expansive plan to divide the army to accomplish both military goals, assuring him that the campaign in France can be won and England can remain secure. Since no war can be just if soldiers are being sacrificed without hope of victory (and a victorious campaign in France at the cost of losing England would be futile), the nobles' reassurance makes the French invasion seem viable.

Only after law, church, and nobility have virtually directed Henry to attack France does the king seem able to make up his mind:

> Now are we well resolved; and by God's help
> And yours, the noble sinews of our power,
> France being ours, we'll bend it to our awe
> Or break it all to pieces (1.2.222–25)

The final episode of the scene, the French insult to the king, therefore seems to leave him no choice—instead of bending, they have chosen not only to reject Henry's demands but to mock him personally by suggesting that he to stick to tennis rather than engage in warfare. However, Henry throws the dauphin's taunt back on the French:

> And tell the pleasant Prince this mock of his
> Hath turned his balls to gunstones, and his soul
> Shall stand sore chargèd for the wasteful vengeance
> That shall fly with them; for many a thousand widows
> Shall this his mock mock out of their dear husbands,
> Mock mothers from their sons, mock castles down,
> And some are yet ungotten and unborn
> That shall have cause to curse the Dauphin's scorn.
> (1.2.282–89)

The affront to the king's personal honor thus becomes the final stimulus pushing Henry to initiate a war that has already been validated and demanded by church and state. Furthermore, just as the king has laid moral responsibility for the war on the archbishop of Canterbury's legal judgment, the dauphin (and the French monarchy for which he stands) is indicted, morally and spiritually, for the crime of war that England is about to unleash.

On one hand, Shakespeare has done his best in this scene to present Henry as a reluctant warrior exercising his legal rights and carrying out the will of the nation against an enemy that has irresponsibly chosen to defy his just demands. However, the very intensity and specificity of legal, moral, and strategic claims forces readers to take them seriously also. If they do, they will see that Henry and the English have just declared a war of aggression, have justified it by reference to French legal chicanery and personal insults, and have preemptively saddled the French with exclusive moral responsibility for all the death and destruction that will ensue after they have been attacked. While the justification for the war may seem preposterous when viewed in this way, the scene illustrates the crucial importance of justification, even for aggressors and their supporters, whether they are Shakespeare, his audiences in the late 1590s, or modern audiences who will be encouraged to admire Henry's heroic victories on screen or on stage.

Henry V provides a remarkable assortment of subsequent scenes and episodes that force readers and audiences to consider the moral realities of war even as they may enjoy Henry's triumph. Whether these episodes validate or call into question Henry's righteousness continues to be a matter of debate in the large number of recent studies of war plays that appeared on the Elizabethan stage during the late 1580s and the 1590s. Blaming or praising Henry or his creator, much of the focus of previous criticism of *Henry V*, seems less crucial (in an age when American students have seen their country involved in drawn-out Middle Eastern conflicts) than allowing the text to raise questions that deserve to be considered even if they cannot be answered to readers' satisfaction. Several scenes and episodes call for moral interrogation.

In act 3, scene 3, Henry threatens the governor of Harfleur with the slaughter of all children and the rape of all "maidens" because he will be unable to restrain his soldiers from such crimes if they have to take the town by storm. In addition, he denies his own moral responsibility and blames the governor for any crimes inflicted on his own people if he continues to be "guilty in defense." Conversely, he issues orders to insure the citizens' safety once the town has surrendered.

In act 3, scene 6, lines 19–112, Bardolph (one of Prince Hal's former friends and companions) is hung by the Duke of Exeter for stealing a sacred object from a French church. Henry not only validates the execution ("We would have all offenders so cut off" 3.6.106) but also uses it to outlaw all abuse of the French, whether through acts of thievery or even through words, since "when lenity and cruelty play for a kingdom, the gentler gamester is the soonest winner" (110–12).

In act 4, prior to the beginning of the battle, the chorus, some of Henry's soldiers, the king, and the French herald acknowledge that his "ruined band" is heavily outnumbered by the enemy, which will not let them simply withdraw from France. On the evening and morning of Agincourt, the king seems to have led his men to imminent destruction, since the army has been devastated. Saccio notes that "casualties, desertions, and dysentery" (82) had cost Henry one-third of his personnel by October 24, and Holinshed would have informed Shakespeare that fifteen hundred soldiers had already died of illness alone (78). Henry, therefore, wants to abandon his campaign, but the French have trapped him and are about to attack with overwhelming numbers.

In act 4, scene 1, lines 35–226, Henry, moving incognito among his troops the night before the battle to investigate their state of mind, encounters three common soldiers, uncertain about whether or not the king's cause is just, who nonetheless agree that "if his cause be wrong, our obedience to the King wipes the crime of it out of us" (131–33). Forced to respond, their disguised leader simply denies his moral responsibility for any crimes of war committed by individual soldiers. In act 4, scene 1, lines 233–80, the king, evidently disturbed by the conversation, reflects to himself about the joyless burdens of command responsibility and how his anxious vigilance to "maintain the peace" (283) goes unappreciated by his lowly subjects. In act 4, scene 1, line 286, turning in the end to the "God of battles," Henry prays to Him to "steel [his] soldiers' hearts" (289) and then enumerates the pious offices he has undertaken to gain God's pardon for his father's "fault" (293) in deposing King Richard II.

In act 4, scene 3, lines 18–67, recovering magnificently with his prebattle exhortation on St. Crispin's Day, Henry rallies his "happy few," converting the odds against them into a cause for national commemoration "from this day to the ending of the world" (58), whether they live or die. In act 4, scene 4, as the battle begins, Pistol, one of the king's former dissolute companions, threatens his disarmed French prisoner with death unless his captor is given a ransom. After Pistol extracts his two hundred crowns and leads "Monsieur le Fer" (26) off to captivity, readers learn that Nym, one of Pistol's comrades, has been hanged, presumably under the edict issued by King Henry in act 3.

In act 4, scene 5, line 21, a troupe of French nobles, shamed by the collapse of their battle line, rouse themselves to attack the enemy. In act 4, scene 6, Henry and his train enter with French prisoners who are escorted offstage; he is given an account of the heroic death of the Duke of York. Hearing the sounds of a French rally, however, he gives orders to cut the throats of his prisoners.

In act 4, scene 7, finding that the boys who were guarding the king's otherwise undefended camp have been killed by the French, Fluellen condemns them for an action that is "expressly against the law of arms" (2). His English comrade Gower commends Henry for ordering his French prisoners to be killed in reprisal. When the angry king enters the scene with more prisoners, he sends a warning to the French that he will kill all prisoners until and unless they either fight him or withdraw from the field. The French herald, Mountjoy, enters to tell Henry that he has won the battle and to ask that the French be allowed to identify and bury their dead.

As relayed in the epilogue, the outcome of the war—peace between England and France to be sealed by a united monarchy—fell to pieces within two years, and England lost all of France but Calais by the end of the Hundred Years' War (1453). In 1558, Calais was reabsorbed by

France. As judged by a third principle of just war theory, *jus post bellum,* therefore, Henry's wars did not result in a just settlement, and the French took back their country within thirty years. Not only did Shakespeare's audiences know all of these details, but also some may have seen Henry's victories come to naught in *Henry VI, Part One* less than ten years earlier.

However, Shakespeare's audiences in 1599 had more urgent reasons to look back to Agincourt. In 1596, three years before the play may have inaugurated the opening of the Globe, Shakespeare's new theater and the site of his plays for the rest of his career, the Spanish took Calais from the French. As Nick de Somogyi has documented (132), the occupation left the army of the most powerful nation in Europe, England's mortal foe, so close that when the city fell that spring, the noise of the cannonades could be heard in Greenwich. Rumors of a new Spanish armada convulsed the country in 1599, and when a rebellion broke out against the English colonialists in Ireland that spring, the Earl of Essex led an English army across the Irish Sea to put it down. Essex's campaign (which turned out to be a failure) is directly compared to Henry's successful invasion of France in the final chorus of Shakespeare's play.

In its own time, therefore, the play may have been written in response to a crisis (that eventually passed), and that crisis may explain two striking features of its celebratory urgency and need to justify English wars abroad. Henry directly follows his threat to turn tennis balls into cannon balls with an appeal to the ultimate arbiter of justice:

> But this lies all within the will of God,
> To whom I do appeal, and in whose name
> Tell you the Dauphin I am coming on
> To venge me as I may, and to put forth
> My rightful hand in a well-hallowed cause. (1.2.290–94)

Ultimately, the rightness of the English cause is God's call, and Henry consistently invokes divine judgment throughout the play, which culminates in a miraculous victory for which Henry, again, is not responsible: "O God," he proclaims, stunned by the final disproportionate tabulation of French and English losses, "thy arm was here; / And not to us but to thy arm alone / Ascribe we all. . . . Take it, God, / For it is none but thine" (4.8.107). Englishmen and women in 1599 must have felt the need for a similar intervention.

The splendid choruses of the play, which begin every act with patriotic invocations of king and country, function to enlist the support of the audience's imagination to transform the playhouse, the players, and the play into something more grand than an afternoon at the theater. In fact, at the beginning of act 3, the chorus is enlisting many of them, as English patriots, to "Follow, follow!" (17) the heroic king not only imaginatively but perhaps also more substantially: "For who is he, whose chin is but enriched / With one appearing hair, that will not follow / These culled and choice-drawn cavaliers to France?"—or to Ireland, perhaps (chorus act 3, lines 22–24)

Most of the significant episodes discussed involve problems of *jus in bello*—whether or not soldiers "fight well" in war and whether their moral conduct adheres to the war convention as closely as possible. In fact, when confronted in act 4 with soldiers worried that they will not "die well" if the king's war is unjust, Henry switches the conversation to issues of *jus in bello*: Anyone who does not "die well" because of any war crimes he may have committed has only himself, not the king, to blame. Moreover, the discussion both narrows and elevates itself to considering any soldier who is in a state of sin for any reason: If he does not "die well," the king is not to blame; the final decision about his fate is God's to make, in any case.

Taking the play's serious involvement with just war issues as a whole, Shakespeare seems to present an unjust war that is waged justly by the king, but not without serious consideration of moral dilemmas about how the war is fought or without attempting to justify an invasion as a holy war. Scholars, students, and readers of the play may disagree in analyzing these episodes; taking them seriously, as the play does, in order to analyze war as a field of moral decision making is more valuable than judging Shakespeare or Henry (either Shakespeare's or history's).

Differences in evaluating Henry and his wars are dramatically evident in the most significant filmed versions of *Henry V*: Laurence Olivier's celebratory and comic film of 1944; Kenneth Branagh's dark and somber representation of war and heroism in 1989; and Michael Bogdanov's more subversive production of the play, filmed during a performance at the Grand Theatre in Swansea, Wales, in 1990, just after Argentina and the United Kingdom had reestablished diplomatic relations following the Falklands War of 1982.

The two classic and award-winning films are particularly resonant subjects for just war analysis in relation to the text of the play. Olivier turns the Salic law speech into a farce scene and eliminates half of the episodes and speeches involving moral ambiguities, including Henry's bloodthirsty threat at Harfleur, the hanging of Bardolph, the king's guilt-tinged prayer to God the evening before Agincourt, and both orders to kill prisoners. Nym and Bardolph are still alive at the end of the play, and even the foiling of treason in act 2, scene 2 is eliminated. Branagh includes all these scenes, with varying emphasis. The Salic law scene is played with deadly seriousness. Bardolph is not only hung but also done so in front of Henry, who gives the order for the execution and suffers emotionally from the anguish of such a decision (Shakespeare simply includes a report of the execution, which does not occur onstage). He suffers palpable guilt and grief over his father's deposition of Richard during his prayer to God. Olivier's virtual excision of moral problematics actually calls attention to the significance of such scenes and may be related to the date of the production, when Allied forces were initiating a just invasion against German-held Western Europe, a circumstance that curiously recalls the national crisis faced by Shakespeare's England in the year that *Henry V* first appeared on stage.

Olivier's film also finds parallels with both the American *Band of Brothers* series and World War II. The HBO series also seriously considers not only the camaraderie, heroism, and suffering of its citizen soldiers but also moral questions that arise even in a just war. Returning readers (and viewers) to the source of their fraternal and patriotic motto, can valuably reorient the teaching of Shakespeare in an age when the United States seems to be engaged in wars without end.

Works Cited

Barker, Simon. *War and Nation in the Theatre of Shakespeare and his Contemporaries*. Edinburgh: Edinburgh UP, 2007.

Bogdanov, Michael, dir. *The Wars of the Roses: Henry V.* Windmill Lane, 2005, DVD.

Branagh, Kenneth, dir. *Henry V.* Renaissance, BBC Curzon, 1989, Film.

De Somogyi, Nick. *Shakespeare's Theatre of War.* Brookfield, VT: Ashgate, 1998.

Hazlitt, William. *Characters of Shakespeare's Plays.* London: Oxford UP, 1955.

_____. *Henry's Wars and Shakespeare's Laws: Perspectives on the Law of War in the Later Middle Ages.* Oxford: Clarendon, 1994.

Holinshed, Raphael. "Henry V." *Holinshed's Chronicles as Used in Shakespeare's Plays.* London: Dent, 1951. 71–89.

Keegan, John. *The Face of Battle: A Study of Agincourt, Waterloo, and the Somme.* New York: Viking, 1976.

King, Ros, and Paul J. C. M. Franssen, eds. *Shakespeare and War.* New York: Palgrave, 2008.

Mattox, John Mark. *Saint Augustine and the Theory of Just War.* New York: Continuum, 2006.

Meron, Theodore. *Bloody Constraint: War and Chivalry in Shakespeare.* New York: Oxford UP, 1998.

_____. *Henry's Wars and Shakespeare's Laws: Perspectives on the Law of War in the Later Middle Ages.* Oxford: Clarendon, 1994.

Olivier, Laurence, dir. *Henry V.* 1944. Two Cities Films, Film.

Pugliatti, Paola. *Shakespeare and the Just War Tradition.* Burlington, VT: Ashgate, 2010.

Saccio, Peter. *Shakespeare's English Kings.* New York: Oxford UP, 1977.

Shakespeare, William. *Henry V.* Ed. T. W. Craik. 2005. Walton-on-Thames, Eng.: Thomas Nelson, 2007.

Quinn, Michael, ed. *Shakespeare, Henry V: A Casebook.* London: Macmillan, 1969.

Taunton, Nina. *1590s Drama and Militarism: Portrayals of War in Marlowe, Chapman, and Shakespeare's Henry V.* Burlington, VT: Ashgate, 2001.

Walzer, Michael. *Just and Unjust Wars: A Moral Argument with Historical Illustrations.* 3rd ed. New York: Basic Books, 2000.

American Literature of the Nuclear Age _____

On December 10, 1950—a little more than three months after the Soviet Union tested its first atomic bomb and the nuclear arms race began—author William Faulkner traveled to Stockholm, Sweden, to receive the Nobel Prize in Literature "for his powerful and artistically unique contribution to the modern American novel" (Faulkner). In his acceptance speech, Faulkner spoke frankly about literature's relationship to the great military conflict of his day, the Cold War. "Our tragedy today is a general and universal physical fear so long sustained by now that we can even bear it," he observed. "There are no longer problems of the spirit. There is only the question: When will I be blown up?" For Faulkner, the apocalyptic nuclear threat that defined the Cold War was also a threat to the era's literature: "Because of this, the young man or woman writing today has forgotten the problems of the human heart in conflict with itself which alone can make good writing because only that is worth writing about" (649). Faulkner urged the authors of the nuclear age to resist sounding "the last dingdong of doom" in their work and instead use their craft to "help man endure by lifting his heart" (650). Literature, he argued, must also fight for survival in the nuclear age.

The Cold War

Students of American literature may certainly find that the fiction written after the World War II remains focused on issues of human character and "the human heart in conflict with itself." Nonetheless, that literature is indeed also a reflection of the Cold War. The Cold War was a decades-long technological, military, and political conflict between the United States and the Soviet Union that loomed over the art of the era, resulting in a literature that is deeply contextual and politicized in many ways. Authors of the time felt compelled to comment on issues of foreign policy, national security, and military strategy. Cold War

American Literature of the Nuclear Age **53**

foreign and domestic policies became symbolic and thematic elements of works of literature. The nuclear threat spawned a new tradition of nuclear-war storytelling, while stories about nuclear war became important parts of the national debate over nuclear weapons. In these ways and more, the Cold War was fought within the nation's literary culture.

In geopolitical terms, the Cold War is generally understood to have been a contest between the two kinds of global economies—capitalism and communism—supported by the United States and the Soviet Union, respectively. The Cold War arguably began at the close of World War II as the war's victors negotiated for control of the postwar world. The Soviet Union won economic and political control over the nations of Eastern Europe and parts of Asia, while the United States secured the power to redevelop Japan and the nations of Western Europe as politically friendly capitalist states. The two superpowers then squared off against each other for the following half century.

The defining feature of the Cold War is its so-called coldness: It never became an armed conflict between the superpowers. This was in part a result of the tens of thousands of nuclear weapons that were built by both sides, any one of which could destroy a city. Massive nuclear arsenals were argued to be a deterrent to war. According to the policy of nuclear deterrence that developed over the Cold War, each superpower's security hinged on its ability to destroy the other superpower, even after it had already been destroyed in a nuclear attack. As nuclear weapons became instruments of Cold War politics, the world experienced a decades-long buildup of terrifying bombs that could destroy civilization many times over. Hence, the Cold War is also seen as giving rise to a historical era called the "nuclear age," an era in which the existence of nuclear technology shapes foreign and military policies. Instead of breaking out in a devastating nuclear war, the Cold War instead erupted in smaller proxy wars on the Korean Peninsula and in states ranging from Vietnam to Grenada. The Cold War ended with the dissolution of the Soviet Union in 1991, leaving indelible marks on the literature written over its long and often harrowing course.

Containment

The Cold War was engaged directly between the superpowers through acts of espionage and propaganda. Much of the confrontation between the Soviet Union and the United States was, in fact, symbolic. Nuclear arsenals and civil defense plans served as deterring symbols of each state's willingness to fight a third world war. American politicians even used domestic technologies such as washing machines and televisions as symbols of the superiority of American capitalism over Soviet communism. During what has come to be called "the kitchen debate" of 1957, then vice president Richard Nixon and Soviet premier Nikita Khrushchev actually stood inside a model American kitchen built in Moscow and used the kitchen's various appliances to argue over whose social system best served its peoples.

The politicized symbols with which the Cold War was fought also became a part of the nation's literature, appearing in a diverse range of texts that includes canonical works such as Ralph Ellison's *Invisible Man* (1952) and J. D. Salinger's *The Catcher in the Rye* (1951), ecological and journalistic monographs such as Jonathan Schell's *The Fate of the Earth* (1982) and John Hersey's *Hiroshima* (1946), and popular thrillers and works of science fiction such as Eugene Burdick and Harvey Wheeler's *Fail-Safe* (1962) and Russell Hoban's *Riddley Walker* (1980). The Cold War was marked by several important policy documents that defined the conflict between East and West, providing authors with characters, images, themes, and scenarios that penetrated the literature in ways both obvious and subtle. Thus, a true appreciation of the literature of the nuclear age begins with an understanding of policies such as containment and nuclear deterrence that defined the Cold War.

The nuclear age achieved its apocalyptic character through iconic images of mushroom clouds rising above Hiroshima and Nagasaki at the end of World War II, an image of total destruction that was repeated in nuclear tests over the following two decades. The United States' Cold War, however, achieved its distinctively threatened character through a piece of writing: the "Long Telegram" sent from Moscow to

Washington, DC, in February of 1946 by an American diplomat named George Kennan. In his telegram (published anonymously in 1947 in the influential policy journal *Foreign Affairs* under the title "The Sources of Soviet Conduct") Kennan warned his readers of a looming Soviet threat:

> We have here a political force committed fanatically to the belief that with [the] U.S. there can be no further *modus vivendi* [means of getting along], that it is desirable and necessary that the internal harmony of our society be disrupted, our traditional way of life be destroyed, the international authority of our state be broken, if Soviet power is to be secure. (qtd. in Winkler 24)

While Kennan helped define the Soviet Union as a threat with his "Long Telegram," former British prime minister Winston Churchill provided the Cold War with one of its most enduring symbols in a speech he delivered at Westminster College in Fulton, Missouri, in March of 1946. Churchill warned that "an iron curtain has descended across the continent [of Europe]," separating the free peoples of the West from those trapped within the Soviet Union's postwar sphere of influence (qtd. in Winkler 22).

Kennan's and Churchill's concepts of the threatening Soviet character became part of the rationale behind the foreign policy known as "containment" that structured the Cold War conflict. Since, it was argued, the Soviets wanted to impose their communist social system on the rest of the world, their influence had to be contained within that iron curtain and not allowed to spread. The policy of containment led to a vigorous anticommunist movement within the United States, the permanent mobilization of the American military, and the building of thousands of nuclear weapons to keep the Soviets from waging a war and, so it was feared, taking over the world.

Within American society, the policy of containment also became a cultural narrative that defined how dissent and conflict was to be managed domestically. As Alan Nadel argues in *Containment Culture* (1995), "containment equated containment of communism with containment of atomic secrets, of sexual license, of gender roles, of nuclear energy, and of artistic expression" (5). Any part of American culture, or of one's personal life, for that matter—such as prior political affiliations, sexual orientations, and friendships—could become part of the Cold War by being branded a communist threat. Over the first three decades of the Cold War, politicians such as Senator Joseph McCarthy and representatives serving on the House Committee on Un-American Activities (HCUA) interrogated hundreds of Americans, ranging from Hollywood filmmakers to mothers protesting nuclear testing. The narrative of containment thus became as defining a part of Cold War American culture as the nuclear threat.

Many important works of American literature written during the 1940s and 1950s reiterate the narrative of containment in one way or another. Consider, for example, Ellison's powerful representation of American racism in *Invisible Man*. As Thomas Hill Schaub discusses in *American Fiction in the Cold War* (1991), Ellison's novel participates in the anticommunist political discussion that preoccupied liberals and other left-leaning artists and intellectuals in the early Cold War. Those who had once admired the Soviet system and even been members of the Communist Party were urged to confront what many of them now saw as a new reality: the failure of their leftist beliefs. After all, before World War II, Soviet leader Joseph Stalin had sent hundreds of thousands of his own soldiers, peasants, and even Communist Party members to prison for disloyalty during the Great Purge; early in the war he had signed a nonaggression pact with Adolf Hitler; and he was now waging Cold War on the United States. The "new liberals" of the Cold War replaced their once-activist progressive ideology with a newfound "realism" that recognized the inherent fallibility of humanity and thus the futility of grand state planning. In doing so, they limited the aims of their progressive policies and, in effect, worked to contain the power of organized political dissent on the left.

The titular protagonist of *Invisible Man* is in the same situation as the Cold War liberal: He must come to terms with the seeming failure of his political organizations. His first-person narrative is thus a rebuke to the grand planning of ideologically driven states such as the Soviet Union. Invisible Man is a young black man from the American South. He is an idealist who wants to make a grand contribution to his country. He travels across a spectrum of professional institutions and African American politics over the course of his life, from a Tuskegee Institute-style school to a paint factory, a mental hospital, a communist-style Brotherhood, and a violent Black Nationalist organization. The lesson he repeatedly learns is that belief in organizations is naive, for all institutions (political, scientific, medical, industrial) are corrupt and fail both him and the people they allegedly serve.

Invisible Man repeatedly confronts institutions that purport to be rational, unambiguous, and accurate in what they do. However, his experience of these institutions, be they schools or political parties, is the exact opposite. Identity is little more than an act, he realizes, as he is repeatedly mistaken for a stranger named Rinehart simply by wearing a simple disguise. Contradiction, not clarity, is the way of the world. "The world moves . . . [n]ot like an arrow, but a boomerang," Invisible Man observes in his prologue (5). By novel's end, he has given up on "learn[ing] a lesson for history" and instead vows to "try belatedly to study the lesson of my own life" (432), a difficult task for a man who sees himself as having been not a person but merely a black body pushed around by others his entire life.

While Ellison's novel is a part of the culture of containment through its dramatization of the inherent failure of leftist politics, other early Cold War novels such as Salinger's *The Catcher in the Rye* (1951) reflect the anticommunist methods of HCUA. During the years when Salinger was revising the manuscript of his novel for publication, Nadal discusses in *Containment Culture*, HCUA held public hearings designed to both expose communist propaganda in Hollywood and to root out communists in the government. HCUA's hearings resulted most famously in the blacklisting of filmmakers accused of being under communist influence and the imprisonment of Alger Hiss, a former communist and government official.

"Uncovering duplicity was the theme of the day," Nadel observes, and this theme is paramount in Salinger's novel as well (75). Salinger's teenage protagonist, Holden Caulfield, is waging a personal war not against communists but against hypocritical people he repeatedly calls "phonies." Nevertheless, as Nadal argues, his war against phonies bears many similarities to the era's anticommunist crusades. Caulfield's first-person narrative reads much like the transcripts of former communists testifying against former comrades before HCUA, for the veracity of his narrative is based on admissions of his lies. "I'm the most terrific liar you ever saw in your life," Caulfield confesses early in the novel. "It's awful. . . . It's terrible" (22). Even the color of Caulfield's hat symbolizes the culture of containment. Communists are colloquially called "Reds" and exposing people's affiliations with communism is called "red hunting." Soon after confessing to be a liar, Caulfield purchases a "red hunting hat" (24) that he wears throughout most of the novel.

Caulfield's character reflects aspects of both the Cold War's hunters and hunted. Witnesses brought before HCUA were required to promptly "name names" of former communists in order to demonstrate their credibility and exonerate themselves. Caulfield also participates in this Cold War ritual of naming names to demonstrate his innocence, peppering his narrative with names that "include people, places, days, months, countries, novels, cars, and cold remedies" (Nadel 78). Caulfield's sister, Phoebe, too, becomes a symbolic agent of containment when she is cast as an infamous American traitor in a school play who, like a witness in a loyalty hearing, is called to confess his former treachery. "It stinks," she tells her brother, "but I'm Benedict Arnold. I have practically the biggest part. . . . It starts out when I'm dying. This ghost comes in on Christmas Eve and asks me if I'm ashamed and everything. You know. For betraying my country and everything" (210).

For Caulfield, the adult world seems to be mostly full of such traitors and phonies.

Like Invisible Man, Holden Caulfield ultimately finds himself in a similar situation as the chastened American liberals and former communists in the Cold War. On one hand, he has acted like a good red hunter, exposing the nation's phonies, but on the other hand, he has been an ideologically driven critic of American society demanding perfection in human nature. Following the narrative pattern of containment, Caulfield must reassess his youthful ideals. He had imagined himself to be a protector of innocence—a catcher saving falling children in a field of rye (Salinger 224). Through his story, he had tried to speak a simple truth in a world full of hypocrites. Yet his quest to drop out of high school and live true to his ideals leads to his incarceration in a mental asylum. Assessing the story of his life, Caulfield starts to sound like an adult by book's end: "If you want to know the truth, I don't *know* what I think about it. I'm sorry I told so many people about it." He concludes his story by giving the reader advice fit for a Cold War spy: "Don't ever tell anybody anything" (277).

Invasion

The policy of containment was necessary because the Soviet Union was believed to be an implacable and, indeed, evil foe. The Soviet Union was "demonized" in Cold War American rhetoric and security strategy, routinely described as a wicked and threatening enemy of American values; metaphorical variants of the demonized Soviet, in turn, became recurring characters in American literature. American national security strategy during the Cold War was based on top-secret documents written by the National Security Council (NSC) that prominently feature a demonized Soviet. After the Soviet Union tested its first atomic bomb in 1949, the NSC, in 1950, produced for President Harry S. Truman National Security Council Document 68 (NSC 68). NSC 68 served as a blueprint for national security for the remainder of the Cold War. NSC 68 reiterated Churchill and Kennan's earlier analyses about the existence of the iron curtain and the need to contain Soviet ambitions, but now in blatantly apocalyptic terms fit for the nuclear age. "The issues that face us are momentous," NSC 68's introductory analysis concludes, "involving the fulfillment or destruction not only of this Republic but of civilization itself" (qtd. in May 26).

NSC 68's primary author, Paul Nitze, based his argument for containment upon a demonized concept of Soviet character. Nitze describes the Soviet Union as "animated by a new fanatic faith" based on the values of slavery as opposed to the values of freedom associated with the United States (May 25). Since it is "the implacable purpose of the slave state to eliminate the challenge of freedom," the United States had no choice but to continually build up its military forces so as to deter the Soviet Union (May 27). Nitze describes Soviet intentions with language once used to describe Nazi Germany:

> Being a totalitarian dictatorship, the Kremlin's objectives in these policies [i.e., the isolation of Soviet people from the outside world] is the total subjective submission of the people now under its control. The concentration camp is the prototype of the society which these policies are designed to achieve, a society in which the personality of the individual is so broken and perverted the he participates affirmatively in his own degradation. (May 33)

The concept of the Soviet Union as, essentially, a large concentration camp that brainwashed prisoners into its willing subjects guided American–Soviet relations throughout the Cold War. As late at the 1980s, President Ronald Reagan, in his public speeches, described the Soviet Union as an "evil empire."

The demonized Soviet became an inspiration for numerous tales of invasion written throughout the Cold War, especially in the popular genre of science fiction. Books and films from the Cold War about invading aliens and giant insects reflect the era's fear of invasion by both enemy aircraft and secret agents, a sentiment often called "Cold War paranoia." In science fiction novels such as Robert A. Heinlein's *The Puppet Masters* (1951), sluglike aliens from another world wage a war of subversion within the United States much as Soviet agents were imagined to be doing in the real world. Literally attaching themselves to people's backs and hiding under their clothing, Heinlein's aliens secretly convert Americans into agents under the control of their distant slave state. "One of us looks human but is an automaton, moving at the will of our deadliest enemy," the book's chief of secret intelligence observes at one point (37). Heinlein's alien agents are good examples of Cold War paranoia because they look like average Americans, driving home the theme that anyone can be a traitor to one's country.

Similarly, in Jack Finney's *The Body Snatchers* (1955), pods from deep in outer space land on a farm and convert the residents of a small American town into soulless, group-thinking duplicates of themselves. The only goal of Finney's pod people is to spread their alien pods across the Earth. To many, Finney's converted Americans acted a lot like communists. In these and several other science-fiction tales, the Soviet Union is metaphorically transformed into a communally thinking monster that rejects individuality, acts strangely, and threatens the existence of not only the United States but also the entire human race.

The invasion scenario was not limited to works of strategy and science fiction. It also became a thematic element of works of literature whose concerns seem at first far afield from the threats of the Cold War and the nuclear age. Such is the case with the regional literature of the American South and Georgia author Flannery O'Connor in particular. Regarded as one the finest American practitioners of the short-story form, O'Connor is most commonly associated with the regional literary tradition of the Southern Gothic and the religious tradition of Catholic writing. However, as Jon Lance Bacon discusses in *Flannery O'Connor and Cold War Culture* (1993), O'Connor bases many of her regional stories on the global threats of the Cold War era. As O'Conner observes in her essay "The Nature and Aim of Fiction":

It's well to remember that the serious fiction writer always writes about the whole world, no matter how limited his particular scene. For him, the bomb that was dropped on Hiroshima affects life on the Oconee River [in central Georgia], and there's not anything he can do about it. (*Mystery and Manners* 77)

O'Connor's gruesomely funny Southern tales about confidence men, impoverished farmers, disabled intellectuals, juvenile delinquents, and unreconstructed racists speak volumes about what she considered the fallen (postlapsarian) human condition. However, O'Connor delivers that grand theme in narratives that also reflect national fears of Soviet invasion and nuclear attack. She uses a Cold War invasion scenario in a half dozen of her short stories, Bacon argues, setting her tales on farms that are attacked by often friendly looking foes.

O'Connor writes in a narrative pattern Bacon calls "the invaded pastoral": "Someone or something enters the pastoral setting and disrupts or destroys the lives of its residents" (8). Four stories in O'Connor's first short-story collection, *A Good Man Is Hard to Find* (1955), concern farms that are invaded by outsiders. And two stories from her second collection, *Everything That Rises Must Converge* (1965), feature farms invaded not by people at all but rather by inhuman creatures. For example, O'Connor's short story "Greenleaf" begins with a bull one night invading the property of a farmer named Mrs. May. The bull simply belongs to the neighboring Greenleaf family. However, as it eats a shrub outside the sleeping Mrs. May's bedroom window, it becomes something greater in Mrs. May's dream, a Cold War monster that threatens to consume her entire farm:

She had been aware that whatever it was had been eating as long as she had had the place and had eaten everything from the beginning of her fence line up to the house and now was eating the house and calmly with the same steady rhythm would continue through the house, eating her and the boys (*Collected Stories* 311–12).

Mrs. May sees the bull as a symbol of how the neighboring Greenleafs, whom she considers her social inferiors, are taking over her property and her way of life. Her fears of invasion prove well founded by the story's end as the bull gores her when she attempts to catch it herself.

O'Connor's short story "A Circle in the Fire" is another example of an invaded pastoral that features imagery drawn from the era's nuclear threat. In this story a farmer named Mrs. Cope lives on an isolated farm protected from the outside world by a stand of trees. Mrs. Cope takes great pride in her personal fortune, favorably comparing her life to those of people persecuted inside the iron curtain: "Every day I say a prayer of thanksgiving," she tells a farmhand. "Think of all we have. Lord . . . we have everything. . . . Why, think of all those poor Europeans . . . that they put in boxcars like cattle and rode them to Siberia" (*Collected Stories* 178). The one thing Mrs. Cope fears is that her trees will catch fire. Like many Cold War Americans, she "keeps watching the skies" for threats, fearfully eyeing the "swollen and flame-colored" sun that "hung in a net of ragged cloud as if it might burn through any second and fall into the woods" (*Collected Stories* 184). Three juvenile delinquents soon invade Mrs. Cope's farm and confirm her worst fears by setting fire to the woods. O'Connor's last image of Mrs. Cope is of a woman who has been conquered, her face bearing the same look of "misery" as that found on Europeans sent to Siberia (*Collected Stories* 193).

Nuclear War

In addition to fearing subversive Soviet attacks from within American society, Americans feared a nuclear attack. With each successive year of the Cold War, the nuclear threat grew more destructive. In 1951, the United States started building a new kind of nuclear weapon, a hydrogen bomb based on the physics of atomic fusion. Hydrogen bombs can be hundreds of times more powerful than the uranium bombs that destroyed Hiroshima and Nagasaki. In 1951, President Truman also established the Federal Civil Defense Administration (FCDA), a government agency responsible for developing plans to protect Americans during a nuclear war. The FCDA produced films designed to grow awareness about the nuclear threat such as the animated short "Duck and Cover" (1952), in which a cartoon turtle named Bert shows children how to hide under desks or newspapers to protect themselves from an atomic blast. In 1953, as part of his economizing "New Look" policy for national defense, President Dwight D. Eisenhower decreased the number of troops in the army and shifted much of the burden of Soviet containment onto the nation's ever-growing nuclear arsenal. The threat of a nuclear war thus became the cornerstone of American national security in the Cold War.

Unlike the millions of veterans returning home from combat after World War II, Americans did not have any direct experience of nuclear warfare, and their notions of a nuclear war derived instead from films such as "Duck and Cover" and from works of literature. As the philosopher Jacques Derrida pointed out at a 1984 symposium at Cornell University, nuclear war is unique because it is:

> a phenomenon whose essential feature is that of being *fabulously textual*, through and through. . . . For the moment, a nuclear war has not taken place: one can only talk and write about it. . . . Unlike the other wars, which have all been preceded by wars of more or less the same type in human memory . . . nuclear war has no precedent. It has never occurred, itself; it is a non-event. The explosion of American bombs in 1945 ended a "classical," conventional war; it did not set off a nuclear war. The terrifying reality of the nuclear conflict can only be the signified referent, never the real referent (present or past) of a discourse or a text. At least today apparently. (23)

Throughout the Cold War, the policy of nuclear deterrence relied upon the apocalyptic imagination. In the Cold War's "delicate balance of terror," nuclear weapons could be effective defenses only if each superpower's leaders and citizenry believed that fighting a war with them would be too destructive to win. This belief could never be proved in practice; nuclear war could be fought only in the imagination, experienced only in texts such as scientific reports, works of fiction, and civil-defense films. As the policy of nuclear deterrence developed over the Cold War and arsenals grew to "overkill" levels, critics of the nation's nuclear defense policy coined a phrase meant to challenge nuclear weaponry's role as defenses in the national imagination, dubbing nuclear deterrence "Mutual Assured Destruction," or MAD for short.

Decades before it was invented, the atomic bomb was described in a work of the imagination: a novel written in 1914 by British author H. G. Wells entitled *The World Set Free*. Wells's novel describes how wars in the future will be fought with cataclysmic bombs. "Before the last war began," Wells writes, "it was a matter of common knowledge that a man could carry about in a handbag an amount of latent energy sufficient to wreck half a city" (104). Wells intended his novel to be a cautionary tale of things to come. The United States' atomic bomb was built partly in response to a cautionary work of the imagination as well. Physicists Albert Einstein and Leó Szilárd wrote a letter to President Franklin D. Roosevelt in 1939 urging him to fund research into creating an atomic bomb. After informing the president about the new physics of nuclear fission, they describe an imaginary atomic attack:

> This new phenomenon would also lead to the construction of bombs, and it is conceivable . . . that extremely powerful bombs of a new type may thus be constructed. A single bomb of this type carried by boat and exploded in a port, might very well destroy the whole port together with some of the surrounding territory. (Einstein 40)

The tale of nuclear war remained a cautionary political fiction in the Cold War. In 1951, the editors of *Collier's* magazine produced a special October issue devoted to describing what a nuclear war fought in the year 1960 would be like, titling their special issue *Preview of the War We Do Not Want*. Although the war they dramatize entails the destruction of much of the United States and the Soviet Union, the editors of *Collier's* saw their special issue as supporting the policy of nuclear deterrence. They wrote it to prove in fiction something that could never be proven in reality: "to demonstrate that if The War We Do Not Want is forced upon us, we will win" ("Operation Eggnog" 6).

Americans' fear of nuclear attack was realized in hundreds of books and films created throughout the Cold War that depict how the nation and the world would be destroyed in a future nuclear war. Works of fiction such as Pat Frank's *Alas, Babylon* (1959) and Walter M. Miller's *A Canticle for Liebowitz* (1960) present their readers with a now-familiar scenario: the disintegration of civilization after a nuclear war. Frank's novel, set in the small Florida town of Fort Repose, is a variant of the invaded pastoral scenario. After nuclear bombs destroy the major cities and military bases of Florida, turning them into irradiated craters, society in the small town of Fort Repose disintegrates. Banks fail, people die of radiation poisoning, buildings burn, food runs short, and bandits prowl the roads. The residents of Fort Repose must rebuild their society in a dangerous new world. In *A Canticle for Liebowitz*, Miller takes the apocalyptic scenario several steps further. He sets his novel in a succession of distant futures—the twenty-sixth, thirty-second, and thirty-eighth centuries. In each of these centuries, civilization destroys itself in nuclear wars after reacquiring the scientific knowledge needed to build nuclear bombs.

Representations of nuclear war's destructiveness are not limited to works of fiction. Works of creative nonfiction offered Americans perhaps their most compelling visions of what a nuclear war would be like, in particular, two books initially published in the literary journal the *New Yorker*: Hersey's *Hiroshima* and Schell's *The Fate of The Earth*. Hersey interviewed six survivors of the world's first nuclear attack to write their personal stories of the day the bomb was dropped on Hiroshima. Each survivor recounts a parade of horrors that followed the attack, from the total physical destruction of the city to hideous burns that caused people's skin to slough off. One of Hersey's survivors recounts how "He reached down and took a woman by the hands, but her skin slipped off in huge, glovelike pieces" (60).

In 1982, Schell published *The Fate of the Earth,* a landmark of antinuclear literature that looked at nuclear war from an ecological perspective. Through a careful analysis of nuclear science and strategy, Schell debunks the policy of nuclear deterrence and explains how nuclear weapons are a threat not only to nations and people but also to all life on earth. "Nuclear weapons are unique in that they attack the support systems of life at every level," Schell explains (23). While built to defend the American republic, Schell argues that the only thing left after a nuclear war would be "a republic of insects and grass" (1). By the 1980s, scientists had learned that a nuclear war would also cause a mass extinction. Ash from burning cities would blot out the sun, leaving the world in a state of "nuclear winter" for years.

Since the beginning of the nuclear age, nuclear weapons have been the subject of political debate. The scientists who first built the atomic bombs in the Manhattan Project knew that nuclear weapons were different from all other weapons. They debated whether or not such terrible weapons should be used against human beings; many hoped that their existence would prompt the formation of a peaceful world government after the war. Nuclear-war stories themselves are always political, be they demonstrations of national resolve or calls for nuclear disarmament. They can do the political work of deterrence by demonstrating the horrors that will be visited upon all combatants should such a war occur, much as the editors of *Collier's* intended—or they can convince people to organize in antinuclear protests by detailing the totality of the nuclear threat, as Schell intended his book to do.

As the Cold War continued through the 1950s and into the 1960s, a sense developed that nuclear weapons had, in some fundamental way, taken on a life of their own and become uncontrollable. To many, the logic behind nuclear deterrence—building tens of thousands of weapons capable of destroying civilization many times over in order not to fight a war with those very same weapons—began to look increasingly dangerous and even absurd. Around the time of the 1962 Cuban Missile Crisis, stories and films about nuclear wars starting by accident seized the nation's imagination. Accidental nuclear-war stories fueled a national debate over the wisdom of nuclear deterrence that continued throughout the Cold War.

Accidental-nuclear-war novels such as Burdick and Wheeler's *Fail-Safe* and films such as director Stanley Kubrick's *Dr. Strangelove or: How I Learned to Stop Worrying and Love the Bomb* (1964) question the logic behind nuclear deterrence. Many poised the question of what would happen if, given the size and technological complexity of the world's nuclear arsenals, something broke or malfunctioned in a bomb. In Kubrick's darkly comic film (based on a 1958 British novel about an accidental nuclear war by Peter George titled *Red Alert*), an insane air force general orders an unstoppable nuclear attack on the Soviet Union while the US president's advisors, hiding underground, shrug off the impending deaths of tens of millions of Americans. In *Fail-Safe*, military leaders assure visitors to the nuclear "War Room" in Omaha that "This system is infallible" (43). However, it is not infallible: "in Machine No. 6 a small condenser blew. It was a soundless event. There was a puff of smoke no larger than a walnut that was gone instantly" (44). That "minor" malfunction sends an American nuclear bomber to destroy Moscow. In order to prevent a Soviet nuclear counterattack, the American president orders the atomic bombing of New York City. Several prominent novels about World War II, including Joseph Heller's *Catch-22* (1961), Kurt Vonnegut's *Slaughterhouse-Five, or The Children's Crusade: A Duty-Dance with Death* (1969), and Thomas Pynchon's *Gravity's Rainbow* (1973), reflect a nuclear-age sentiment as well, presenting modern warfare as fundamentally out of control and absurd.

In the final decade of the Cold War, President Reagan proposed eliminating the nuclear threat by building a Strategic Defense Initiative (SDI), a network of satellites that could shoot down enemy missiles and aircraft. Reagan's proposal, like nuclear warfare itself, was an act of the imagination. SDI was far beyond the capabilities of the science and engineering of the 1980s. Critics of Reagan's plan called it "Star Wars." However, even a "Cold Warrior" such as Reagan had come to see the limits of nuclear deterrence. A nuclear war would be not only a military disaster but also a cultural disaster, erasing human history.

In tale after tale about nuclear war, the broken society that follows the war is merely a shadow of civilization. Such is the case in Hoban's postapocalyptic novel *Riddley Walker*, set two thousand years after the social and ecological catastrophe of a nuclear attack. Even after millennia, Hoban's humanity remains in a medieval state. Hoban's protagonist, Riddley Walker, delivers his first-person narrative in a crude form of English, compelling the reader to learn a new form of broken culture. Riddley's sense of history is little more than myth:

> *Riddley we aint as good as them befor us. Weve come way way down from what they ben time back way back.* May be it wer the barms what done it poysening the lan or when they made a hoal in what they callit the O Zoan. Which that O Zoan you cant see it but its there its holding in the air we breave. You make a hoal in it an Whoosh! No more air. Wel word ben past down thats what happent time back way black. (125)

Postapocalyptic authors such as Hoban explore the implications of the Cold War between the United States and the Soviet Union, thinking the unthinkable: What happens after nuclear deterrence has failed? The postapocalyptic literature of the nuclear age provides the most fully realized sense of what a world after a nuclear war would be like. Art and science, cities and industries, whole histories and societies would not survive.

The very existence of such a literature also illustrates one of the ironies of the Cold War and indeed of history itself: Social and cultural conflict, no matter how potentially destructive, shape social and cultural production. In science and industry, the Cold War's permanently militarized economies funded the development not only of devises that can destroy civilization, such as nuclear weapons, but also of objects that have become valued parts of civilization, such as computers. In literature, the threat of nuclear war produced a complex tradition of postapocalyptic storytelling whose authors explored the values and limits of civilization itself. Cold War fears of invasion gave authors a way to structure conflict in their plots while the troubling domestic politics of the Cold War inspired authors to examine the relations of both politics to identity and the individual to society. In these ways and more, the threats and fears of the Cold War became a part of the story of American literature.

Works Cited

Bacon, Jon Lance. *Flannery O'Connor and Cold War Culture*. New York: Cambridge UP, 1993.

Burdick, Eugene, and Harvey Wheeler. *Fail-Safe*. New York: McGraw, 1962.

Derrida, Jacques. "No Apocalypse, Not Now." *Diacritics* 14.2 (Summer 1984): 20–32.

Einstein, Albert. "Letter to President Roosevelt, August 2, 1939." *The Nuclear Predicament: A Sourcebook*. Ed. Donna Gregory. New York: St. Martin's, 1986. 39–40.

Ellison, Ralph. *Invisible Man*. New York: Random House, 1947.

Faulkner, William. "Address upon Receiving the Nobel Prize for Literature." *The Portable Faulkner*. Ed. Malcolm Cowley. New York: Penguin, 2003.

Heinlein, Robert A. *The Puppet Masters*. New York: Signet, 1951.

Hersey, John. *Hiroshima*. Rev. ed. New York: Knopf, 1985.

Hoban, Russell. *Riddley Walker*. New York: Summit, 1980.

May, Ernest R., ed. *American Cold War Strategy: Interpreting NSC 68*. New York: St. Martin's, 1993.

Nadel, Alan. *Containment Culture: American Narratives, Postmodernism, and the Atomic Age*. Durham, NC: Duke UP, 1995.

O'Connor, Flannery. *The Complete Stories*. New York: Farrar, 1971.

_____. *Mystery and Manners: Occasional Prose*. New York: Farrar. 1969.

"Operation Eggnog." *Preview of the War We Do Not Want*. Spec. issue of *Collier's* 27 (October 1951): 6, 8, 10.

Salinger, J. D. *The Catcher in the Rye*. Boston: Little, 1951.

Schaub, Thomas. *American Fiction in the Cold War*. Madison: U of Wisconsin P, 1991.

Schell, Jonathan. *The Fate of the Earth*. New York: Knopf, 1982.

Wells, H. G. *The World Set Free*. London: MacMillan, 1914.

Winkler, Allan M. *The Cold War: A History in Documents*. New York: Oxford UP, 2000.

Walt Whitman, Emily Dickinson, and the Civil War: Inventing the Poetry of Mass Death _____

Ed Folsom

The American Civil War was the country's first confrontation with mass death and injury on a scale previously unimaginable. Quintessentially American poets Walt Whitman and Emily Dickinson were among the first to wrest with the horrific details of the war at an artistic level.

At the start of any war, many political and military leaders think the war will be over quickly. Many Americans still remember what Secretary of Defense Donald Rumsfeld said on the eve of the Iraq War in 2003: "It is unknowable how long that conflict will last. It could last . . . six days, six weeks. I doubt six months" (Rumsfeld). Vice President Dick Cheney agreed that "it'll go relatively quickly . . . weeks rather than months" (qtd. in Moyers). Whitman and Dickinson experienced the same false hope at the beginning of the Civil War. Like the president's advisers blithely predicting that the Iraq War would be a "cakewalk" and would be over within a few weeks, most contemporary observers predicted the Civil War would be a brief and clean war and be over in a matter of weeks, if not days (Adelman). "A great and cautious national official," Whitman recalled, "predicted that it would blow over 'in sixty days,' and folks generally believ'd the prediction" (Whitman *Prose Works* 1.26). Civil War histories are full of stories of people who packed picnic lunches and sat on the hills to watch the Battle of Bull Run, only to be shocked into horror as the Northern troops beat a retreat into Washington, DC (Catton 460). "Where are the vaunts, and the proud boasts with which you went forth?" Whitman asked, "Where are your banners, and your bands of music, and your ropes to bring back your prisoners? Well, there isn't a band playing— and there isn't a flag but clings ashamed and lank to its staff" (*Prose Works* 1.27).

A year and a half later, Whitman was at the war front, in Fredericksburg, Virginia, looking after his injured brother (who was a Union soldier) and wondered how long the bloody quagmire would last. As he approached the mansion used as a hospital, he passed by "a heap of amputated feet, legs, arms, hands, &c., a full load for a one-horse cart" (*Prose Works* 32). It was the first indication he had that this would be a war of amputation, eventually severing an entire generation of American males from the country's future. That pile of body parts Whitman encountered, like some grotesque parody of the life-affirming poetic catalogs that were so characteristic of his prewar poetry, became the stubborn reality he learned to incorporate in his radically altered post–1860 poetry. Instead of absorbing an ameliorative, evolving, progressive, expanding self, nation, and cosmos into the affirmative song that he sang in his 1855 and 1856 editions of *Leaves of Grass*, he began cataloging mass death.

The grisly catalog of death eventually expanded to more than 600,000 casualties. (Projected as a percentage of the nation's population, that death toll would amount to nearly seven million dead young men by modern standards.) For Whitman, a poet of the body, who believed the soul only existed when it took on flesh and bone, the war was an attack on the American soul, leaving a generation of American men dead or disfigured.

Whitman had published three editions of his life's work, *Leaves of Grass*, before the Civil War, and he publish three more after the war. Before the war, he saw his book as an effort to hold the country together, to catalog its vast diversity into unifying poems that would celebrate contradiction and teach Americans to live with these contradictions. However, once the United States was torn apart by war, Whitman's poetry changed. At this point, instead of cataloging the vast variety of life in the nation, he began cataloging a seemingly endless accumulation of deaths.

Pieces of this catalog can be found throughout Whitman's wartime poetry, collected in his book *Drum-Taps* (1865), but perhaps never so effectively expressed as in his prose *Memoranda during the War* (1875), in which he writes the longest sentence he would ever compose. In it, he invents a syntax of mass death, an undiagrammable utterance that wanders the ruined nation to gather up "the infinite dead," pausing continually to absorb the horror, the details, and the unimaginable numbers of dead young men whose bodies eluded the grave and were composted into the landscape. The sentence is so long and so intricate that Whitman originally wrote it out as a poem, lined so as to create one of his characteristic poetic catalogs ("The Dead in This War," *Walt Whitman Archive*). The sentence buries seven parenthetical insertions among its approximately thirty dashes, creating a jagged syntactical field sliced with phrasal trenches. This astonishing sentence ends up, after its nearly four hundred words, being a sentence fragment. There is no way, Whitman discovered, to predicate the subject: "The dead in this war." These numberless dead are beyond animation, as they are but fragments of bodies, amputated selves, that have so "saturated" American land that the living are fated to reap a harvest of death, with blood in every grain eaten:

The dead in this war—there they lie, strewing the fields and woods and valleys and battle-fields of the south—Virginia, the Peninsula— Malvern hill and Fair Oaks—the banks of the Chickahominy—the terraces of Fredericksburgh—Antietam bridge—the grisly ravines of Manassas—the bloody promenade of the Wilderness—the varieties of the *strayed* dead, (the estimate of the War department is 25,000 national soldiers kill'd in battle and never buried at all, 5,000 drown'd—15,000 inhumed by strangers, or on the march in haste, in hitherto unfound localities—2,000 graves cover'd by sand and mud by Mississippi freshets, 3,000 carried away by caving-in of banks, &c.,)—Gettysburgh, the West, Southwest—Vicksburgh—Chattanooga—the trenches of Petersburgh—the numberless battles, camps, hospitals everywhere—the crop reap'd by the mighty reapers, typhoid, dysentery, inflammations—and blackest and loathesomest of all, the dead and living burial-pits, the prison-pens of Andersonville, Salisbury, Belle-Isle, &c., (not Dante's pictured hell and all its woes, its degradations, filthy torments, excell'd those prisons)—the dead, the dead, the dead—*our* dead—or South or North, ours all, (all, all, all, finally dear to me)—or East or West— Atlantic coast or Mississippi valley—somewhere they crawl'd to die, alone, in bushes, low gullies, or on the sides of hills—(there, in secluded spots, their skeletons, bleach'd bones, tufts of hair, buttons, fragments of clothing, are occasionally found yet)—our young men once so handsome and so joyous, taken from us—the son from the mother, the husband from the wife, the dear friend from the dear friend—the clusters of camp graves, in Georgia, the Carolinas, and in Tennessee—the single graves left in the woods or by the road-side, (hundreds, thousands, obliterated) —the corpses floated down the rivers, and caught and lodged, (dozens, scores, floated down the upper Potomac, after the cavalry engagements, the pursuit of Lee, following Gettysburgh)—some lie at the bottom of the sea—the general million, and the special cemeteries in almost all the States—the infinite dead—(the land entire saturated, perfumed with their impalpable ashes' exhalation in Nature's chemistry distill'd, and shall be so forever, in every future grain of wheat and ear of corn, and every flower that grows, and every breath we draw)—not only Northern dead leavening Southern soil—thousands, aye tens of thousands, of Southerners, crumble to-day in Northern earth. (*Prose Works* 1.115)

Whitman entitled this section of his *Memoranda* "The Million Dead, Too, Summ'd Up," using his characteristic contraction-apostrophe, which creates a haunting ambiguity, because the sentence, with all its embedded statistics, sums up Civil War dead; also, however, the contraction also invites readers to fill in a few more letters, and the death sentence literally "summons up" the dead, reminding readers' of the war dead's physical presence throughout the landscape and on their emergence in everything that grows from the soil into which they dissolve. Whitman's catalog is a summing and a summoning, The summons is of not only the dead but also the living, who are being summoned to witness this mass death and, grotesque as it may seem, ingest it, live off of it, and make a future out of it. These dead soldiers reemerge—in actual physical and chemical transformation—in "every future grain of wheat and ear of corn," in the very "breath we draw." The act of staying alive necessitates the inhalation of the atoms of the dead.

The writer Whitman most revered, Ralph Waldo Emerson, left his Unitarian ministry over his refusal to administer what Whitman called the "conventional communion service" (*Prose Works* 1.350). In some essential ways, Whitman's poetry is based on his own radical reconception of a democratic communion more stunning than any that religion has imagined. It was not just Christ's body and blood that were endlessly recycled and ingested, as is the case in conventional Christian communion. Instead, Whitman suggests, all life and death are an endless cycle of composting communion: "I do not talk of the beginning and the end" (*Leaves of Grass* 30). He first expressed this faith in the first published version of *Leaves of Grass* in 1855: The soul is an endless process of compost, breaking down and reforming.

The Civil War forced Whitman to expand his radical spirituality further than he ever had before. Mass death made him imagine a kind of wildly unconventional democratized communion, one in which every citizen who survived the war would take and eat of the soldiers whose bodies had merged with and saturated the land. For Whitman, every one of the more than 600,000 soldiers who died became as significant of Christ, as potent a symbol of loss and rebirth as any in history. In his *Drum-Taps* poem called "A Sight in Camp in the Daybreak Gray and Dim," Whitman lifts the blanket from a dead soldier to realize that "this face is the face of the Christ himself, / Dead and divine and brother of all, and here again he lies" (*Leaves of Grass* 307). Thus, Whitman expresses his uncanny vision of communion.

Following his long sentence about death in *Memoranda during the War*, Whitman notes how many of "these countless graves" contain "the significant word Unknown." "In some of the cemeteries," he writes, "nearly all the dead are unknown" (*Prose Works* 1.115). Returning to battlefields and cemeteries ten years after the war, Whitman writes of how these soldiers have left little trace because of the relentless fertility of nature:

> From ten years' rain and snow, in their seasons—grass, clover, pine trees, orchards, forests—from all the noiseless miracles of soil and sun and running streams—how peaceful and how beautiful appear to-day even the Battle-Trenches, and the many hundred thousand Cemetery mounds!" (*Prose Works* 1.323).

Like the missing letters in his suggestive contraction "summ'd," much will always be missing in this summoning.

Meanwhile, in Amherst, Massachusetts, the other great nineteenth-century American poet, Emily Dickinson, was experiencing the mass death of the Civil War in a different, but no less horrific, way. Bound to her family home for her entire life, Dickinson, like most nineteenth-century women, experienced the war from a distance, but no less intensely. Instead of a pile of amputated limbs, she saw the seemingly endless lists of the dead and wounded that American newspapers printed. As the lists got longer, mass death came to be anonymous death. The lists of names on the vast black slabs of the Vietnam Memorial in Washington, DC, capture what Dickinson would have experienced as the newspaper arrived each day, invading her home with these lists of names severed from their physical identities. It was from such a list of casualties in the *New York Herald* that Whitman picked out his brother George's name, the name itself mangled (Whitmore instead of Whitman) like the soldier it indicated, that led Whitman to the Fredericksburg battlefield and changed the course of his life and his poetry (Loving 13). Dickinson's response to the litany of names was no less unsettling than Whitman's:

They dropped like Flakes—
They dropped like Stars—
Like Petals from a Rose—
When suddenly across the June
A wind with fingers—goes—

They perished in the Seamless Grass—
No eye could find the place—
But God can summon every face
On his Repealless—List. (Dickinson 194–95)

This poem was probably written around the time that Whitman read his brother George's name in the newspaper, went to Fredericksburg to experience the accumulating death firsthand, and then stayed in Washington, DC, to catalog in his notebooks the thousands of wounded and dying soldiers that he visited in the hospitals there. Where Whitman describes mass death as eventually composting the soil so that it grows up in flowers, grain, and corn and perfumes the air, Dickinson describes a world, a universe, dropping things in masses, each individual death like a snowflake lost in the vast accumulation of snow, like a falling star disappearing amid the millions, or like petals stripped from a rose by a cold wind in a warm month. Like Whitman's mass of unknown graves that eventually compost into leaves of grass, the dead in Dickinson's poem perish in the seamless grass, which grows over and closes the seam of the grave, leaving the dead now seamless (the dead now *seem less*). No eye could find the place: The living, as Whitman reminds readers, have trouble remembering, and the dead, as their numbers proliferate, have less identity. "Nearly all the dead are unknown," Whitman reminds readers (*Prose Works* 1.115).

What sounds like a conventional and comforting religious conclusion to Dickinson's poem is, as is always the case with her poetry, more ambiguous than it first may seem. Dickinson's God always seems, to her, "careless" with life (which is, to him, a thing as easy to "efface" as to "invent"), more concerned, as she says in one poem, with his "Perturbless Plan" than with the murmuring "Perished Patterns":

> It's easy to invent a Life—
> God does it—every Day—
> Creation—but the Gambol
> Of His Authority—
>
> It's easy to efface it—
> The thrifty Deity
> Could scarce afford Eternity
> To Spontaneity—
>
> The Perished Patterns murmur—
> But His Perturbless Plan
> Proceed—inserting Here—a Sun—
> There—leaving out a Man. (Dickinson 355)

In "They Dropped Like Flakes," a poem about lists, God seems to have a big list, as if those expanding lists in the newspapers were some journalistic equivalent of God's "Repealless List," his supposedly complete registry of all of mankind's dates of "effacement." What comfort to the living is God's summons? What comfort to the living is it that God can recall each face as he effaces it, if the living eye cannot find a trace? The poem is not focused on God's summons alone: Like Whitman's poem summoning up the million dead, Dickinson's poem ends on its own kind of contraction, as she inserts a dash between "Repealless" and "List," leaving what seems to be a noun hanging at the end of the poem, where it suddenly doubles as a verb, summoning readers to "Listen" and "List."

In William Shakespeare's *Hamlet* (1603), the ghost of Hamlet's father, in a chilling moment, demands his son to "List, list, oh list!" (1.5) Dickinson, too, often listens to the dead and tortures herself by what she cannot hear: "The Living—tell— / The Dying—but a Syllable— / The Coy Dead—None" (Dickinson 194). In "They Dropped Like Flakes," "List" as a command interrupts the conventional comforting statement that seems to be forming the conclusion of the poem and asks readers instead to use their senses to listen to the silence of the dropping flakes, the muteness of the list of names of the dead.

As a result of such profound silences, Dickinson says, as she does in another poem about the mass death of the Civil War, "It feels a shame to be Alive— / When Men so brave—are dead" (Dickinson 213). For her, the dissolving of soldiers into the landscape is every bit as horrifying as it is for Whitman, but it comes for her without his serene ecological faith in the power of compost to turn death to life again. For Dickinson, the process is even more violent, a mortar-and-pestle procedure, where God seems the implied agent of grinding, as the living look on:

> Are we that wait—sufficient worth—
> That such Enormous Pearl
> As life—dissolved be—for Us—
> In Battle's—horrid Bowl? (Dickinson 213)

In "When Lilacs Last in the Dooryard Bloom'd," Whitman sees "battle-corpses, myriads of them, / And the white skeletons of young men" and casts them all as "the debris and debris of all the slain soldiers of the war," recognizing that these now "dissolved" beings "suffer'd not," but rather "The living remain'd and suffer'd" (*Leaves of Grass* 336). Like Dickinson, Whitman questions whether the living were "worth" the sacrifice of mass death, and much of the rest of his life was dedicated to trying to imagine a United States worthy of the sacrifice of a generation of young men. However, he never put this sacrifice in the stark economic terms Dickinson did:

> The price is great—Sublimely paid—
> Do we deserve—a Thing—

> That lives—like Dollars—must be piled
> Before we may obtain? (Dickinson 213)

Whatever the unspecified "Thing" for which these mass deaths have paid cannot be worth the price paid, in Dickinson's estimation. Dickinson seems to wonder how one can go when the corpses are viewed as payment for something to be obtained.

The poem ends with one of Dickinson's most enigmatic stanzas:

> It may be—a Renown to live—
> I think the Man who die—
> Those unsustained—Saviors—
> Present Divinity. (Dickinson 213)

As with Whitman's view of each dead soldier as "Christ himself," Dickinson slips from the singular "Man," which incongruously takes on a plural verb ("die" instead of the singular "dies") and blurs the one soldier into an overwhelming host of "unsustained—Saviors," as it becomes difficult to hang onto the significance of any single death in the face of hundreds of thousands. These endless dead soldiers multiply Christ, and their "Renown" outshines any that living heroes might accrue, as they bring one close to God—become God, precisely because they are now unseen but nonetheless sustain the living. They "Present Divinity" to the living by their very absence. In the parlance of religion and war, the living live because the soldiers died; they died so others may live. Dickinson seems to ask her readers if, with such an overwhelming accumulation of death, they can live with that knowledge.

Photography emerged at the same time that Whitman and Dickinson were writing poetry. The Civil War became the first American war to be photographed. Photography is a technology that grew up with the emerging military technologies that administered mass death; it is no mistake that photography shares the diction of weaponry: A camera is "aimed," and "shots" are taken; from the beginning of the art in the late

1840s, many Americans found it threatening and intrusive and worried that each photograph somehow uncannily stole a piece of one's life. Susan Sontag and others have demonstrated just how enmeshed photography and war have been ever since the Civil War was shot on film (Sontag).

Because of the state of camera and film technology at the time, photography could not absorb actual battle (exposure times blurred quick action; cameras were large and bulky and had to be placed on tripods; plates had to be prepared and quickly developed, requiring darkroom carts to be dragged along with the photographer), and so the visual depiction of the Civil War is based on those aspects that mid-nineteenth-century photography could capture: the preparations and aftereffects of battles. Echoing Whitman's long prose sentence about the harvest of death, one of the most familiar photos of the Civil War, taken by one of Mathew Brady's assistants, is titled "Harvest of Death," and it shows the Gettysburg battlefield, also a farm field, strewn with corpses. Only black-and-white photography was possible at the time, and the dark exposures create an almost moonlit cast in many Civil War shots. Whitman, who knew Brady and was a good friend of Brady's assistant Alexander Gardner, who took many of the war shots, wrote a powerful poem that seems to put into words the dim-lit black-and-white fields strew with corpses.

> Look down fair moon and bathe this scene,
> Pour softly down night's nimbus floods on faces ghastly, swollen, purple,
> On the dead on their backs with arms toss'd wide,
> Pour down your unstinted nimbus sacred moon. (*Leaves of Grass* 320–21)

Whitman does not flinch from looking at the swollen ghastly faces, but he uses the light to create a kind of halo over the scene. On the other hand, Dickinson, in a poem that seems to respond to the same photographic scene, looks hard and close at the ghastly swollen faces and notes the ways that the mouths are frozen open in a final moan, the fragments of papers (often prayers or religious tracts from the soldiers' pockets) strewn over the field, and the rolled-up eyeballs in the gaping eyes. Her battlefield scene, like Brady's,

> 'Tis populous with Bone and stain—
> And Men too straight to stoop again,
> And Piles of solid Moan—
> And Chips of Blank—in Boyish Eyes—
> And scraps of Prayer—
> And Death's surprise,
> Stamped visible—in Stone. (Dickinson 316)

The photograph "stamps" Death "visible," and the stone stillness of the photograph sculpts the dead into unbending, blank, silent forms, as does the excruciating sculpting of Dickinson's imagery, creating a poetic rigor mortis. It is different from, and more unyielding than, Whitman's mass dead, who are still in motion, as nature's chemistry casts a nimbus around them and then transforms them.

An attribute of Whitman's poetry that distinguishes it from Dickinson's, as it relates to the mass death of the Civil War, is that it hoped to create a future from the countless corpses. For Whitman, the obligation of those who survived the Civil War was to make a future that would be worthy of that vast sacrifice. Perhaps this is why Whitman had a lifelong fascination with doctors: The poet and the physician both confront pain and death with a belief that confronting it is worth the effort and that something positive can emerge from it. That is why, in Whitman's Memoranda during the War, the surgeons were, with few exceptions, heroic:

> I must bear my most emphatic testimony to the zeal, manliness, and professional spirit and capacity, generally prevailing among the surgeons, many of them young men, in the hospitals and the army . . . [for these were] the best men, and the hardest and most disinterested workers. . . .

They are full of genius, too. I have seen many hundreds of them and this is my testimony. (*Prose Works* 1:84)

The doctors were "disinterested," and that disinterest steadied their nerves, allowed them to confront the horror and get to work. However, they, too, were overwhelmed by the unimaginable scope of the slaughter and unable to help more than a fraction that cried out for it:

> Of all harrowing experiences, none is greater than that of the days following a heavy battle. Scores, hundreds of the noblest men on earth, uncomplaining, lie helpless, mangled, faint, alone, and so bleed to death, or die from exhaustion, either actually untouch'd at all, or merely the laying of them down and leaving them, when there ought to be means provided to save them. (*Prose Works* 1:85)

There is something heartbreaking in Whitman's small but telling phrase, "actually untouch'd at all": The worst horror is not to die in excruciating pain but to die untouched.

Whitman devoted one of his most powerful war poems, "The Wound-Dresser," to evoking the power of touch and to capturing the importance of "disinterest"—maintaining an exterior calm while the horror of the slaughter burns deep into the soul. The poem imagines a wound-dresser in a Civil War hospital making his rounds:

> I dress the perforated shoulder, the foot with the bullet-wound,
> Cleanse the one with a gnawing and putrid gangrene, so sickening,
>   so offensive,
> While the attendant stands behind aside me holding the tray and pail.
> I am faithful, I do not give out,
> The fractur'd thigh, the knee, the wound in the abdomen,
> These and more I dress with impassive hand (yet deep in my breast a
>   fire, a burning flame). (*Leaves of Grass* 311)

The final parenthetical phrase separates itself from "the impassive hand," as if the "fire" of his emotions cannot be fully acknowledged or given voice, for fear it would overwhelm him and leave him useless amid the horror to which he is attending. The wound-dresser's hand must remain "impassive," in control, disinterested, and able to do its grisly work without wavering; the "burning flame" within the wound dresser's breast, the fire of impassioned response to the horrors he witnesses, has to be kept "deep" below the surface in order to allow the hand to keep functioning and to prevent the flame from consuming him. Finally, he knows, as he wanders among the dying, that the best he can do is offer them a touch:

> The hurt and wounded I pacify with soothing hand,
> I sit by the restless all the dark night, some are so young,
> Some suffer so much, I recall the experience sweet and sad,
> (Many a soldier's loving arms about this neck have cross'd and rested,
> Many a soldier's kiss dwells on these bearded lips.)
> (*Leaves of Grass* 311)

This is how the poem ends, on a statement wrapped in parentheses, expressing (with some half-suppressed combination of amazement, guilt, and gratitude) the affection the poet has managed to wrest from the horror, the moments of tender touch that allow him to draw something "sweet" from an experience so "sad."

After the Civil War, as Reconstruction staggered toward conclusion and Whitman began to see that the reemerging nation was not, in fact, one that seemed worth those nearly million dead, he turned once again to his association with doctors to unflinchingly diagnose the disease afflicting the United States. "I say we had best look our times and lands searchingly in the face, like a physician diagnosing some deep disease," he wrote at the beginning of *Democratic Vistas*. "Never was there, perhaps, more hollowness at heart than at present, and here in the United States" (*Prose Works* 2.369). The physician diagnosing the disease becomes, for Whitman, the role of the poet in his culture, not there to celebrate so much as to diagnose, always assessing what measures can be taken to restore the body politic to health, or assessing if the disease has in fact progressed too far. This will always be the challenge: Confronting pain, suffering, and death, one must ask oneself: What can be made of this? What art—indeed, what future—can rise from it? Writers in the twentieth century would work endlessly to discover how they could make the horrors of war writable, but Whitman and Dickinson, facing the bloodiness of the Civil War, invented the poetry of mass death.

Works Cited

Adelman, Kenneth. "Cakewalk in Iraq." *Washington Post* 13 February 2002. A27.

Catton, Bruce. *The Coming Fury*. New York: Doubleday, 1961.

Dickinson, Emily. *The Complete Poems of Emily Dickinson*. Ed. Thomas H. Johnson. Boston: Little 1960.

Loving, Jerome. *Walt Whitman: The Song of Himself*. Berkeley: U of California P, 1999.

Moyers, Bill. *Bill Moyers Journal* 2 May 2008. Public Broadcasting Service.

Rumsfeld, Donald H. "Secretary Rumsfeld Town Hall Meeting at Aviano Air Base." 7 February 2003. US Department of Defense News Transcript.

Sontag, Susan. "Looking at War: Photography's View of Devastation and Death." *New Yorker* 9 December 2002.

The Walt Whitman Archive. Eds. Ed Folsom and Kenneth M. Price. 4 Feb. 2012.

Whitman, Walt. *Leaves of Grass: Comprehensive Reader's Edition*. Eds. Sculley Bradley and Harold W. Blodgett. New York: New York UP, 1965.

_____. *Prose Works 1892*. Ed. Floyd Stovall. 2 vols. New York: New York UP, 1963–64.

CRITICAL READINGS

Testaments of Youth: Writing the US War in Vietnam

Philip Beidler

"Use kids to fight a war—if you're going to use anybody," reads one of the anonymous testimonies in Mark Baker's *Nam* (1981), a well-known American oral history of the Southeast Asian conflict, in which the United States was officially involved from 1965 to 1975. "They're the best. They're still learning. They can hump the hills. They can take it. And they don't take it personal," Baker's account continues.

Add to that the fictional words of a general to a civilian journalist in James Webb's novel of US Marine combat *Fields of Fire* (1978): Who are they, the correspondent inquires, the combat soldiers of Vietnam? The general replies. "You know. They are the best we have. But they are not McNamara's sons, or Bundy's. I doubt they're yours. And they know they're at the end of the pipeline. That no one cares. They know." (Secretary of Defense Robert McNamara and National Security Advisor McGeorge Bundy were both early proponents of the war.) Call it a Vietnam cliché, a conscripted army of "rock and roll kids" as Martin Sheen's Captain Willard puts it in *Apocalypse Now* (1979), "with one foot in the grave." Many clichés derive from some sort of truth. The ideas behind these quotes can be applied to the Vietnam War experience.

Regarding the literature of the American conflict in Vietnam, the peculiar politics and demographics of war must be discussed. As one war is always different from the last, the last will always prove different from the next. This can be true in terms of the age of soldiers. The average American combatant in World War II was in his midtwenties, demonstrably older than his counterpart in Vietnam. In contrast, with the involvement in Afghanistan and Iraq of National Guard and Army Reserve troops (in addition to regular forces) and the significant numbers of officers and enlistees with professional statuses, the age demographic would surely show a turn upward. The fact remains that most

Americans who wound up serving militarily in Vietnam—and, more particularly, in combat units in the field—were young; aside from officers and noncommissioned officers (NCOs), they were largely from blue-collar or urban and rural poverty-line backgrounds. They were in large measure draftees, frequently of ethnic, racial, and economic minorities, and, at various times, disproportionately African American, Hispanic, and poor white. They were frequently high school graduates, although this often meant that, among other things, they were not politically and economically well-connected enough to get college and graduate-school draft deferments, or, failing that, perhaps affluent or politically savvy enough to find physicians willing to write them phony medical and psychiatric exemptions.

Beyond that, whatever the statistics, the idea of the Vietnam conflict as a young people's war will always remain part of a larger, more generalized national mythology of generational conflict and change from the 1960s onward, a mythology symbolized, rightly or wrongly on the idea of a culture of youth. At the outset of the 1960s, elite military units such as the US Army Special Forces (the Green Berets) and newly developed quick-strike formations such as the First Air Cavalry Division were heralded as specialists in unconventional warfare, of fighting totalitarian aggression in what were called in those days "third world conflicts" or "wars of national liberation."

A corresponding opportunity for idealistic civilian service likewise presented itself in the much-publicized establishment of the Peace Corps, in which American volunteers, many of them young, devoted themselves to projects of international assistance and development. In the domestic life of the nation, popular culture marketed the generation of love, hope, and youth. As the war ground on, and idealism waned on both the military and domestic fronts, young people turned to political activism across a radical spectrum, embracing the civil rights, women's rights, students' rights, draft-resistance, and antiwar movements. Meanwhile, a broader youth culture expressed itself in clothing, music, movies, literature, sexual freedom, recreational drug use, and experiments in communal living. What the late 1960s and early 1970s Richard Nixon-Spiro Agnew contingent called "the silent majority" (those who felt themselves somehow bypassed by all the color and excitement of the decade) were just that. It was the youth culture that got all the pictures and the press, which, both at home and abroad, often seemed to center on the war.

Moving from generalized cultural contexts to more specifically literary endeavors oriented on the Vietnam War, one may see that the title of this essay is actually associated with another highly controversial and destructive war of fifty years earlier and on the other side of the globe. The war in question is World War I and the specific references are to both the British experience of the war of the trenches on the Western European front and the title of a book, written in by a young British woman named Vera Brittain, who had served as a nurse in the casualty stations and surgical hospitals in France and, by the time the war ended, had suffered the loss of both her fiancé and her beloved brother, both young British officers. In a broader sense, the titular reference also quickly becomes one to a vast canon of generational literature of the war about fighting and dying young.

One of the great soldier poems of World War I is Wilfred Owen's "Anthem for Doomed Youth." The war testament of youth is a spirit that became a more generalized Anglo-European and American theme, with further exemplary figures in literature ranging from the British Robert Graves and Siegfried Sassoon to the French Henri Barbusse, the German Erich Maria Remarque, and the Americans John Dos Passos, William March, and Ernest Hemingway. By way of Gertrude Stein, who took the term from a French garage mechanic lamenting a younger cohort so damaged in body and spirit by the war, such figures came to constitute "a lost generation." Accordingly, the writing of the lost generation is the body of literature from which many of the American writers of the Vietnam War, at least initially, seemed to take their marching orders. It is a literature of disillusionment, betrayal, and sellout by the politicians and the arms makers, who are the masters of war and the merchants of death. It is also a body of text that frequently contrasts sharply with the literature of the previous generation's, which struggled victoriously against fascist totalitarianism in World War II.

To be sure, in depictions of the war against Adolf Hitler's Nazi regime and the Japanese imperialists there exist great visceral novels of combat that depict the horror and alienation of twentieth-century warfare. However, even in such texts as Norman Mailer's *The Naked and the Dead* (1948), Irwin Shaw's *The Young Lions* (1948), and James Jones's *The Thin Red Line* (1962), soldier protest and outrage seem finally subsumed in a culture of victory. (It remains highly significant, for example, that the two most accomplished writers about the literature of twentieth-century wars, Paul Fussell and Samuel Hynes—both of them World War II combatants, without illusions about that conflict—ultimately refer to World War I as the template for American literary responses to the Vietnamese War and its cultural aftereffects.)

Even works of absurd exposé, such as *Catch-22* (1961), by Joseph Heller, or *Slaughterhouse-Five* (1969), by Kurt Vonnegut, that achieved notoriety among youthful opponents of the Vietnam War, are consigned largely to the experimentalist academic canon. If the model of all such texts was the ur-classic of earlier American literature, Stephen Crane's *The Red Badge of Courage* (1895), with its central character named Henry Fleming, or, more aptly, "the Youth," and his double-edged initiation into "the red sickness of battle," the latest Vietnam-era renditions seem to pay special attention to the consequences for such initiates in a new age of post–Vietnam American disillusionment and malaise. For the generation of young American writers emerging from the experience of the Vietnamese War, Hemingway generally seemed to have it right about their perspective on life as he spoke of a previous generation. In his "A Way You'll Never Be," the implication is that to try to tell one's story is to accept a kind of life sentence to solitary confinement.

This essay examines five fairly well-known texts written by young people who experienced the Vietnam War. Four of the texts were written by Americans: Philip Caputo's *A Rumor of War* (1977), the account of a young, college-educated marine lieutenant's experiences as an infantry officer during the 1965–66 opening phases of the war; Larry Heinemann's *Close Quarters* (1977), a novel written from the perspective of the blue-collar enlisted soldier about US Army mechanized infantry combat at the 1968–69 height of the war; Robert Mason's *Chickenhawk* (1983), the personal narrative of a warrant-officer helicopter pilot serving in the First Air Cavalry during the 1967 big-unit campaigns of the Ia Drang; and Lynda Van Devanter's *Home before Morning* (1983), a US Army nurse's account of her 1968–69 experiences in the medical evacuation and surgical hospitals of the American main bases. The fifth novel is Vietnamese, Duong Thu Huong's *Tiểu thuyết vộ đề* (1991; *Novel without a Name*, 1995) written by a Vietnamese female veteran who served as a support soldier and propaganda entertainer during the war, but centering on the ten years' experience of jungle warfare and survival for three young male Vietnamese combatants.

These narratives have been chosen to cover an intentionally large chronology, geography, and breadth of experience, revealing the myriad Vietnam War experiences. A further principle of selection involves the degree to which they all address the aftermath of the war upon the participants. As opposed to the many discussions concentrating on literary or political representations to the exclusion of historical and biographical detail, this essay concludes by briefly addressing the authors' subsequent lives.

Also implicit in the title, is a concern for directness of experiential statement. In this sense, this essay departs from that body of scholarly writing about the literature of the Vietnam War centered on interesting questions of style, structure, voice, authority, representation, and textuality. Instead, this essay focuses on the visceral questions: How was it? What was it like? How did it feel?

When considering the American war alone, one must address the myriad possibilities of the individual experience between and among several polarities: American versus Vietnamese, male versus female, combatant versus noncombatant, white soldier versus African American and Hispanic soldier, and enlisted soldier/draftee versus NCO and officer professional. The garish, comic-book-like adventures depicted in Robin Moore's *The Green Berets* (1965), for example, are distinctly pre-1965, before major American combat unit commitments. In contrast, Tobias Wolff's *In Pharaoh's Army* (1994), an account of the author's tour of duty as a Special Forces junior officer adviser in the far southern Vietnam delta, deals almost exclusively with civic action. *We Were Soldiers* (1992), both book and film, depicts the first main-force engagements between major US and North Vietnamese formations in the Central Highlands in 1967—big-unit engagements of size and duration never to be substantially repeated in the course of the war. In contrast, Gustav Hasford's *The Short-Timers* (1979)—the film adaptation of which, *Full Metal Jacket* (1987), was directed by Stanley Kubrick—centers on US Marine small-unit combat during the 1968 Tet Offensive and, in the latter parts of the film, the grim, extended, World War II-like house-to-house urban battle to recapture the former imperial capital of Hue.

The film *Platoon* (1986) takes place in the jungle region of III Corps on the Cambodian border, variously referred to as the Iron Triangle or the Parrot's Beak. The well-known works of former army infantryman Tim O'Brien—*If I Die in a Combat Zone* (1973), *Going after Cacciato* (1978), and *The Things They Carried* (1990), are all set in 1969 in the northern coastal Americal Division area of operations centering on Quan Ngai province (made notorious by the My Lai massacre). One of the earliest novels of major US combat operations, a neglected work by Josiah Bunting, *The Lionheads* (1972), gives one of the few militarily detailed and graphic depictions of US combined-force riverine operations in the delta. In 2010, *Matterhorn*, by marine combat veteran Karl Marlantes, returns to the I Corps/DMZ region during the period of intense battle centering on such famous strongholds as the Rockpile and Con Tien and culminates in the late 1967 and early 1968 siege of Khe Sanh.

The earliest of the texts highlighted in this essay, both in chronological setting and date of publication, is Caputo's *A Rumor of War*, the autobiographical account of the author's experience as part of a US Marine Corps landing force. The combat region is the same for *Fields of Fire*, by Webb, a highly decorated marine officer, eventual secretary of navy, and US senator from Virginia; *The Short-Timers*; the film *Full Metal Jacket*; and, perhaps most famously, the bestselling memoir (and source of the award-winning film script) *Born on the Fourth of July* (1976), by marine infantryman Ron Kovic. The young lieutenant Caputo, born of the post–World War II middle class, has been a son of the suburbs, recipient of "VA loans" (4), and attendee of Saturday-afternoon showings of the 1949 film *Sands of Iwo Jima* (6). By the mid-1960s he has become a college-educated junior officer. Amid general peace and plenitude, he knows the young people under his command to be the leavings of "the ragged fringes of the American Dream" (27). Having survived officer-candidate school, Caputo is deployed to Okinawa, where, in turn, he and his rifle platoon become part of the Marine Expeditionary Brigade sent to Vietnam as part of the earliest buildup of American ground units in the country. Coming ashore at Da Nang, and awarded flower necklaces by beautiful girls in flowing *ao dais*, the marines settle initially for what one of them calls a "splendid little war" (66). (The phrase, describing the 1898 American intervention in Cuba, actually belonged to Secretary of State John Hay.) A static interlude follows as Caputo's marines fill sandbags and stand guard as a security force for American bombing missions over the North. Eventually, commanders devise reconnaissance and security missions.

Caputo learns the conjoined exhilaration, frustration, and exhaustion, mental and moral, of the junior officer in close combat. After a brief leave, he loses his platoon and is rotated out of the field. Assigned to graves registration duty on brigade staff, he becomes the officer in charge of the dead. Soon he is marching in his own nightmares with the maimed and dismembered, all with the faces of real men he has known.

Returned by his own request to a line company, Caputo once again inhabits "Death's Grey Land." In a brief interlude, the young lieutenant, a college English major, finds a copy of Dylan Thomas's poetry. He reads "And Death Shall Have No Dominion" and concludes that Dylan Thomas could not possibly have been in a war. Deeper into war and madness, Caputo, the officer, gives a go-ahead to a political assassination mission. His squad kills the wrong man. Tried and nearly convicted, he is forced to leave the Marine Corps. There remains an appended ending. Caputo, now a foreign correspondent, returns to witness the fall of Saigon. Lifting off in a helicopter with a bunch of evacuees, in type and image of a botched, unraveled, pointless mission, the splendid little war has come full circle. "Americans di-di?" asks a Vietnamese cohort—roughly, "Americans bug out?"— All he can say in return is "Yes, Americans di-di" (343).

Heinemann's *Close Quarters* takes place in the jungles of the Cambodian border patrolled by III Corps and about three years after Caputo's experience as a marine. The novel highlights the US Army major-unit war, the world of traditional infantry combat depicted in novels such as Winston Groom's *Better Times than These* (1978) and in big documentaries such as Eric Bergerud's *Red Thunder, Tropic Lightning* (1993). The setting is also shared with that of Oliver Stone's *Platoon*; coincidentally, the last battle scenes in both the film and Heinemann's novel are based on the Tet 1968 firebase defense at Suoi Tre, involving the units of both Stone and Heinemann. In general, *Close Quarters*, like *Platoon*, centers on small-unit combat in the jungles of the III Corps region near the Cambodian border. Further, the point of view is also that of an enlisted rifleman, Philip Dosier, like Stone's Chris Taylor, a perceptive, intelligent, blue-collar draftee who earns an education as a Vietnam grunt.

As with Caputo, in Heinemann one senses the pull of distinct literary analogies, many of them of recognizable earlier twentieth-century origin. The scared, boyish, and profane enlisted soldiers experiencing Vietnam War combat in Heinemann's book seem similar to the primary characters in *Im Westen nichts Neues* (1928; *All Quiet on the Western Front*, 1929) Barbusse's *Le Feu* (1916; *Under Fire*, 1917), or Dos Passos's *Three Soldiers* (1920). The book also nods to writers of World War II such as Jones and Mailer. At the same time, the time frame is notably mid-twentieth-century America. To use the economic terms of critic Christian Appy, the characters in *Close Quarters* are the newest blue-collar soldiers, war workers in the fullest sense. The unit is itself industrial: It is a mechanized infantry with armored cavalry assault vehicles with crudely designed rolling-gun platforms, each with a .50-caliber machine gun facing forward and two M60 infantry machine guns to the rear on both sides. Nonetheless, even with such hot, deadly machines, crewed by the infantry, the war remains essentially one of the patrol, the sweep, the outpost, the night defense position, and the ambush.

Dosier's narrative of initiation into combat becomes basically a traditional "buddy" story, with two spiritual guides, Cross and Quinn, both equally maddened, hopeless, and profane, helping to chart Dosier's journey deeper into war. The chapter titles tell the story: "Ugly Deadly Music," "Moon of Atevo," "Torque." Cross goes home; Atevo dies. Dosier kills a man with his bare hands. Rest and recreation (R and R) in Japan is "The Perfect Room." Back in Vietnam, the battles go on "By the Rule." Dosier murders a prisoner in cold blood. He makes it through the climactic battle at Suoi Cut. The new order of the day is "Going Home High." Dosier knows better. "Nobody goes home from here," he writes toward the end.

> Come on, fuck with me. I killed one dude with my bare hands, I broke a couple of bones in his throat and squeezed until his eyes bugged out and pounded him into the mud until I could hardly lift his head and the son of a bitch clucked and jiggled his arms, and died. I don't care—one more, ten more, a thousand more, it doesn't mean anything. (278)

This sentiment remains, even after all the letters home to the college girl, the eventual return, and the attempt to take up life again. No one wants to look you in the eye, and disguise does not matter either.

> "I would buy a pair of dark glasses," he imagines, "the darkest lenses I could find, and save myself the trouble of people leaning close to me and whispering, 'Dosier You know, you've got the oddest, strangest look in your eyes. Why is that, hey? What have you seen?" (295)

The gaze comes to possess Dosier, the look of the ambush; "the thousand-meter stare cranked down to fifty or five" won't leave (294). He returns home to his mother and father suddenly grown old; to a shot at domesticity with Jenny, the college girl; and a last visit to Quinn, the universal soldier, ironically killed in a truck wreck. "God damn you, Quinn," he says. "God damn, you" (336).

In *Chickenhawk*, the autobiographical account of a one-year tour in Vietnam as an American helicopter pilot, Mason tells another story of an American boy. From the outset, Mason knows he is born to fly; he rides his bicycle to the outskirts of his town to see daredevils in air shows. He is smart, but not book smart or school smart. He is brave, steady, and competent, but no hero. He is the antihero, Chickenhawk. The book charts his life as he goes through flight school, advanced training, and eventual deployment to Vietnam as part of the First Air Cavalry Division, the first fully airmobile major US infantry unit. Mason's tale moves at a hurtling pace, from his first experiences of combat, as he flies deeper into confrontation with benumbing fear, horror, and death. Even though the book seems to be an unassuming narrative, the education of a helicopter pilot, at some point, readers realize that Mason has flown in the great campaigns of the Ia Drang. He has survived the war in the Central Highlands.

The general history surrounding Mason's experiences comes later. Most of the narrative is about flying out of forward bases—Rifle Range, Golf Course, Happy Valley, the Turkey Farm; of call signs—

Deacon, Doc, Ringknocker, Sky King; and of crazy orders and even worse missions. The day-to-day work becomes increasingly dangerous, almost suicidal. The rear-area tensions pit warrant-officer pilots against military careerists of traditional officer rank, with the latter frequently incompetent both as commanders and as individual pilots. One by one, unit members with whom Mason has arrived are injured or killed; others crack up or get taken off flight status. When Mason begins to have dreams, then nightmares, then hallucinations, there is nothing spectacular about the trauma: He just knows he is starting to go crazy. On a last short-timer R and R to Hong Kong he is so troubled by his dreams that he returns to Vietnam after three days.

Eventually Mason gets to go home. His wife is waiting. Now all that is left is a question. "Epilogue:" he writes. "And then what happened." As it turns out, a lot happened. "My days were good; my nights were hell. I had been back from Vietnam for over a year. The dreams still oppressed me, and the unseen fear kept me bouncing out of bed." He gets grounded as an instructor pilot and decides to leave the army. He drinks and tries tranquilizers. He tries going back to college. Business deals fail. He quits his job. Ten years after Vietnam, the bills begin piling up. He gets involved in a drug-smuggling deal and is sentenced to five years in prison. "No one is more shocked than I," he writes in a last sentence (339). It seems prison is where his life had been heading since the Ia Drang.

In stories of the Vietnam War written by American men, women seem invariably consigned to traditional roles: wives, sweethearts, prostitutes, and R and R mistresses. Van Devanter represents the first of two major strains of women's in-country narratives of the Vietnam War: that of military nurses. (The other, represented by writers such as Gloria Emerson and Frances Fitzgerald, is that of correspondents.) At the time of the Vietnam War, being a nurse was a woman's most visible military experience. Van Devanter's narrative tells mainly of her journey toward and experiences within the system of evacuation and surgical hospitals, where the wounded of Vietnam were treated and frequently died. Like the youth narratives of Caputo, Heinemann, and Mason, Van Devanter's is also one of its time and place, an archetypal gender story of post–World War II young American women. Van Devanter is conventional, middle class, and Catholic. She is a product of the suburbs—in this case, Washington, DC, Maryland, and Virginia. Like many young women of the era, she earns her RN in a typical hospital nursing program. Her journey from army induction, medical corps training, and deployment to Vietnam reads like a 1960s women's road-trip film.

Vietnam changes everything in Van Devanter's life. She is assigned to the network of dust-off and evacuation units treating badly wounded soldiers brought in directly from the field. She finds herself in the worst of it at Pleiku in 1969, amid continuous heavy fighting between the First Cavalry and 101st Airborne and the North Vietnamese army regulars. Within days of their arrival, Van Devanter and her fellow nurses begin living their nightmares, with endless waves of broken, mutilated, screaming boys, mostly in their late teens or early twenties, coming in on helicopters with their legs and arms blown off, their bowels ripped open, or their brains dripping from their skulls. Relief comes predictably in alcohol, drugs, wild off-duty partying, casual sex, and serial affairs. Van Devanter eventually succumbs to her numb loneliness and has an affair with Carl, an older married surgeon, and later has another with Jack, a young doctor. Van Devanter writes an utterly conventional story but irredeemable in its everyday horror. The nurse becomes the American-girl diarist, writing letters home depicting the gruesomeness with which she is surrounded. "The Lynda I had known before the war was gone forever," she concludes (171).

After her tour of duty, Van Devanter goes home and tries to hitch a ride to the San Francisco airport. Still in uniform, she gets spit on and called a "Nazi bitch." Somebody yells, "Welcome home, asshole!" (212). Back with her family, she is assigned to Walter Reed Army Medical Center. Home again as well, Jack tells her good-bye. Van Devanter tries nursing in Los Angeles. Her technical skills are fine, but she is reduced by depression to speaking in monosyllables (258). She counts how many pills it would take to kill herself, but cannot go through with the act. "I was too afraid of dying," she says.

Toward the end, Van Devanter is nursing and married to Bill, who is working on a documentary on veterans' problems for an organization called Vietnam Veterans Against the War (VVAW). She deals with the emergent concept of post-traumatic stress disorder (PTSD). In the penultimate chapter, as of 1980, she is engaged in the VVAW women's project. "It has been a long, dark night," she writes, "but I'm finally reaching home" (303). Finally, with a veterans' group, she goes back to Vietnam. Together, the group celebrates Memorial Day while there. "Another memorial day for us," she concludes, "in Vietnam" (315).

In turning to *Novel without a Name*, the text of a young Vietnamese soldier's experience of the war as part of the communist liberation army, reflecting on names is beneficial. What Americans call the Vietnam War, the Vietnamese call the American War. Americans have also called the war the Ten-Year War. It became fashionable among American military theorists to say that, in Vietnam, the United States fought a one-year war ten times. The reference shows how integral to American experiential narratives of the war the one-year tour of duty was. The archetypal young American soldier begins his or her year at war as a "fucking new guy" (FNG). Somewhere in the middle of the tour, he or she takes a trip away from the combat zone for R and R. After the midway point of the tour, the soldier becomes a "short-timer." All that remained then was to survive and go home.

In *Novel without a Name*, all the categories, experiential and literary, are challenged. During the major period of the Vietnam conflict, Duong was a North Vietnamese female warrior, serving in a support unit specializing in propaganda and morale. The experiences in the text are those of communist forces in the combat zone. The text has a narrator, who relays the experiences of three soldiers, boyhood friends from the same village, and covers settings such as jungle base camps, bunkers, and tunnel complexes. The story is told in a recognizable first-person present tense but is combined with dreams, memories, flashbacks, fantasies, and nightmares. In many ways, the world of *Novel without a Name* has become the postmodern precinct of *The Forever War* (1974), eerily imagining a science-fiction counterpart to the world of Joe Haldeman. At the same time, the narrator's quest becomes much like a Vietnamese legend. The nomenclature of the title registers both the work's literary reflexiveness and its homage to ancient conventions of the classical Asian form. Its inhabits a landscape of culture and experience intensely physical, terrifying, highly spiritualized, and full of mysterious presences.

Quan, the narrator and the commander of a small fighting unit, is twenty-eight; He has been fighting the war for a decade, as have his two cohorts, Luong and Bien. Luong, a political soldier, has been elevated to a staff-officer position; Bien, the biggest and strongest of the village boys, has either gone insane fighting the war or is feigning insanity to achieve a psychiatric discharge. Luong assigns to Quan the mission of traveling through the dangerous war zone to investigate Bien's situation. As a reward, he will be allowed to travel home for a visit to his village, which would be his first since he marched away, singing patriotic songs, ten years earlier.

Novel without a Name is a deeply political novel. From the outset, Quan is compromised by the powerful status of Luong. He may have to betray Bien. For this, he will be rewarded with a visit home. He finds himself compromised by Bien also, who may be feigning insanity. Meanwhile, Quan's odyssey through the war zone takes on its own mysterious, dreamlike character. Relieved from command of his unit in a hideous zone of the war called the Gorge of Lost Souls—where a group of rotting women's bodies lie—he travels a network of trails presided over by shadowy watchers. He survives a random B-52 strike. He has sex with a hideously ugly female liaison agent. He finds refuge with a mysterious elder and his beautiful young granddaughters. He finds Bien in a filthy cage. They part when Bien is assigned to a unit in the deep jungle, crafting wooden coffins.

Whatever the work, Quan realizes, it is a kind of acceptance of death-in-life. "*Who knows?*" he says of the coffins being carried through the mountains to the front. "*Perhaps one of them is for me.* Like the other soldiers, I was prepared to accept this strange gift. Fighting and dying; two acts, the same indescribable beauty of the war" (192). In the village he has loved a young woman named Hoa. She is pregnant by another man. Returning to his unit, he finds a letter more than eight years old waiting for him, in which she has expressed her love and pleaded for his safe return.

In the unit, the fighting continues. Bien is reported dead. Luong admits to political cynicism. At the end, they have captured a Vietnamese base left behind by the Americans, with its boundless supplies, including whole shelves of priceless vitamin B_{12} serum. The soldiers begin firing wildly, mad to destroy every bit of bounty in sight. An American prisoner is taken. At a drunken victory banquet, a comrade sings a traditional peasant song: "I'm climbing on Mount Quan Doc, / I'm writing at the foot of the banyan tree." Quan reflects:

A mournful change we had wedded to the lament of a two-string guitar. . . . Chant of the months, of the years spent in the Truong Son mountains. Soldier, the dawn is icy. You fall under the bullets. On the white of the parachute cloth, I see your blood spreading. (288–89)

Whether written from the American perspective or the Vietnamese perspective, the books discussed in this essay seem to reach the same conclusion. The Vietnam War did incalculable damage to young people on both sides. The narratives traverse the abyss of memory and history to become portraits of a lost world. For the young Americans—Caputo, Heinemann, Mason, and Van Devanter—they left the stable world of prewar assumptions and values in Vietnam. For Duong's novel, as with Bao Ninh's *The Sorrow of War* (1995), the outcome is structurally and morally same as the outcome for the Americans. Gone is the Vietnamese world of the *xa*, a word for which there is no adequate English translation. In Vietnamese, it means something like "where people come together to visit the spirits."

For the authors who have written about the Vietnam War, one finds that fighting and writing about the war continue. Caputo and Heinemann have become major writers of their generation. Caputo is a journalist-novelist who explores the Conradian dark places of the world, while Heinemann won a National Book Award for *Paco's Story* (1986), the searing account of a Vietnam veteran's survival and return. After spending time in federal prison, Mason wrote a follow-up text of recovery, *Chickenhawk: Back in the World* (1993). His wife has become a prominent figure in veterans' counseling activities. For the two woman writers whose work is examined in the essay, the costs of remembering and writing have been high. When *Home before Morning* appeared, other nurse veterans complained, objecting to its sensational content. Van Devanter, after a lifetime of PTSD and intermittent alcoholism, died at forty-seven, most likely of war-related connective tissue disease. Duong, the author of several other novels critical of the postwar politics in the Socialist Republic of Vietnam, has served a jail term as an enemy of the state. American and Vietnamese, the authors were young people during the war willing to "pay any price, bear any burden," as John F. Kennedy said in his inaugural address. For many Americans who fought in the Vietnam War, the nation to which they returned seems not all that different from what the Vietnamese veteran described in one of Duong's other novels. The old hardliners prevail, she writes. To live at all is to inhabit the paradise of the blind.

Though the fighting ground might be different, the themes of modern war remain. Certain terms may have changed: Armies conscripted by economic and educational status are called "all-volunteer"; civilian casualties are "collateral damage"; "Unconventional" warfare has become "asymmetrical" combat. In the age of terror, one can argue that wars are increasingly fought by, on one hand, ideologically fanatical irregular fighters and, on the other, by highly trained, professional national-defense forces. No matter what, the young people of each generation are the ones who pay the heaviest price when it comes to war. As the poet Owen wrote in "Anthem for Doomed Youth":

> Not in the hands of boys but in their eyes
> Shall shine the holy glimmers of goodbyes.
> The pallor of girls' brows shall be their pall;
> Their flowers the tenderness of patient minds,
> And each slow dusk a drawing-down of blinds. (10–14)

As is known to many students of the history and literature of World War I, Owen was killed in the last week of combat. His parents received the news on the day of the armistice.

Works Cited

Caputo, Philip. *A Rumor of War*. New York: Holt, 1977.
Duong Thu Huong. *Novel without a Name*. New York: Penguin, 1995.
Heinemann, Larry. *Close Quarters*. Farrar, 1977.
Mason, Robert. *Chickenhawk*. New York: Viking, 1983.
Owen, Wilfred. "Anthem for Doomed Youth." *The Collected Poems of Wilfred Owen*.
      New York: New Directions, 1964. 44.
Van Devanter, Linda. *Home before Morning*. New York: Beaufort, 1983.

Other Worlds, Other Wars: Science Fiction Reinvents War _____

Tim Blackmore

> This is fictional life based on factual death.
>> (Samuel Fuller, director of *The Big Red One*)

Beyond merely forecasting how future wars might be fought, military science fiction (SF) addresses themes facing all writers of war fiction and considers whether the military is a beneficial or a detrimental societal force; whether individuality is strengthened or lost when one joins the military and joins a mass of others; if there is respite for individuals who, used to the rights guaranteed a democratic citizen, find themselves facing an uncaring chain of command that treats them as widgets rather than as human beings; if gender is erased by the military; and if gender might be the cause not only of militarism but also of war itself.

The Present's Future: A Survey of Military Science Fiction

Once composed of a relatively small group of science-fiction novels, military SF has become a thriving subgenre. Some military SF strives to resolve the conundrums facing democratic citizens who forfeit their freedom when they join a group that is by nature authoritarian and unitary. However, the bulk of military SF is absorbed with tales of combat, adventure, and what are supposed to be the valuable qualities of military life and discipline. Military SF concerned with philosophy and science, rather than adventure, attracts the attention of the military, research-and-development departments, the Pentagon, think tanks, and military schools.

While H. G. Wells's *War of the Worlds* (1898) is one of the most famous SF war books, no book in the genre has surpassed the popularity of Robert A. Heinlein's *Starship Troopers* (1959); Joe Haldeman's

The Forever War (1974) and Orson Scott Card's *Ender's Game* (1985) follow closely behind. *Starship Troopers* arrived propitiously before John F. Kennedy's 1961 call on the United States to "pay any price, bear any burden" in order to rescue the world (Kennedy 19). In *Starship Troopers* Juan "Johnnie" Rico joins the Mobile Infantry. There are two stories: One describes the Mobile Infantryman fighting "the bugs" (an alien hive intelligence) in his powered armor; the second concerns classes in history and moral philosophy taught by Johnnie's veteran mentor, who tells him that "the noblest fate that a man can endure is to place his own mortal body between his loved home and the war's desolation" (Heinlein 74). Only those who sign up to serve may become citizens and vote.

Ten years after the release of *Starship Troopers*, when combat veteran Haldeman returned from his tour in Vietnam, the United States was in the throes of social revolution. (Haldeman is one of the few combat veterans to write military SF; others include Jerry Pournelle, David Drake, and Elizabeth Ann Scarborough. For the most part, noncombatants or civilians have produced the canonical work—a fact worth pondering.) Haldeman's novel has a much more bitter tone than Heinlein's does. Protagonist William Mandella is drafted into a 1,143-year war with an alien race, and, with his integrated male–female, heterosexual–homosexual army, is sent on pointless and brutal missions during which "relativity traps us in the enemy's past; relativity brings them from our future" (Haldeman 105). Haldeman's characters are shocked out of their own time by a horrific future of endless war. The veterans of decades, then hundreds of years of war, remain physically young but are infinitely aged by war trauma. In Card's novel, humanity fights the "Buggers" (or "Formics"), an antlike race of hive minds. Ender and his teen commanders discover, upon slaughtering the alien race, the games they have been playing are real. Ender leaves Earth in search of an enemy, Hive Queen, so he can make amends for his genocide. These books form the tripod upon which rests all other contemporary military SF (Rabkin 19).

While Heinlein's promilitary, prowar novel was specifically answered by Harry Harrison's famous satire *Bill, the Galactic Hero* (1965), representing the beginning of decades of fictional and critical arguments about Heinlein's book (Stover 49), the most striking, if indirect, responses to *Starship Troopers* came from feminist SF writers like Ursula K. Le Guin, James Tiptree Jr. (pseudonym of Alice Bradley Sheldon), and Sheri S. Tepper. Stavia, the protagonist of Tepper's *The Gate to Women's Country* (1988), lives three hundred years in the future in a United States spotted by war–produced toxic "desolations." The known world is divided into the walled towns of Women's Country, outside of which are male-only warrior garrisons. Boys of fifteen are given a chance to return through the eponymous gate; if they do, they become women's servitors. Not slaves, the boys who have chosen to leave the garrisons apparently reject war in favor of peace and cooperation: Only these men are allowed to breed.

Tepper's attack on a patriarchal culture of violence and militarism caused her partially utopian novel (Abbott 524) to be itself much pilloried (the attacks would, ironically, come from within the feminist and queer academic communities as a response to her short but nasty attack on homosexuality as perversion to be bred out of the race). Her novel was shortly followed by Lois McMaster Bujold's *Barrayar* (1991), which, while told from the vantage point of an enlightened, supercompetent woman named Cordelia, is relatively sympathetic to a masculine, warlike feudal culture that employs high technology.

Scottish novelist Iain M. Banks's *Look to Windward* (2000) considers what it is to survive and remember the war dead. This novel is another entry in Banks's Culture novels about a future advanced human society run by artificial intelligences (AIs) and follows an alien suicide bomber, Quilan, whose mate has been killed in a war inadvertently caused by the Culture. He is set up for revenge by a group of old soldiers who live in a kind of afterlife: For Quilan's comrades to be allowed into heaven, he must kill five billion Culture subjects. This is a requiem for, and memory text about, those who have died in war.

Although it arrived nearly ten years after the end of the Persian Gulf War, the book, through its dedication ("For the Gulf War Veterans," referring to the 1991 Desert Shield and Desert Storm), announces itself as a commentary on that conflict, without specifying whether "veterans" encompass the hundreds of thousands of civilians and enemy soldiers who, like British and other coalition partners, also followed orders. The novel's dedication launches a text about terrorism, suicide bombers (an eerily prescient vision of the 9/11 terrorist attacks drives the narrative), and war's victims who are damaged to one degree or another.

Science-fiction romances emerged in the United States after the tradition of westerns had solidified. "Horse operas" and, later, "soap operas," were joined by "space operas": stories of romanticized, idealized, and often two-dimensional heroes, usually produced in series. In contrast, military SF tends to be hard-nosed, gritty, even cynical, and focused on combat, combat-related trauma and injury, and the quotidian reality of military life. Space opera is no longer a pejorative term, and includes much-loved works such as George Lucas's *Star Wars* films and David Eick and Ronald D. Moore's *Battlestar Galactica* television series, in which character development and interaction comes to the fore. However, contemporary military SF and military space opera overlap so much that attempting to separate them further into subgenres distracts from the political and moral issues the genres share.

Increasingly, women are writing military SF with female heroes (Bonner 4), which has not had an impact on what Chris Hables Gray calls the "deluge of future-war sf books [published] since 1980 that includes at least eight free-standing anthologies and seven anthology series, over 30 volumes altogether," that has served to strengthen "themes of male bonding, fatherhood, and especially the inevitability of war" (322). There is an enormous appetite for military SF (enough to sustain an entire publisher, Baen Books), whether or not the United States is at war (Connors 34). Some critics have argued that the success of military SF is directly related to what the United States considers its manifest destiny: "Sf . . . has been driven by a desire for the imaginary transformation of imperialism into Empire, viewed not primarily in terms of political and economic contests among cartels and peoples, but as a technological regime that affects and ensures the global control system of denationalized communications" (Csicsery-Ronay 232). Readers must consider if military SF is a superior, attractive form of national power fantasy.

No matter how alien it seems, SF is always about the human race and about human points of view. It is unclear how much SF is responsible for creating the battlefields of today or tomorrow. During World War II, famous writers of "hard" (scientifically and technologically accurate) SF, including Isaac Asimov and Heinlein, worked closely with the US military, sharing a kind of language and worldview (Gray 320). Charles E. Gannon notes that the creation of the think tank SIGMA in 2007 formalized the collaboration between numerous SF authors and military agencies (198). Rather than predict or create the future, SF imagines it: What happens afterward is dependent on the political, scientific, class, gender, and racial values of the times.

Soldier's Pay: Military Values, Valued Militaries?

This section considers how each novel constructs the military as a social force. While most military fiction in the early twentieth century is pro-military and often pro-war, things have not always been that way. Each novel sees the military's role in society differently. In *Starship Troopers*, the military creates discipline, respect, and obedience through agreement and ensures that society is governed by those who have willingly offered themselves as sacrifices. Retired Strategic Air Command B52 navigator and noted professor H. Bruce Franklin describes *Starship Troopers* as a reflection of a corporate United States in the late 1950s "that was attempting to hold and expand a worldwide empire against a rising tide of global revolution" (Franklin 112). In Heinlein's vision, the military is the foundation for everything valuable. He introduces three kinds of government, then chooses one, dismissing his contemporary US democracy because it has been over-powered by "junior hoodlums who roamed their streets [and] were symptoms of a greater sickness; their citizens (all of them counted as such) glorified their mythology of 'rights' . . . and lost track of their duties. No nation, so constituted, can endure" (Heinlein 96). He also attacks the bugs' hive mind. Fearful of authoritarian communism it saw operating in the Soviet Union and China, the United States embraced the Cold War (c. 1946–89) SF metaphor of ants, wasps, or bees for human communist collectives. This is seen in Heinlein's *The Puppet Masters* (1951); Jack Finney's *The Body Snatchers* (1955) and its four cinematic adaptations, including *Invasion of the Body Snatchers* (1956); and James Cameron's *Aliens* (1986). The government Heinlein chooses is run by veterans for the good of all.

Haldeman's military controls everything, too, but rather than being Heinlein's wholly benevolent force, Haldeman's army is a bureaucratic horror. The military determines who is worth sustaining: Each human's value is measured in kilocalories. All citizens are, as one of them later sums up, "Born, raised and drafted" (Haldeman 172). Heinlein's stern-but-fair paternalistic military becomes, in Haldeman's formulation, a ruthless organism that pursues its own survival at any cost (including the destruction of the human race). Published in the mid-1970s, when Americans confronted a perjured president whose regime was arguably guilty of war crimes in other countries (the secret bombing of Cambodia [Operation Menu]; the destruction of a democratically elected government in Chile) and realized that multinational corporations (Dow Chemical, IBM, Lockheed) partly governed the planet, *The Forever War* rang true to a generation that felt swindled by those in power. Betrayed yet again by the military, Mandella's lover complains to him: "It's so dirty"; he shrugs and answers, "It's so army" (Haldeman 160), an exchange unthinkable in *Starship Troopers*.

Even by 1985, Card's novel remained leery of the military as a force for good. The military repeatedly lies, cheats, re-creates truths, and puts Ender in mortal danger in order to test him. The military not only manipulates Ender and his family but also corrupts his sister Valentine, the unalloyed sign for good in the novel. Rather than being protected by Heinlein's enormous caring parental force, twelve-year-old Ender is made to learn cold truths familiar to Asian military historians. When Ender's tutor tells him: "I am your enemy, the first one you've ever had who was smarter than you. There is no teacher but the enemy. No one but the enemy will ever tell you what the enemy is going to do" (Card 262–63), one hears echoes of classic military texts like Miyamoto Musashi's *Gorin no sho* (c. 1643; *The Book of Five Rings*, 1974), Tsunetomo Yamamoto's *Hagakure* (1716; *Hagakure: The Book of the Samurai*, 1979), and Sun Tzu's *Ping-fa* (5th century BCE; *The Art of War*, 1905). The amoral military commits crimes, breaks taboos, and reduces Ender to an object in order to achieve its goals: "You had to be a weapon, Ender. Like a gun . . . functioning perfectly but not knowing what you were aimed at. *We* aimed you. We're responsible" (Card 298).

Tepper's resistance to the military as a societal organization is rooted in both the feminism and pacifism of the early 1970s. Tepper identifies the military not only as a source of masculine planetary destruction but also as the creator of a worldview that demands the ownership of women for the purposes of breeding, sex, or rape (Tepper 260, 209, 237). The garrisons' warriors understand women to be slaves who, while they think they run things, wind up doing all the work (Tepper 66–68). Tepper's utopia posits that "penis worship" (295) and the military way of life are so snarled as to be inseparable. The penis "doesn't exist independently," one character argues, "except to warriors" (Tepper 58–59), and so both the symbolism of the penis and the military must be eradicated. Tepper's utopian satire provokes readers to consider other ways of thinking about military power.

By the time Bujold wrote *Barrayar*, the US armed forces had changed significantly: It had become an all-volunteer military and was moving toward allowing women into combat (the United States accepted women into aviation combat in 1993). Although *Barrayar's* Cordelia questions the military, she has been a soldier and, thus, honors other soldiers. Bujold's novel arrived at a time when most Americans, exhilarated by the one-hundred-day victory over Iraq, agreed with then President George H. W. Bush's famous statement: "By God, we've kicked the Vietnam syndrome once and for all" (qtd. in Toner). Bujold's novels honor the soldier and military service, if not the war. The Vorkosigan series also makes the reader comfortable with Barrayar's deeply military culture. While Cordelia has no use for mindless heroics ("Suicidal glory is the luxury of the irresponsible" [Bujold 335]), her son Miles amasses every military honor its culture can bestow on him. The Barrayaran military and Miles's own private army are all painted in warm, friendly hues, and are repositories of both high moral values and one's best friends and lovers.

Although *Look to Windward* was published before 9/11, it addresses the complexity of a benevolent empire that, despite its best intentions, commits atrocity in the name of human rights. The book is narratively, philosophically, and politically complex, and treats military ethics with great care—the ambiguity and problems faced by characters in Haldeman and Tepper's novels are brought to their full aching reality here. None (except the very loud, vengeful alien dead) is convinced the wars they have fought have been worthwhile. *Look to Windward* condemns thoughtless action based on blind certainties and dogma. When the old soldiers gather at the end of the novel, they join in a lament and make what peace they can, part of which involves rejecting the military's codes and moral guides. The reader could hardly have come further from Heinlein's near-Manichean certitudes: everything in Banks's novel shades into complexity.

Militarism: What War Is Good For

Part of the issue in representing war, whether on film or in prose, poetry, or graphics, is that it may become attractive no matter what its intended message. Militarism informs not only the culture in which it exists but also the texts used to sustain society's myths. For Franklin, "*Starship Troopers* imagines and applauds a future in which the imperialism of

Earth has become virtually cosmic" (Franklin 112), a future based on the United States' mythic vision of itself as a model "city on a hill," according to Puritan divine John Winthrop (41). In Heinlein's world, peace is a figment of the pacifist's befuddled imagination, a view echoed by his staunch follower Pournelle, who claims that "peace is a purely theoretical state of affairs" (Pournelle viii). Pournelle's truism is much repeated in the world of military SF that subsists, after all, on endless stories of war. Haldeman's protagonist has a slightly different viewpoint: Mandella recognizes that wars have "often accelerated social reform, provided technological benefits, even sparked artistic activity," but he knows that "This one, however, seemed tailor-made to provide none of these positive by-products" (138). The human race comes to a cultural halt and stagnates, leaving Mandella to conclude that "the most important fact about the war to most people was that if it ended suddenly, Earth's economy would collapse" (139). In Heinlein's world, war exists for the good of humanity; in Haldeman's, war exists for itself.

Between these two extremes oscillates *Ender's Game*: Card accepts military necessity but is unwilling to wholly cede power to any group. One of Ender's friends warns him that "The Battle School didn't create us, you know. The Battle School doesn't create *anything*. It just destroys" (109). This is not quite true, since the Battle School is the instrument that transforms the children into an unbeatable army. Michael Collings argues convincingly that *Ender's Game* is deeply ambiguous: "If Ender were intended simply as a Heinleinian juvenile hero, and if the narrative were nothing more than an unsophisticated exercise in highly commercialized 'sci fi,' the action of the novel would logically conclude" with Ender's victory (Collings 108).

Ambiguity has little place in Tepper's enraged, sorrowful book about male violence. The novel equates masculine violence and militarism with planetary ecological destruction, the near-genocide of the human race and other living species. While Tepper's solution is brutal, it is also possibly satirical, and certainly belongs to the kinds of warnings issued in both utopias and dystopias. Wendy Pearson argues that

Tepper's text is as guilty of hatred and anger as any pro-war text (218–20); its undeniable homophobia seems at odds with its overall message (76). While the women of Women's Country act ruthlessly when necessary, they refuse all forms of militarism. Although Bujold's *Barrayar* valorizes Miles ("soldier" in Latin) Vorkosigan's exploits and membership in the military family, the novel shows less patience for a world built solely on military honor: "She nailed Vordarian's men by eye, as they backed from the table. 'Officers, I recommend that when this conference resumes, you surrender unconditionally. . . . I'm tired of your stupid war. End it'" (Bujold 354–55). Cordelia's rage, that of a mother who has saved four children, prevails. However, war is ended by Cordelia's own romantic, unbelievable, melodramatic derring-do—it is all splendid clever action, luck, and staging.

There is no romance about the "light of ancient mistakes" that bathes *Look to Windward* (25), which is ambivalent about militarism (particularly military intervention in other countries), as are Banks's other Culture books. Banks pays close attention to all the victims, each death suffered. None is more important than another, and all must be remembered. In the face of a mass death, refining one's view is infinitely difficult. Paying attention to victims is not enough to satisfy some of Banks's critics who feel that the Culture excuses imperialism (Hardesty 43), although some are more sympathetic to Banks's politics (Duggan 567).

Most military SF naturalizes or romanticizes military culture and militarism. There is no subgenre that focuses on "peace SF" or "conflict resolution SF." As Gray puts it: "The majority of pro-war stories [have] a more basic claim that war is a necessary aspect of human nature and/ or manhood, that it is natural and inevitable, and that humans will need to fight nasty aliens someday besides" (315–16). What objections there are to militarism come largely from two ideas: The first proposes that humans will save themselves because they ultimately prefer to be individuals rather than lose themselves in a faceless military crowd; the second suggests that as humans evolve away from misogyny and intolerance, they can also set aside their fascination with, and belief in, war.

Individualism and Gender: Putting "I" before "War"

Soldiers, particularly, find themselves caught in the conundrum of having to forfeit their personal rights in order to protect the rights of others. Two themes with which military SF deals in depth are individualism and gender. Each seems to propose a way out of militarism, possibly of war. The American individual is both created and supported by the Constitution and the Bill of Rights. Anxiety about individual identity continues to grip American cultural imaginary, as films such as *The Matrix* franchise (1999–2003) and television shows such as the 2004 iteration of *Battlestar Galactica* demonstrate. There is a constant struggle between a powerful belief in the individual's supremacy and the sense that societal welfare comes first. Wars (declared or undeclared) against communist countries (North Korea, North Vietnam, Cambodia) made Americans question whether their communist enemies were human; they fought in massed waves, seemed to care little or nothing for their own safety, and sacrificed themselves for paltry military objectives. The same puzzlement struck Western troops facing suicide bombers in Iraq and Afghanistan: Are enemy soldiers separate thinking beings or mindless slaves herded to slaughter by inhuman commanders? Heinlein's Johnnie Rico explains the Cold War anxiety implicit in an apparently endless horde of (communist) bugs:

> Every time we killed a thousand Bugs at a cost of one M.I. [Mobile Infantry trooper] it was a net victory for the Bugs. We were learning, expensively, just how efficient a total communism can be when used by a people actually adapted to it by evolution: the Bug commissars didn't care any more about expending soldiers than we cared about expending ammo. (121)

Johnnie is reassured that even if he has surrendered himself to the military, he and his fellow soldiers are independent entities with their own biological futures (Stover 50). In *The Forever War*, Mandella discovers the savage irony of fighting for human individuality only to have it erased by the new clone identity that is: "over ten billion individuals but only one consciousness" (Haldeman 260).

Because he assumes responsibility for all his actions, whether or not the military exonerates him, Ender staggers under the burden of individuality. Horrified, he learns that the alien queens thought they "were the only thinking beings in the universe, until we met you . . . who cannot dream each other's dreams. How were we to know? We could live with you in peace. Believe us, believe us, believe us" (Card 321). The hive mind understands only what it knows: Groups of singular intelligences present a contradiction to the Buggers. Card overwhelms militarism when he suggests that the warrior must love the enemy if the enemy is to be destroyed. That love is part of war is foreign to most military SF. Card pours enormous responsibility into the individual's hands, trusting personal morality over militarism's certainty. It is the individual, Ender, who triumphs over not only the alien queen but also the Battle School's world of war.

The United States' much-loved charismatic maverick gunslinger—the tall-walking, slow-talking man of action (e.g., John Carter, Luke Skywalker, Neo, Batman)—may provide a cover for how Americans actually behave. Civilians who become soldiers may be deeply worried about losing their identity. However, there can also be comfort and pleasure in joining the military, because the group confers identity and distributes responsibility for its behavior. The maverick represents the idea of a person who cannot be bent to the populace's will, who adheres to his or her own code of honor but who is true to American ideals. While few may have the emotional, psychological, and physical wherewithal to play the role, the myth that each person is like this at heart is seductive: The gunfighter is a consummate "professional man of arms, cool, isolated, self-sufficient, capable of self-defense under any circumstances, who measures all things and all men by the canons of his calling" (Slotkin 438). Corollary to the solitary maverick is the horde of bugs in the alien army. Fears inherent to the human mass are then transferred to the alien: They are the ones who join without thinking, fight without knowing whether the cause is just, and die without purpose because they have not chosen their own future.

Just as Ender must bear responsibility for an unintentional genocide, Tepper's characters assume the full burden of the breeding program in which they engage and will break most of their own laws to complete their long-term plans (291). Arguably, the women of Women's Country are as bloody-minded as Card's military. Unlike Heinlein's military, however, the governors of Women's Country have planned their own eradication. Stavia represents the new, troubled breed of individuals who question their every action.

The individual appears to be the whole story in Bujold's Vorkosigan books. Miles thrives because his charm and quick intelligence make him a likable hero. The Vorkosigan series is deceptively attractive because readers cheer on a culture that, despite its apparent wish to set aside warfare and espionage, embraces militarism. Bujold creates a czarist court replete with class division of labor, serfs, women as second-class humans, and war as a grand game through which both individuals and their culture prosper. This is no grim picture of the military life; rather, the individual is utterly fulfilled by swearing oaths of loyalty to beneficent (or clearly monstrous) masters. Sylvia Kelso argues that Bujold writes from "the anti-war, 'pro-people' stances common to the peace movement and to many feminists" (10), ultimately concluding, somewhat weakly, that Bujold argues for the individual and against the military. Frances Bonner has argued, however, that Bujold's work "is feminized rather than feminist and, far from challenging the conventions which limit space opera, it eagerly embraces them" (Bonner 6). Both Kelso and Bonner's comments lead to the reconsideration of militarism through gender's lens: War texts written by women about women are not necessarily feminist or pacifist (consider Elizabeth Moon's *Serrano* series).

Two texts stand in stark opposition to each other when it comes to gender: *Starship Troopers* and *The Gate to Women's Country*. In the first, women serve as starship pilots, which makes them even more revered as beautiful, unattainably pure angels for whom men die (Johnnie calls them "the ultimate reason you are fighting" [Heinlein 125]). Johnnie's overbearing oedipal mother, who writes him emasculating letters, is soon killed, freeing Johnnie's father to "prove to myself that I was a man. Not just a producing-consuming economic animal . . . but a *man*" (Heinlein 136). In *Starship Troopers*, a man knows himself by acting on the will to fight and die. In Tepper's novel, biology is destiny. War is twisted into the strands of men's DNA and must be unthreaded if humans are to survive the war gene. The myth governing Women's Country is that women are helpless before the male garrisons, that they are, as in Heinlein's text, precious creatures to be fought over and protected. However, the reality is that the women are playing roles (much of the novel involves a reworked version of Euripides's play *Trōiades* [415 BCE; *The Trojan Women*, 1782], which provides metatextual commentary) and are engaged in unblinking social and biological engineering. There is no space for disagreement in Women's Country: It is run by a committee's iron hand (one that ultimately organizes an entire garrison's slaughter). Tepper's novel is useful as a thought experiment because it suggests social engineering might allow society to choose life over war. The women in Tepper's novel are up to their elbows in making the present and the future: They are not precious beings, nor do they need to prove themselves through killing.

Finally, it is Haldeman's *Forever War* that first saw so clearly into the struggle over gender in future war. Haldeman's novel proposed an army divided evenly between male and female soldiers: The genders, made equal by virtue of the armored fighting suits, no longer provide an excuse for exempting women from combat. Soldiers are encouraged to sleep with each other in nonmonogamous relationships so as to vent their battlefield frustrations through mindless sex. The ominous quality of these couplings emerges when Haldeman tells us that the women are "compliant and promiscuous by military custom (and law)" (45). Haldeman understood military logic in 1975 (no soldiers were to be wasted in a culture of total war) would result in full conscription. He even saw ahead to an entirely lesbian and queer army that carries out its orders as well as any heterosexual male army has ever done.

Cultural critics were not far behind on the same issues. Cynthia Enloe identifies that it is "by taking women's experiences of militarization seriously . . . that we are most likely to understand it fully. . . . [Militarization] tends to insinuate itself into ordinary daily routines where it is rarely heralded or even deemed noteworthy" (3). In *The Forever War* the collapse begins when the genders merge and are then equally devalued by the military forces that govern the human race. Enloe methodically retraces the paths Haldeman took in his thought experiment, much as Marilyn Waring does in her famous book *Counting for Nothing* (1999; originally published as *If Women Counted*, 1990). Waring ably demonstrates that war, which produces staggering human and environmental destruction, is considered by economists to be of enormous economic worth, in a system in which women and children (true producers, for Waring) have little or no monetary value (139). Like Tepper, Enloe, and Waring, other scholars are studying both the specific impact of war on the environment and the prospect that "the earth can no longer absorb the punishment of war, especially on a scale and with a ferocity that only the wealthiest, most powerful country in the world—no, in history—knows how to deliver" (Sanders 21). The ground has shifted in these last paragraphs from a stark disagreement about the role of men and women in warfare and peace work to the proposal that soon all humans will be as valueless in the eyes of the military and to a final question about the fate of the planet. This chain of themes is inextricable, as Tepper argued.

Science Magic: Narratives of Progress

While readers might expect that military SF will privilege both progress and high technology, that is not always so. Some military SF is committed to the advancement of military science, but much military SF rides on old technology or imagines technologies that parallel those current in the late eighteenth or the early nineteenth centuries (for example, David Weber's Honor Harrington series proposes galactic naval vessels that fight much as British, French, and Spanish armadas did in the Napoleonic Wars). Some SF seems to be almost antitechnology, or chooses low technology over high. Military SF continues to be militarist, to follow templates laid by Heinlein, and to portray the military as a largely functional, happy family. Part of the security offered readers by military SF is that the world appears to operate according to enlightened rationalism, progress, and merit. The military is a stern, fair, parental (usually father) figure that rewards those who perform well (implicitly, performing well means performing good deeds).

Heinlein was the first to discuss in detail how a mechanized suit of battle armor (combined space suit and weapons platform) would be operated by the user. The US government's Defense Advanced Research Projects Agency (DARPA) has been working on a mechanized suit for decades (Blackmore *War X*, 45–50). Heinlein's suit withstands tactical nuclear bombs: So great is Heinlein's belief in engineers and engineering, so staunch his faith in the narrative of American progress, that the most feared thing then, in an era of melting nuclear power plants, becomes a footnote in a battle: Johnnie casually tosses around nuclear rockets and grenades on the battlefield (13). Equally, Heinlein believed that prosthetics necessitated by battlefield amputations would allow humans to continue to function perfectly in both war and peace (35). He missed what Haldeman understood: The person who is part machine, or cybernetic organism (cyborg), is also no longer fully human. Lost body parts cost most soldiers part of their psychological selves as well.

In Haldeman's eyes, scientific advances bring war full circle to the invention of what he calls a "stasis field" that slows time and stops electricity. After nearly a millennium of warfare, human and Tauran technology forces hand-to-hand combat. *The Forever War*'s final battle starts when Mandella, fully equipped with the best powered armor centuries of war can develop, "drew [his] sword and waited" (251). Haldeman's experiences in Vietnam taught him that high technology does not guarantee victory: Both sides may be losers if they invest in an ongoing arms race that beggars everyone. However, for DARPA, many American scientists, and other interested parties, the technology in both Heinlein and Haldeman's novels represent a desirable future.

In the American imagination, attitudes toward war technology have been complex. Often films, television shows, novels, and graphic novels side with a guerrilla force that is undermanned and must rely on relatively unsophisticated technologies. The Ewoks of Lucas's *Return of the Jedi* (1983), humans in Cameron's *The Terminator* films (1984, 1991) and his 1986 *Aliens*, the crew of the *Nebuchadnezzar* (and, by extension, community of Zion) in the Wachowskis' *Matrix* films, and the Na'vi of Cameron's *Avatar* (2009), all show indigenous (often a code for "primitive") populations overcoming forces far superior in number and advanced weaponry. Although the United States was defeated in such a war in Vietnam and has been tied down in two such wars in Iraq and Afghanistan (in all three cases arraying the most advanced of information, weapons, and signal systems of any military in history to fight relatively untrained, badly armed, and poorly fed troops), it continues to see itself as the underdog, siding with the Ewoks of Endor against the Emperor's malign forces. As in other cases, science fiction helps to smooth over rough truths that society may wish to avoid.

Conclusion

It may be comforting to accept military fantasies as reality, particularly when stories are presented as innocent military romances. However, there does not seem to be such a thing as an innocent war romance. Heinlein's *Starship Troopers*, in successfully fusing the bildungsroman, the hard-science military adventure, and what Richard Slotkin has identified as the American gunfighter myth (16), has created a narrative in form and content that still has astonishing power. Military SF and military space opera have built on and continued Heinlein's work: Korean war veteran Pournelle wrote a famous and popular series about a heroic mercenary soldier (John Christian Falkenberg); Drake, a Vietnam War veteran, has also made a living writing military SF that does much to glamorize war (his *Hammer's Slammers* series). The grittier these texts, the more believable and attractive they are to readers. Pournelle and Drake have fostered generations of military SF writers, just as they were influenced by Heinlein. Interest in war does not necessarily make militarist readers, but as one critic notes: "Unfortunately, there are many [readers], according to Drake's Web site, who don't understand 'the difference between description and advocacy, or who deny that there is a difference'" (Connors 34). Drake's implication that he writes war description rather than pro-war SF seem disingenuous: One piece of military SF or military space opera tends to breed another. All texts, particularly military SF, attempt to persuade the reader of something. Most military SF is written with both deep passion for the military and a belief in the righteousness of a militarist worldview. However, belief does not necessarily make something so. If nothing else, war has revealed such a truth.

Works Cited

Abbot, Philip. "Utopian Problem-Solving: *The Great Divorce* and the Secession Question." *The Journal of Politics* 62.2 (2000): 511–33.

Banks, Iain M. *Look to Windward*. London: Orbit, 2000.

Blackmore, Tim. "Save Now [Y/N]? Machine Memory at War in Iain Banks' *Look to Windward*." *Bulletin of Science, Technology and Society* 30.4 (2010): 259–73.

_____. *War X: Human Extensions in Battlespace*. Toronto: U of Toronto P, 2005.

Bonner, Francis. "From the Female Man to the Virtual Girl: Whatever Happened to Feminist SF?" *Hecate* 22.1 (1996): 1–11.

Bujold, Lois McMaster. *Barrayar*. New York: Baen, 1991.

Card, Orson Scott. *Ender's Game*. New York: Tor, 1994.

Collings, Michael R. *In the Image of God*. Westport, CT: Greenwood, 1990.

Connors, Scott. "The Politics of Military SF." *Publishers Weekly* 7 Apr. 2008: 34–35.

Csicsery-Ronay, Istvan, Jr. "Science Fiction and Empire." *Science Fiction Studies* 30 (2003): 231–45.

Drake, David. "Introduction." *Hammer's Slammers*. New York: Ace Books, 1979.

Duggan, Robert. "Iain M. Banks, Postmodernism, and the Gulf War." *Extrapolation* 48.3 (2007): 558–77.

Enloe, Cynthia. *Maneuvers*. Berkeley: U of California P, 2000.

Franklin, H. Bruce. *Robert A. Heinlein: America as Science Fiction*. New York: Oxford UP, 1980.

Gannon, Charles E. "Imag(in)ing Tomorrow's Wars and Weapons." *Peace Review: A Journal of Social Justice* 21.2 (2009): 198–208.

Gray, Chris Hables. "'There Will Be War!': Future War Fantasies and Militaristic Science Fiction in the 1980s." *Science Fiction Studies* 21 (1994): 315–36.

Haldeman, Joe. *The Forever War*. New York: St. Martin's, 2009.

Hardesty, William H. "Mercenaries and Special Circumstances: Iain M. Banks's Counter-Narrative of Utopia, Use of Weapons." *Foundation the International Review of Science Fiction* 28.76 (1999): 39–47.

Heinlein, Robert. *Starship Troopers*. Berkeley: Berkeley, 1968.

Kelso, Sylvia. "Loud Achievements: Lois McMaster Bujold's Science Fiction." *Three Observations and a Dialogue: Round and about SF*. Seattle: Aqueduct, 2009.

Kennedy, John F. "Inaugural Address of John F. Kennedy." *Current* 510 (Feb. 2009): 19–20.

Mauldin, Bill. *Up Front*. 1945. New York: Norton, 2000.

Pearson, Wendy. "After the (Homo)Sexual: A Queer Analysis of Anti-Sexuality in Sheri S. Tepper's *The Gate to Women's Country*." *Science Fiction Studies* 23 (1996): 199–226.

Rabkin, Eric S. "Reimagining War." *Fights of Fancy*. Eds. George Slusser and Eric S. Rabkin. Athens: U of Georgia P, 1993. 12–25.

Sanders, Barry. *The Green Zone*. Oakland: AK, 2009.

Slotkin, Richard. *Gunfighter Nation*. New York: Atheneum, 1992.

Stover, Leon E. *Robert A. Heinlein*. Boston: Twayne, 1987.

Tepper, Sheri S. *The Gate to Women's Country*. New York: Bantam, 1989.

Toner, Robin. "Phases of War: Politics; Did Someone Say 'Domestic Policy'?" *The New York Times* 3 Mar. 1991. 8 June 2011.

Waring, Marilyn. *Counting for Nothing*. Toronto: U of Toronto P, 2004.

Winthrop, John. "A Model of Christian Charity." *The Norton Anthology of American Literature*. 3rd ed. Eds. Nina Baym, et al. 1989. 41.

Women Writing War: Female Voices from the Combat Zone

Catherine Calloway

War has traditionally been considered a male-oriented discourse. When one thinks of war writing, the literary works that most frequently come to mind are those written by men, works such as Stephen Crane's *The Red Badge of Courage* (1895), Erich Maria Remarque's *Im Westen nichts Neues* (1928; *All Quiet on the Western Front*, 1929), James Jones's *The Thin Red Line* (1962), Norman Mailer's *The Naked and the Dead* (1948), Joseph Heller's *Catch-22* (1961), Michael Herr's *Dispatches* (1977), Tim O'Brien's *The Things They Carried* (1990), and Sebastian Junger's *War* (2010). The list of male accounts is endless; however, all too often, the war narratives of women are overlooked. Certainly, women have always been a part of the war experience, whether as active participants in the combat zone or as holders of other roles on the home front. As Linda Grant De Pauw so aptly states, "Women have always and everywhere been inextricably involved in war, [but] the roles of women in war are hidden from history. . . . During wars, women are ubiquitous and highly visible; when wars are over and the war songs are sung, women disappear" (xiii).[1]

In their study *Hell Hath No Fury: True Stories of Women at War from Antiquity to Iraq* (2010), Rosalind Miles and Robin Cross call attention to some of the many female figures throughout history who have actually served in combat. These include Japanese samurai warrior Tomoe Gozen (4, 22), Arabic princess Khawlah bint al-Azwar al-Kind'yya (2, 9), Frankish empresses Fredegund and Brunhilde (15), the Egyptian queen Cleopatra VII (19), the Vietnamese Trung sisters (1), American Revolutionary War soldier Deborah Sampson (80), British army soldier Flora Sandes (82), various Amazon women (5), and suicide bombers (11).

Joshua S. Goldstein in *War and Gender* (2001) reminds readers that in "the eighteenth- and nineteenth-century Dahomey Kingdom of West

Africa . . . a large-scale female combat unit . . . functioned over a long period as part of a standing army" (60). Helen Zenna Smith reveals in *Not So Quiet . . . Stepdaughters of War* ([1930] 1989) that British women drove ambulances along the front lines in World War I. Also, during Nazi Germany's invasion during World War II, the Soviet Union suffered a shortage of both workers and soldiers and began to draft women, first as part of the labor force and then as military workers (Goldstein 64–65). Nearly "500,000 [Soviet women] served at the front" (Goldstein 65). Female guerrilla fighters have existed in a variety of countries as well, including Northern Ireland, South Africa, Israel, Argentina, Vietnam, and Iran (Goldstein 77–78). Furthermore, Joan of Arc, who rallied the French army to defeat English forces during the Hundred Years' War, is well-known throughout history and is cited in most studies of women and war, including those of Miles and Cross (4, 22) and Goldstein (116–17).

Despite the prevalence of women in the war zone, Miles and Cross note, "the reality of the woman fighter, taking up her weapons for war and staking her life on her strength and skill, has proved hard to accept" (2). A fictional example from the Vietnam War illustrates this lack of acceptance. In O'Brien's story "Sweetheart of the Song Tra Bong," a chapter in *The Things They Carried*, soldiers have to deal with the experience of an American woman who becomes absorbed into the "heart of darkness" of the combat zone. When one soldier, Mark Fossie, arranges for his girlfriend, Mary Anne Bell, to travel to Vietnam, he never expects her to take a keen interest in the war. Before the distraught Fossie realizes what is happening, the blonde-haired, blue-eyed Mary Anne sheds her white culottes and pink sweater and starts going on patrols with a group of Green Beret soldiers, camouflaging herself, carrying a weapon, and wearing "a necklace of human tongues" (O'Brien 110). "She had crossed to the other side," O'Brien writes. "She was part of the land. . . . She was dangerous. She was ready for the kill (116). O'Brien uses the example of Mary Anne Bell to point out that war changes everyone, regardless of gender: "What happened to her . . . was what happened to all of them. You come over clean and you get dirty and then afterward it's never the same" (114).

An example such as O'Brien's that illustrates the absorption of women into the war experience naturally raises important questions: Why do women desire to experience combat and choose to actively participate in warfare? How do the voices of women who have experienced combat and who have exchanged the traditional feminine role of life-giver for that of life-taker provide an alternative history to a long culture of male-driven wars? Also, once having undergone the experience, why do these women feel compelled to write of war? Since each individual war experience is unique, the reasons vary.

The American Civil War generated some of the first memorable accounts by women who chose to participate in warfare.[2] Some women believed strongly in supporting the cause, whether it was Confederate or Union. Others did not want to be separated from their male family members, especially their husbands.[3] Still others wanted to serve as nurses or domestic workers. However, most of these women's written accounts of the war did not receive immediate publication. While Sarah Emma Edmonds's *Memoirs of a Soldier, Nurse and Spy: A Woman's Adventures in the Union Army* was published in 1865 at the end of the Civil War, other accounts such as *A Woman Doctor's Civil War: Esther Hill Hawks' Diary* and *An Uncommon Soldier: The Civil War Letters of Sarah Rosetta Wakeman, Alias Pvt. Lyons Wakeman, 153rd Regiment, New York State Volunteers, 1862–1864* were not discovered until years later. Hawks's three-volume diary, begun in 1862, was not located until 1975, when Mr. and Mrs. Eldon Porter accidentally found it in trash left behind during the renovation of an Essex County, Massachusetts, building (Schwartz vii). Wakeman's letters, written between November 24, 1862, and April 14, 1864, were quietly saved by family members for over a century before they were shared with Lauren Cook Burgess, a female Civil War reenactor, who edited them for publication in 1994 (Burgess xv) and photocopied and placed them in the Library of Congress (Burgess vxii).

Both Edmonds and Wakeman masqueraded as men in order to participate in the Civil War. However, since Edmonds's memoir is, as Elizabeth D. Leonard notes, written mainly for entertainment and is "a romanticized, much embellished" (xxi) account, then perhaps Wakeman's straightforward letters that were addressed solely to her family and not intended for publication are more relevant to a study of war and gender.

Sarah Rosetta Wakeman enlisted in the Union army in 1862, citing her age as twenty-one instead of nineteen and her name as "Lyons" Wakeman.[4] She had previously worked in other traditionally male roles, first as a farmer and then as a boatman (Burgess 9–10). In her letters, which reveal her lack of formal education in their deviation from standard English usage,[5] Wakeman indicates that she received encouragement to enlist in the Union army by soldiers whom she encountered through her work on the Chenango Canal who emphasized the financial benefits of soldiering available only to men. "I got 100 and 52$ in money," Wakeman writes to her family in a November 24, 1862, letter, in which she recounts the news of her enlistment (18). Throughout her epistles, she expresses her interest in offering financial aid to her family—her parents and eight siblings—who struggled economically.

In the November 24, 1862, letter, Wakeman adds, "All the money i send you i want you should spend it for the family in clothing or something to eat. Don't save it for me for i can get all the money i want " (18). Furthermore, Wakeman comments in a March 29, 1863, epistle that she hopes that she will survive the war so that she can continue to support her family. "When I get out of the service," she writes, "I will make money enough to pay all the debts that you owe" (25), an ambitious undertaking for a woman of the mid-1800s. As Burgess notes in her introduction, "Like other women before her who faced similar family situations or worse, Rosetta realized that one of the only ways open to finding an honorable position that paid enough for her to assist her indebted family was by dressing and acting the part of a man" (9). In fact, she considers "re-enlis[ting] for five years" because she would receive "eight hundred dollars bounty" (58) from the government, an amount that would have been a small fortune in the 1800s.

It is apparent that Wakeman enjoyed her masculine role and the freedom that came from masquerading as a man. She writes that she does not mind the hard life of a soldier, which required her to sleep on boards on the ground and "to use the floor for a table" (22). In addition, she implies that she found her feminine role at home oppressive. Wakeman informs her parents, "I can tell you what made me leave home. It was because I had got tired of stay[ing] in that neighborhood. . . . I will Dress as I am a mind to for all anyone else [cares], and if they don't let me Alone they will be sorry for it" (31). She also expresses interest in owning a farm someday, perhaps "in Wisconsin. On the Prairie" (31), but makes no reference to desiring marriage or to sharing her farm with a husband. Wakeman's independence is emphasized throughout her letters. She describes herself "as independent as a hog on the ice" (42) and speaks of herself in masculine terms: "I am the fattest fellow you ever see" (27) and " tough as a bear" (48).

Civil War accounts such as Wakeman's indicate the relative ease with which women can transition from one gender role to another. Life as a soldier seems to suit Wakeman. In a letter to her father, she tells him that she doesn't mind where her regiment goes or what they encounter in warfare. "I don't fear the rebel bullets nor I don't fear the cannon" (25), she writes, then adds, "When you think of me think where I am. It would make your hair stand out to be where I have been. How would you like to be in the front rank and have the rear rank load and fire their guns over you[r] shoulder? I have been there my Self" (26–27).[6]

As Burgess notes, Wakeman takes pride that her military prowess matches that of the men in her unit (12). She "like[s] to drill," she confesses: "I [c]an drill just as well as any man there is in my regiment" (48), and she is adept at handling her weapon. She also reveals that she has been in one fight with a male soldier, Stephen Wiley, and won, having "give[n] him three or four pretty good cracks" (60). Most of the other soldiers she finds likable, but she expresses scorn for male officers whose only goal in the war is to make enough money to resign.

While Wakeman does not appear to serve with other women in the Union army, she reveals an awareness of those women who, in their masculine dress and actions, are involved in gender blurring. In one undated letter, she tells of three women who are incarcerated at Carroll Prison. While two are captured rebel spies, the third woman is "a Major in the union army [who] went into battle with her men" (44). The major's incarceration appears to be connected with her gender because, Wakeman notes, "when the Rebels bullets was acoming like a hail storm she rode her horse and gave orders to the men" and was confined "for not doing a[c]cordingly to the regulation of war" (44), a suggestion that the major had usurped her assigned gender role. Other men, however, knew that women were among the ranks, for Wakeman receives a pass to visit Perry Wilder, her second cousin, and Henry Austin, a friend from home, who were stationed near Georgetown. As Burgess notes, Wakeman was likely wearing her uniform at the time, and Wilder and Austin were aware "that she was serving in the army under an assumed male identity" (51). At the same time, both Wakeman and her family seem to be ashamed of Wakeman's masquerading as a man. Burgess interprets Wakeman's remark in a December 28, 1863, letter that she is "'aShamed to Come' home" as "a reference to her fear of what home folks would think of her unconditional adventures" (12) and attributes the storing of her letters in a family attic for more than one hundred years to the family's view of Wakeman as "somewhat of a black sheep and her adventures in male attire a bit strange" (1).

Whatever her family may have thought of her gender blurring, Wakeman's relationship with her family is a strong one and is her reason for writing. Her letters express concern for her family and frequently begin with the reassurance that she is fine and in good health.[7] Her letters also inform her family of her whereabouts, whether she is serving in Alexandria, Virginia; Washington, DC; or Louisiana. She also expresses the hope of seeing her family again someday, if not on earth, then in heaven; however, as the war progresses and she travels further south, this hope of survival becomes more pessimistic. Indeed, of the three women writers focused on in this study, Wakeman is the only one who does not survive her war.[8]

There is a vast difference between the letters of Wakeman and *The Horror Trains: A Polish Woman Veteran's Memoir of World War II*, the personal narrative of Wanda E. Pomykalski, who served in the Polish military during World War II, not only in the type of war in which they were involved but also in their purposes for writing. Pomykalski was part of the military during a worldwide war, not a civil war within one nation, and she writes for the world, not for her family only (as Wakeman does). Also, since Wakeman is writing during her war experience, her letters are more immediate. Pomykalski writes decades after the end of World War II.

The more than fifty-year lapse in time between World War II and the publication of *The Horror Trains* in 1999 naturally raises questions about the veracity of memory. How accurate is Pomykalski's account? In what ways have her memory of World War II changed with the passing of time, and how has the general historical perspective of the war evolved? Also, Pomykalski was not a participant in every event that she writes about, a reminder that World War II was a vast war that spanned continents over a number of years. As Bronislaw S. Szykier, who also served in the Polish army in World War II, notes in his prologue to *The Horror Trains*, while Pomykalski's narrative deals with personal events, "she also writes about events that required research because she was not personally involved in them. These include the Warsaw Uprising, the actions of the Polish First Armored Division in France and the Netherlands, and the brave deeds of the Polish Air Force pilots in the Battle of Britain" (xii-xiii).

Pomykalski is a naïve eighteen-year-old when she begins to be aware of the threat from Adolf Hitler's Nazi regime. At that time, military training and war seem "just a picturesque exercise" (23). However, when Germany suddenly attacks Poland and the city of Warsaw (where Pomykalski works) on September 1, 1939, war begins to become a reality. For Pomykalski, going to war has nothing to do with gender or even finances—she has no desire to masquerade as a man or to take on male roles as Wakeman had; instead, going to war has everything to do with necessity and duty. Working in an office for a Polish army captain while waiting to begin college, Pomykalski is given the choice of staying with the captain's unit in Warsaw or returning to her family home. She decides to stay to help the officer destroy military records and then later to accompany the captain to south Poland until their allies enter the war. Since her home town of Cieszyn has been overrun by Germans, Pomykalski cannot return home. She states, "My duty was with Poland, and there was nothing else" (38), only an uncertain future. Her life becomes a series of questions: "'Why am I going? . . . Where am I going? What is to become of me and my brothers, my parents and the life I have known? Why am I leaving Warsaw'" (38)? The question will later become, "How does one continue to cope after the world has collapsed?" (190).

Throughout Pomykalski's account, she emphasizes the sacrifices that both men and women make for the future of Poland. It is a joint war effort, and their military superiors make it clear that women are a vital part of the war. Captain Walczak, the group's supervisor, tells one worker, Eva, that he is making her his "'right hand in communication with the fighting forces'" (47). "'You speak several languages,'" he tells her. "'You have executive ability which we need badly'" (47). To Pomykalski, he states, "'You are young, but dependable. I shall have a lot of work for you, too. There will be typing and papers that will have to move quickly'" (47). Much later in the war, when both men and women have spent time in Soviet prisons and the Polish army is in the process of finally being reunited, "the Polish soldiers drilled with sticks and underwent basic training. Female soldiers, along with the men, went on long marches and practiced combat skills" (289). "We sang together," Pomykalski writes, "we learned together, we concentrated on training. We tried to understand the meaning of war" (296).

When they are transferred to Palestine, the women most often engage in clerical work, but the military also decides that women are needed as truck drivers. As Wakeman did, the Polish women take pride in their work "and in being able to endure [their] strange war right beside [their] men" (185).

The book's title, *The Horror Trains*, comes from the many journeys that captured Poles had to make in claustrophobic freight cars for days and weeks at a time. During this time, they are labeled as spies and taken by the Russians to the Soviet Union to serve as slave labor in "the bleak emptiness of Russia" (142). Their first cold trip, taken with little food and water, ends after three weeks when they arrive at a prison in Odessa. Later they endure a three-week journey to Siberia, where they are again jailed. Each time that they are incarcerated, they endure lice, bedbugs, starvation, cramped living quarters, and inhumane treatment. Like Wakeman, Pomykalski writes of the sacrifices that those involved in war must make, whether it be living off less food and other supplies, enduring harsh living conditions, facing separation from family and friends, risking exposure to infection and disease, or possibly dying.

For Pomykalski, there is the urgent need to tell the story, to bear witness to what happened to the Polish people during World War II, especially those who were herded into "the massive slave-labor network" (303) that existed in areas held by the Soviet Union. While Pomykalski is one of the lucky ones who is released and sent to Iran during the war, more than two million Poles were left behind in Russia's bleak, silent deserts; many were never seen or heard from again. Ironically, the British, supposedly a Polish ally, helped the Soviets take over Iran and aided in the spread of propaganda that portrayed Soviet life as wonderful. To the dismay of the Polish people, the Russians were given half of Poland near the war's end, and Joseph Stalin was looked upon as a hero rather than as a murderer. Despite these events, the Polish army continued to fight, losing forty-two hundred soldiers while capturing the elusive Monte Cassino from the Germans in Italy in May 1944, only to have all of Poland given to Russia as part of the spoils of war.

Only the Polish people seemed to understand what this decision meant: "the war which began to save Poland from Nazi occupation ended up as Soviet occupation" (356). While the Nazis were defeated, much of Europe would be ruled by communists, and the Polish people would have no home to return to. It is this story that Pomykalski must write, this gap in history that she must fill, and because of the circumstances, the story could not be told at the time. As Szykier points out, the historical information that Pomykalski relates could not be made public in the 1940s for several reasons:

> One was that [their] "dear ally," the Stalinist Soviet Russia, would be slandered; the other was that no one would believe [their] stories that "alleged" atrocities, hatred, and sadism could exist in the "workers' paradise" [the Soviet Union]. Later, during the Cold War, [they] were given to understand that [they] should not alienate the giant "sleeping bear," ruled by the likes of Khrushchev, Andropov, and Brezhnev. (Pomykalski xi)

Embedded in the larger story of the war is the story of Katyn Woods, which is a gruesome tale of atrocity that Pomykalski feels she must make known to the world. Fourteen thousand Polish leaders and military officers had disappeared when the Soviet Union invaded Poland and were supposedly being held in several labor camps. When the Polish army reformed, the fourteen thousand men never arrived for military duty, and no news was reported of them. Stalin insisted that "'all Poles [had] been released'" (295), denied any knowledge of the whereabouts of the men or their files, and sent "the entire Polish Army to the Near East" (304), perhaps to deflect attention from the thousands of missing soldiers. In 1943, Germany announced that it had found the fourteen thousand missing officers, "'butchered in the Katyn Woods'" (315) apparently in the spring of 1940. All of them had been:

> shot in the back of the head, with hands bound, and their corpses [placed] face downward in a mass grave. . . . The doctors stated that the officers had

been stacked so tightly together that not even one centimeter separated them, and that the anaerobic decay of the bodies' fat gave them a consistency similar to that of glue. (315)

Although the Polish people insisted on an investigation into this horrific Soviet war crime, no justice was served: "The atrocities the Soviets committed were simply blotted out from world consciousness" (359).

Throughout her memoir, Pomykalski is aware that she is a part of "history in the making" (185) and that it is not necessarily a new history. There have always been wars, and people have always been oppressed. She realizes, "This is not the first time. . . . All this has happened to us before . . . besides those accounts I had read in the history books" (185). Her friend Vera reminds her that this latest version of their history needs to be told, especially to counteract the Soviets who have engaged in historical revisionism and have promoted the idea of their country as a "worker's paradise." It is obvious that "the outside world knew nothing" (278). The truth is so hidden in Russia that even the wife of the Siberian prison's commissar is unaware that young women, much less children and the elderly, have been imprisoned. The only hope for telling the story of the Polish people is for writers like Pomykalski to offer their accounts of the truth, even years later.

Kayla Williams offers yet another perspective in her memoir *Love My Rifle More than You: Young and Female in the U.S. Army* (2005), an account of the year that she spent in a war zone in Iraq.[9] Like Wakeman, Williams, who enlisted in the military in 2000, knew that enlistment would mean financial stability and a way "to better [her] career prospects" (41). In addition, the signing bonus was substantial. She would "get fifteen thousand dollars cash for signing plus fifty thousand dollars for grad school" (42) on the condition that she devote five years to the US Army. Williams quickly explains her purpose for writing and, like Pomykalski, establishes a universal audience:

I wanted to write a book to let people know what it *feels* like to be a woman soldier in peace and in war. I wanted to capture the terror, the mind-numbing tedium; and the joy and the honor . . . . The times we were scared out of our minds. The times we were bored out of our minds, too. No one has ever written that book—about what life is like for the 15 percent. (15)

Pomykalski and Williams both seek to fill historical gaps, though in different ways. While Pomykalski wants to expose to the world the atrocities suffered by the Polish people in general during World War II, Williams expresses a desire to focus more on gendered conflict, about what it is like to be a military minority, a woman, in the twenty-first century, whether serving in a war zone or on a military base in peace time.[10]

Indeed, Williams begins her memoir with a discussion of gender—and in a shockingly negative manner. She notes the narrow range of choices that female soldiers confront: to be a "bitch" or a "slut" (13). An army woman who is "distant or reserved or professional" is categorized as a "bitch," while a woman who is "nice or friendly, outgoing or chatty" is labeled a "slut" (15). As De Pauw notes, "This loose use of language to stigmatize women conflates all roles women play in war into that of sexual object and makes accurate assessment of their true activity difficult" (5). According to Williams, "A woman soldier has to toughen herself up. Not just for the enemy, for battle, or for death. I mean toughen herself to spend months awash in a sea of nervous, hyped-up guys who, when they're not thinking about getting killed, are thinking about getting laid" (13). Williams's view of the dilemma of the female soldier is one that is virtually unheard of in the literary works of Wakeman and Pomykalski. Wakeman's fellow soldiers think she is a man, while the men and women that Pomykalski describes were so busy trying to survive in a world where war was viciously sweeping from continent to continent that they did not have the time or the energy to think of sexual matters. Foremost in their minds was supporting the Polish army and the war effort, as the war itself was killing off their friends and family members in droves.[11]

In some respects, Williams is attracted to the "strange sexual allure" (18) of the military. If one is "[a] woman at war," she notes, "you're automatically a desirable commodity, and a scarce one at that. We call it 'Queen for a Year.' . . . After you're in-country for a few months, all the girls begin to look good—or at least *better*. It changes—how should I say this?—the *dynamics* of being deployed" (19). Female soldiers learn to use their gender in a positive instead of a negative way. According to Williams:

> You could get things easier, and you could get out of things easier. For a girl there were lots of little things you could do to make your load while deployed a whole lot lighter. You could use your femaleness to great advantage. You could do less work, get more assistance, and receive more special favors. (20)

Despite the sexual allure, she tires of the male gaze. "In Iraq," she complains, "guys stared and stared and stared" (22). Gender conflict, Williams writes, "was like a separate bloodless war within the larger deadly one" (22). Some of the men with whom she serves offer to pay her to show them her breasts, while others make sexual remarks, recount stories of female soldiers who were sexually promiscuous, or tell rape jokes in her presence. Another soldier makes a direct request for sexual favors, and one man even nicknames her "Boobs" (167). Only one soldier on Williams's tour tries to physically assault her, and when she makes an unofficial complaint against him, he is reassigned. However, he has the audacity to tell other soldiers that Williams initiated the incident. Intimidation also surfaces, as she is "one of [only] four females out of five hundred people" when she serves at Range 54 near Sinjar, Iraq (257). In September 2003, when she is given the responsibility of team leader, it is difficult for men to realize that she is in charge.

Not all of Williams's stories about the opposite sex reveal harassment, though. She also gives credit to the men with whom she served who treated her with respect, such as those in Delta Company, an infantry unit, which, she writes, was composed of "the single best group of soldiers I met. . . . No one made inappropriate comments or stepped out of line" (122–23). In fact, the soldiers from Delta Company 1/187 later awarded Williams an army commendation medal.[12] While Williams received the same type of medal from her own unit, this one meant even more: It "counted. . . . It was from the infantry, and they almost never recognize support elements" (228).

Williams's memoir reveals that she has the same commitment toward her war that Wakeman and Pomykalski have toward theirs. When she joins the Army Reserves in 2000, Williams's intention is to become a translator in the Arabic language. "The thought that I might go to war," she notes "was pretty distant" (41). Although she initially considers the war "wrong [and doesn't] want to go" (14), she chooses to serve in Iraq, even though the necessary surgery for a painful foot condition would have allowed her to escape deployment. "We would go to war," she writes, "because that was the way it worked. We had signed a contract. We had given our word" (61). Once in Iraq, Williams remains committed, despite the foot ailment and the other hardships. For her, war is an ethical issue: "staying was the right thing to do" (230). She knows that Arabic translators and other personnel are desperately needed, and she has "developed a deep commitment to [her] fellow soldiers" (231), stating, "I felt strongly that it would be wrong for me to leave. There were people getting killed and people getting seriously injured—people with *real* problems. I didn't feel comfortable getting out of my commitment for what was a relatively minor concern" (231).

Williams debunks the notion that women are not actively involved in warfare.[13] She classifies the common assumption that women are removed from action and "don't do combat zones" (16) as nonsense:

We are Marines. We are Military Police. We are there as support to the infantry in almost every way you might imagine. We even act in support roles for the Special Forces. We carry weapons—and we use them. We may kick down doors when an Iraqi village gets cleared. We do crowd control. We are also often the soldiers who negotiate with the locals. . . . It's frequently the non-infantry soldiers like us—with fewer up-armored vehicles—who end up getting hit and engaging in combat. (16)

Former marine captain Anu Bhagwati agrees: "The prohibition on women in combat 'is archaic, it does not reflect the many sacrifices and contributions that women make in the military, and it ignores the reality of current war-fighting doctrine'" (qtd. in Jelinek 1A). According to Laura Naylor, a military-police specialist, female soldiers in Iraq are "interchangeable with the infantry. . . . For anyone to say women aren't allowed on the frontline is absurd" (Benedict 135–36). As the accounts of Williams and other women indicate,[14] American women in Iraq endure the hardships of a war zone: for example, the lack of suitable bathroom facilities and adequate health care for women, the dangers of mortar attacks and improvised explosive devices or roadside bombs, the frustration of not knowing who is friend or foe, the lack of training in the Arabic language, the Vietnam-era equipment with which they are expected to work, the accidental killing of children and other civilians, and the dehumanization of the enemy.

An important aspect of the written accounts of women who have served in war is their recognition of the tendency to become morally irresponsible, to shift to what O'Brien touches on in "Sweetheart of the Song Tra Bong": the going to war "clean" and then "getting dirty" (114). Williams acknowledges that war "can turn you. . . . Women are no different from men in their corruptibility" (15). As examples, she cites her participation in interrogations of Iraqi men, which required her to abuse them verbally or to humiliate them sexually by "[r]idicul[ing] the size of [their] genitals" (247).[15] The first time that Williams participates in an interrogation she enjoys the feeling of power it gives her, though she knows that her "sense of pleasure" is "creepy" (205). However, once she has to embarrass a detainee sexually and then witnesses the physical abuse inflicted by the male interrogators, she decides that she will no longer assist in such mockery and reminds a soldier of the

Geneva Convention, which prohibits such acts. However, because she never reports the behavior to her superiors or actively works to stop the abusive interrogations, she questions her own moral culpability. By her own silence, is she as much to blame as those who consistently participate in such behavior? [15]

The ease with which gender roles can be taken on or discarded is a topic that emerges in the literary works of Wakeman, Pomykalski, and Williams. As her letters reveal, Wakeman easily discarded her role as a woman, yet had she survived the war, it is unlikely that she would have wanted to resume a life of femininity. Williams points out that she can easily transition from one gender role to another. As her title indicates, it is as easy to pick up a rifle as to put on mascara:

> In a dress, away from the base, you'd never guess I was a soldier. Always been a girl that catches a guy's eyes. And yet I do fifty-five push-ups in under a minute. Tough, and proud to be tough. I love my M-4, the smell of it, of cleaning fluid, of gunpowder: the smell of strength. Gun in your hands, and you're in a special place. I've come to look forward to that. (15)

In Pomykalski's narrative, she indicates that when the Polish women in the Soviet prisons are incarcerated and removed from their war duties, they turn to domestic tasks such as sewing and knitting. Her friend Wina, a ballerina, never gives up her dream of returning to her dancing career, and another woman, Teresa, wastes no time after leaving prison before acquiring a tan and donning "a white linen suit, her high heels clicking" (Pomykalski 312). Though the Polish women may have lost their ability to be life-bearers—they stop menstruating when they are imprisoned and their female-hygiene needs are ignored—they never lose their feminine desires, even when serving in a war zone.

An Uncommon Soldier, *The Horror Trains*, and *Love My Rifle More than You* offer perceptions of war that are not limited to male experience and, as such, provide insight into war as well as humanity. De Pauw asserts that:

Through the centuries one of the most striking characteristics of women in combatant and combat support roles is that they perform them not as women but as human beings. Gender becomes an issue when history omits the detail that some brave warriors were women, and war stories then reinforce prescribed gender roles and expectations. But history books do not alter the truth of what happens on the day of battle. (xiv)

Wakeman, Pomykalski, and Williams, three representative examples of the many women who have served their countries in the combat zone, are, as Pomykalski so perceptively notes, writers of history, "history [that is] in the making" (185), and of a truth that needs to be shared. Their long overdue versions of war offer an alternative history to the many male war stories, both challenging readers to consider both war and gender in fresh ways and granting insight into life in a combat zone from a female perspective. Miles and Cross assert that "[a] growing female participation both in the world's armies and in the governments that send their fighting forces to war, may be our only hope of reducing, if not ending, the calamitous conflicts that mark the history of the human race" (378). With this participation, more voices such as those of Wakeman, Pomykalski, and Williams are needed to challenge dominant ways of thinking about war.

Notes

1. Interestingly, an Internet ad for the documentary film *Lioness*, which focuses on women combat veterans of the Iraq war, echoes De Pauw, stating, "There for the Action. Missing from History" ("*Lioness*: A Room").

2. According to Elizabeth D. Leonard, the exact number of women who served in the Civil War in male disguise is unknown. Scholarly estimates range from four hundred to one thousand (xiv).

3. Such was the case of Mrs. Betsy "Mother" Sullivan, who went to the Civil War with her husband and ended up serving as a mother figure to all of the men in his company (Elshtain 98–99).

4. As both the letters and Burgess note, later in the war, Wakeman used a second male alias, Edwin R. Wakeman, perhaps as a tribute to Edwin P. Davis, a colonel she respected (12).

5. In her preface, Burgess explains how she edited Wakeman's writing to make it more recognizable to modern readers (xv–xvii).

6. In other correspondence, Wakeman indicates her willingness to fight, stating, "I am ready at a minute's warning to go into the field of battle and take my stand with the rest" (36) and "I hope that our regiment will have to go into the field before it is over. Then I shall be satisfied and not until we have to go" (43).

7. For example, her June 5, 1863, epistle opens with the line "It is with Affectionate love that I Write to you and let you know that I am well at Present" (31).

8. In her epilogue, Burgess states that in June 1864, Wakeman succumbed to "chronic diarrhea, the most deadly disease of the Civil War" after a month-long illness (81–82), a reminder that being killed in battle is not the only way to die in war. In the epilogue to *The Horror Trains*, Pomykalski reveals that, at the end of the war, she moved to England, married, and began a family before immigrating to the United States. She made two return trips to Europe, including to her beloved Poland, in 1984 and 1994 (360–62). Williams returned from Iraq in February 2004. In the final chapters of *Love My Rifle More than You*, she writes of the difficulty of having to live without a weapon and of postwar adjustment in general.

9. As Bettina Hofmann notes, "[a] crucial turning point for the change of gender roles as well as for a change in the military certainly was the Vietnam War" (15). For information on women and the Vietnam War, see Hofmann's study as well as Philip Beidler's essay elsewhere in this volume. Women's accounts from the wars in Iraq and Afghanistan have been slow to appear, although as of January 2011, more than 225,000 women had served in those countries (Jelinek 1A). In addition to *Love My Rifle More than You*, works to consider include Ruff and Roper's *Ruff's War: A Navy Nurse on the Frontline in Iraq*, Browder's *When Janey Comes Marching Home*, Benedict's *The Lonely Soldier*, Holmstedt's *Band of Sisters* and *The Girls Come Marching Home*, and the documentary film *Lioness*.

10. Ironically, Williams's war is fought in Iraq, one of the last, and most peaceful, locations where Pomykalski served. Pomykalski points out the biblical allusions to Iraq, "the land connected with the story of the Garden of Eden" (317).

11. The only allusions to women being viewed sexually in Pomykalski's account involve enemy soldiers. When the Soviet troops go to Berlin after Hitler's suicide, they spend several weeks storming "wildly through what was left of Berlin, killing civilians and raping German women" (355). Also, Pomykalski implies that her friend Halina is a victim of rape at the hands of the Russian soldiers. However, there is no indication in her account that she or any other woman had to worry about sexual threats from the Polish men with whom she served, perhaps because they were so focused on the war effort. Williams acknowledges that when the soldiers in Iraq were in combat, they thought less about sex.

12. Pomykalski received the UK Defence Medal and Italy Star and the Polish Silver Cross.

13. According to Elshtain, "Female bodies have traditionally had purposes incompatible with the imposition of traditional discipline by the army. Women are designated noncombatants because of the part they play in the reproductive process; because women have been linked symbolically to images of succoring nonviolence; because men have had a long history of warrioring and policing" (183).
14. See, for example, the works by Benedict and Holmstedt mentioned above.
15. Wakeman also implies that she did not always act as she should have in the Civil War, but is not specific about what kind of behavior she exhibited. She merely tells her parents that "there is a good many temptations in the army. I got led away into this world So bad that I sinned a good deal" (53) and that she is working on repenting from her sins.

Works Cited

Benedict, Helen. *The Lonely Soldier: The Private War of Women Serving in Iraq.* Boston: Beacon, 2009.

Browder, Laura. *When Janey Comes Marching Home: Portraits of Women Combat Veterans.* Chapel Hill: U North Carolina P, 2010.

Burgess, Lauren Cook, ed. *An Uncommon Soldier: The Civil War Letters of Sarah Rosetta Wakeman, Alias Pvt. Lyons Wakeman, 153rd Regiment, New York State Volunteers.* New York: Oxford UP, 1994.

De Pauw, Linda Grant. *Battle Cries and Lullabies: Women in War from Prehistory to the Present.* Norman: U Oklahoma P, 1998.

Edmonds, Sarah Emma. *Memoirs of a Soldier, Nurse and Spy: A Woman's Adventures in the Union Army.* DeKalb: Northern Illinois UP, 1999.

Elshtain, Jean Bethke. *Women and War.* New York: Basic, 1987.

Goldstein, Joshua S. *War and Gender: How Gender Shapes the War System and Vice Versa.* Cambridge, Eng.: Cambridge UP, 2001.

Hofmann, Bettina. *Ahead of Survival: American Women Writers Narrate the Vietnam War.* Berlin: Peter Lang, 1996.

Holmstedt, Kirsten. *Band of Sisters: American Women at War in Iraq.* Mechanicsburg, PA: Stackpole, 2007.

_____. *The Girls Come Marching Home: Stories of Women Warriors Returning from the War in Iraq.* Mechanicsburg, PA: Stackpole, 2009.

Jelinek, Pauline. "Report: Women Should Be Allowed in U.S. Combat Units." *The* (Jonesboro, AR) *Sun* 15 Jan. 2011: A1.

Lioness. Dir. Meg McLagan and Daria Sommers. Docurama, 2008. Film.

Miles, Rosalind, and Robin Cross. *Hell Hath No Fury: True Stories of Women at War from Antiquity to Iraq.* New York: Three Rivers, 2008.

O'Brien, Tim. *The Things They Carried.* New York: Mariner Books, 1990.

Pomykalski, Wanda E. *The Horror Trains: A Polish Woman Veteran's Memoir of World War II.* Pasadena, MD: Minerva Center, 1999.

Ruff, Cdr. Cheryl Lynn, and Cdr. K. Sue Roper. *Ruff's War: A Navy Nurse on the Frontline in Iraq*. Annapolis, MD: US Naval Institute P, 2005.

Schwartz, Gerald, ed. *A Woman Doctor's Civil War: Esther Hill Hawks' Diary*. Columbia: U South Carolina P, 1989.

Smith, Helen Zenna. *Not So Quiet . . . Stepdaughters of War*. 1930. New York: Feminist P, 1989.

Williams, Kayla. *Love My Rifle More than You: Young and Female in the U.S. Army*. New York: Norton, 2005.

Focus Afghanistan: Deep Documentary Immersion and Genre Debt in *Restrepo, Camp Victory, Afghanistan,* and *Armadillo*

Douglas A. Cunningham

While the aftermath of the September 11, 2001, attacks on the World Trade Center and Pentagon resulted in an almost immediate (November 2001) counterattack against suspected strongholds of Osama Bin Laden in Afghanistan, the US invasion of Iraq in March of 2003 soon stole the spotlight and dominated media attention for the next six years. The period between 2003 and 2009, in fact, produced several deep-immersion documentaries, fiction films, and television programs about the Iraq War: *Gunner Palace* (2004), *Occupation: Dreamland* (2005), *The War Tapes* (2006), and *Brothers at War* (2009) stand among the most visible of the feature-length documentaries, while fiction films and television series such as *In the Valley of Elah* (2007), *Stop-Loss* (2008), *The Hurt Locker* (2008), *Over There* (2005), and *Generation Kill* (2008), among several others, round out Hollywood's accounts of what journalist Thomas E. Ricks has called "the American Military Adventure in Iraq," which is the subtitle of his 2006 book. This brief list of films and programs does not begin to include the myriad reality and documentary television programs associated with these events.

Interestingly, in the wake of the American military's 2007 surge in Iraq under the leadership of General David Petraeus (an effort that did much to stabilize the war-torn country), the focus of many independent documentary filmmakers shifted to the mission of the International Security Assistance Force (or ISAF, for which General Petraeus has also served as commander) in Afghanistan. Although there has not been the same outpouring of work about Afghanistan as there was about the Iraq War, films such as *Restrepo* (2010), *Armadillo* (2010), and *Camp Victory, Afghanistan* (2010) offer early hints of what will certainly become a bevy of films about this conflict; these early offerings have done much to capture the essence of both the combat and training missions in that country. *Restrepo*, for example, chronicles a US infantry company's deployment at a remote mountain outpost in the Korengal Valley. Likewise, *Armadillo*, a Danish production structurally and thematically similar to *Restrepo* in many ways, follows a Danish infantry unit assigned to counterinsurgency patrol duties in Helmand Province. *Camp Victory, Afghanistan*, however, differs from these other films in that it works to capture the ISAF efforts to help train the Afghan army in Herat Province rather than focusing strictly on active combat operations. As of 2012, only *Restrepo* has seen wide art-house distribution in the United States (although *Armadillo* enjoyed a US nonfestival premiere in New York City in 2011), but the success of both *Armadillo* and *Camp Victory, Afghanistan* on the festival circuit testifies to the renewed public interest in ISAF's mission in Southwest Asia.

In her seminal book, *The World War II Combat Film: Anatomy of a Genre* (1986), Jeanine Basinger studies the constitutive elements of films such as *Bataan* (1943), *Air Force* (1943), *Destination Tokyo* (1943), and *Objective Burma!* (1945), to name some of the most representative examples. Although she writes of fictionalized films addressing a different conflict, most of which were also produced within a different historical context, Basinger's theories on the World War II "combat film" can help modern readers understand tropes inherent to documentary films produced during the wars in Iraq and Afghanistan. At first blush, Basinger's book might seem an odd choice when attempting to explore the genre conventions of modern war documentaries; however, these documentaries stand, in many ways, as the contemporary equivalents of the fictionalized films Basinger takes as the objects of her study. This essay, then, explores how Basinger's genre theories might be "repurposed" to account for characteristics of documentary films about the Iraq and Afghanistan wars.

Basinger screened dozens of World War II combat films while writing her book and designed the following model of definitive characteristics for the combat film:

[1] The credits of the film unfold against a military reference. . . . The credits include the name of a military advisor. [2] Closely connected to the presentation of the credits is a statement that may be called the film's dedication. . . . [3] A group of men, led by a hero, undertake a mission which will accomplish an important military objective. . . . [4] The group contains an observer or commentator. [5] The hero has had leadership forced upon him in dire circumstances. . . . [6] [The group of men] undertake a military objective. . . . [7] As they go forward, the action unfolds. . . . [8] The enemy's presence is indicated. . . . [9] Military iconography is seen, and its usage is demonstrated for and taught to civilians [in the film]. . . . [10] Conflict breaks out within the group itself. It is resolved through the external conflict brought down upon them. [11] Rituals are enacted from the past. . . . [12] Rituals are enacted from the present. . . . [13] Members of the group die. . . . [14] A climactic battle takes place, and a learning or growth process occurs. . . . [15] The tools of cinema are employed [to tell the story of the film]. . . . [16] The situation is resolved. . . . [17] THE END appears on the screen. . . . [18] The audience is ennobled for having shared [the combatants'] combat experience, as [the combatants] are ennobled for having undergone it. We are all comrades in arms. (67–70)

Granted, Basinger does not argue that every World War II combat film matches every item on this list; rather, she states, "This 'list' can be put into two forms. . . . As a 'story' of film . . . which becomes what everyone imagines the combat genre to be but which, in fact, does not exist in pure form in any single film. It is this 'story'. . . that filmmakers would later use to create new genre films. . . . [Or as] an outline of . . . characteristics, to be used in analyzing films of the genre" (67).

As Basinger explains, this list does, indeed, prove useful when examining combat films and the ways they manifest some (if not necessarily all) of the constitutive elements she describes. However, Basinger spends the bulk of her book examining fictional(ized) films while devoting little analysis to wartime documentaries such as *Memphis Belle: The Story of a Flying Fortress* (1944), *The Fighting Lady*

(1944), or *San Pietro* (1945), which, no doubt, correspond to many of the same characteristics Basinger notes on her list. She states:

> To consider such documentaries is important, because they influenced the look of the combat film in three ways: home audiences, having seen them, now had an idea of the physical look of combat and thus would expect films about combat to look that way; filmmakers, having the same experience as these viewers, would react similarly and could and would perhaps use some of that same footage in combat films; and those filmmakers who made the documentaries in the field would return to Hollywood to make combat films when the war was over. (113)

Basinger does conduct a brief examination of John Ford's influential documentary short *December 7th* (1943) and some other documentaries, but she does not provide a detailed analysis of how (if at all) these or other wartime documentaries weigh in on her genre checklist (114–15). This omission does not at all reduce the extreme value of her important work on the genre, but the lack of attention to this cross-influence in the academy at large implies a stovepiping effect in which fictional(ized) and documentary war films are assumed to have negligible influences on one another. History itself belies this assumption. The academy has devoted a great deal of attention to the blurred lines between nonfiction works on war and their fictional counterparts; the same work must be done by film scholars to explore the cross influences of fictional(ized) war films and documentary war films. Several fictional(ized) war films are based on actual events and recounted in near documentary fashion (Richard Attenborough's 1977 adaptation of Cornelius Ryan's *A Bridge Too Far* [1974], comes to mind), while, in turn, many documentaries draw on tropes most often associated with fictional films (microlevel attention to one or two persons of interest and/or individual battles rather than to the macrolevel events of campaigns and theaters; highly stylized musical scores that manipulate and direct viewers' emotional investments in "characters" and stories) in order to further dramatize what might otherwise seem to some mere rote recounting of dates, places, and orders of battle. Several of the Iraq War documentaries demonstrate this latter trend; thus, analyzing connections between World War II fictional(ized) combat films and deep-immersion documentaries from the Iraq War can, perhaps, help one to see most clearly these cross influences at work.

Perhaps the first of the high-profile Iraq War documentaries—and certainly the most curious and innovative in terms of style—is Michael Tucker and Petra Epperlein's *Gunner Palace*. Set in Baghdad in the months following the 2003 invasion, the film patches together a portrait of the Second Battalion, Third Field Artillery operating out of a palace once owned by Uday Hussein, a son of Saddam Hussein, former and fallen president of Iraq. Tucker embedded with the Third—affectionately known as the "Gunners"—for two months, and the film he produced with Epperlein bustles with a hip, rhythmic, and streetwise energy.

The soldiers of the Gunners provide much of the diegetic and non-diegetic rapping, guitar riffing, and poetry reading that punctuate the action of the film, which consists primarily of the Gunners patrolling, raiding, joking, partying, and either speaking to—or performing for—Tucker's digital camera. As will be the case with almost all of the Iraq and Afghanistan documentaries under discussion, *Gunner Palace* does not attempt to follow the high-level trajectories of any particular campaign or "at-large" US effort in Iraq; instead, Tucker and Epperlein focus on the more personal aspects of the soldiers' lives, such as their views about army life, the war, and the Iraqis and the ways in which these American men choose to cope with the stressful situations around them.

Tucker's affected, gravelly voice-over for the film (through which he recounts his experiences as an embedded filmmaker while, at the same time, adding historical contextualization to the soldiers and the events highlighted in the film) plays like the hard-boiled narration from films noir such as *Dead Reckoning* (1947) or *The Lady from Shanghai*

(1947). Still, the allusions to the narrative gimmicks of such wartime and postwar crime dramas—others of which so often feature as protagonists the disillusioned, violence-prone veterans turned either detective or patsy—seem appropriate for a film in which war is presented as a piece of gritty, pop-culture adventure in its own right. On the other hand, this voice-over may, in fact, be seeking to capture some of the stateside cynicism and violent behavior (often a symptom of post-traumatic stress disorder) that sometimes carries over into civilian life following a war. Many noir protagonists intoned such narration during the immediate postwar years in no small part because these films told stories of men whose taste for violence—whetted during the war—found new outlets in stateside crime and gangster activity. Tucker's allusions to noir, then, hint that—at least in his opinion—Iraq in 2004 bears some resemblance the darkness and confusion inherent to these postwar crime films.

Tucker's film declares its hip self-consciousness at every turn. While in and around Uday's swimming pool celebrating the success of a recent raid, for example, soldiers dance to a recording of the Temptations singing "My Girl," as if enacting a kind of postmodern homage to the clichés of wartime bonding amid 1960s music in films such as *Apocalypse Now* (1979) and *Platoon* (1986). A silhouetted Gunner with an electric guitar pays tribute to Jimi Hendrix's famous version of "The Star-Spangled Banner" by playing the anthem against the Muslim call to prayers and the golden heat of a setting sun. Scenes such as these seem both poignant and disturbing—for the musical performances, poetry, and duty-bound but biting cynicism of the Gunners reveal they are very aware of the contradictions and ironies inherent to their dangerous work in and around the luxury of Uday's bombed palace.

Following closely on the heels of *Gunner Palace*, Ian Olds and Garrett Scott's film *Occupation: Dreamland* departs sharply from the stylistic snap of its predecessor. Olds and Scott produce a film far less aestheticized (no rap, poetry, or noirish voice-over performances) while, at the same time, present a more diverse field of frank viewpoints about the war in Iraq. At several points throughout the film, the soldiers of the First Battalion, 505th Parachute Infantry Regiment from the Eighty-Second Airborne Division, assigned to counterinsurgency duties in Al Fallūjah, Iraq, in early 2004, voice their deep concerns and beliefs freely to the offscreen filmmakers, their opinions ranging from dutiful rhetoric of support to more nuanced ideas about the reasons for the war, the likelihood of its success, and the contradictory nature of personal politics constantly at odds with national and military policy. (At one point, a noncommissioned officer advises his troops to refrain from expressing their personal political opinions on camera.)

Of all the Iraq War deep-immersion documentaries discussed in this essay, *Occupation: Dreamland* offers the most substantial voice to Iraqis themselves, some of whom accost the filmmakers on the streets of Al Fallūjah and demand time to air their grievances about the US Army's presence and actions in the city. Olds and Scott indulge these demands, and the inclusion of these Iraqi voices (translated via subtitles in the final film) allows for an interesting contrast with the opinions of the 505th soldiers. The scenes of Iraqi outcries occur as the filmmakers accompany the 505th during missions in which the unit is charged with maintaining civil order in Al Fallūjah during Thursday city council meetings. As title cards inform viewers, the mission of the 505th on these Thursdays mandates that the soldiers engage the hearts and minds of the local populace as a way to generate support for US efforts in Iraq in general and in Al Fallūjah in particular. The attempts of a young army lieutenant to converse with the locals who have surrounded him and are demanding answers to pointed questions proves one of the most unsettling sequences in the film. Olds and Scott capture the awkwardness and danger of these moments without flinching, and their bold juxtapositions of US and Iraqi musings throughout the film delivers what is, perhaps, the greatest reward of *Occupation: Dreamland*.

Deborah Scranton's *The War Tapes* implements a unique twist on the deep-immersion format in that she places cameras in the hands of three Army National Guard soldiers, all of whom deploy to Logistics

Support Area Anaconda, Iraq, as members of the 172nd Infantry Regiment (Mountain) of the Eighty-Sixth Infantry Brigade Combat Team. With few exceptions, the soldiers film their experiences themselves, and viewers watch as their attitudes, endurance, and composure change over the course of the year. *The War Tapes* stands apart in the way that its soldiers-filmmakers emerge as very real and vulnerable characters throughout their time in Iraq and their reintegrations into their New England communities upon their return to the United States.

Unlike either *Gunner Palace* or *Occupation: Dreamland*, Scranton's film dances most effectively among its portmanteau assemblage of stories from Sergeant Steve Pink, Sergeant Zack Bazzi, and Specialist Mike Moriarty, enabling the audience to appreciate the arc of development respective to each of the men. Pink's darkening cynicism grows beyond even his already characteristic sarcasm; an Arabic-speaking Lebanese American, Bazzi offers intriguing insights about the futility of war and the ties to corporate interests, but he subordinates his personal opinions to his love of the army; having embarked for Iraq on a personal mission of masculine validation, Moriarty returns from his adventure with deep emotional scars. Scranton's film may be the most personal portrait of American men at war to emerge from the Iraq War.

Jake Rademacher's *Brothers at War* aspires to the heights reached by *The War Tapes*; while it does not attain the same emotional stature as Scranton's film, *Brothers at War* nevertheless tells a compelling story of two army brothers and a third brother—actor-filmmaker Rademacher—who embeds twice with units in Iraq as a way of understanding (and perhaps measuring up to) his brothers' wartime experiences. As a result, Rademacher becomes a central focus within his own investigation of the Iraq War, and much of what drives the novelty of his coverage is the fact that he stands as such a quirky contrast to his two dyed-in-the-wool army brothers—officer Claus (a striking West Pointer and family man, staunchly devoted to the American cause) and enlisted man Isaac (moody and withdrawn since his return from Afghanistan).

Whether intentionally or not, Rademacher's film does much to explore the ways in which socially constructed ideas about "true" masculinity affect choices, relationships, and modes of behavior within a single family. One senses early in *Brothers at War* that at least part of what drives Rademacher's time in Iraq is his yearning for a modicum of the masculine bragging rights accorded his brothers. Although each of the Iraq War deep-immersion documentaries addresses this question in one form or another (most often only briefly by soldiers who couch their decisions to join the army as an effort to live up to some masculine ideal), the exploration of this issue within *Brothers at War* stands as the most overt and intimate.

How do these Iraq War combat documentaries fare against the constitutive elements of Basinger's combat film model? In truth, these documentaries mirror the model quite closely, although the nature of the ensemble "casts" and the obvious fog and friction of war in these films inhibit the kind of pointed, narrative-driven storytelling familiar from World War II combat films. As a result, essential elements such as Basinger's third criterion—"A group of men, led by a hero, undertake a mission which will accomplish an important military objective"—morph into something more akin to: "A group of men, under the direction of their immediate leadership, undertake myriad objectives throughout the duration of their period in country." Similarly, the contingent nature of war (and the Iraq War in particular) and the approaches these filmmakers take to their subjects also necessitate the morphing of other elements: Basinger's fifth criterion, "the hero has leadership forced upon him in dire circumstances," might become "the men struggle to reconcile their senses of duty with their personal convictions and growing disillusionment"; her sixteenth, "the situation is resolved," might become "these men return home and wrestle with their personal demons, but the situation at large continues." Again, rather than aligning one for one, the generic categorization of these deep-immersion documentaries from the Iraq War calls for a retooling of Basinger's original model to account for the differences in form (documentary vs. fiction[alized] film) and conflict (a counterinsurgency war vs. a conventional war of attrition).

Do the films about the War in Afghanistan share similar connections to Basinger's model that Iraq War documentaries seem to? In essence, yes. In fact, Sebastian Junger and Tim Hetherington's *Restrepo* resembles many of the deep-immersion documentaries from the Iraq War: Viewers meet several men at the small-unit level (a platoon of the Second Battalion, 503rd Infantry Regiment) isolated together within a remote and hostile location (in this case, the Korengal Valley of Kunar Province on the Afghanistan-Pakistan border); hear their thoughts and feelings about their wartime experiences, both while they are in country and during interviews following their returns to the United States; watch the soldiers of the 503rd attempt to interact with the locals; and witness the horrors of combat.

As in films such as *Gunner Palace* and *Occupation: Dreamland*, the relationships viewers form with these soldiers feel cursory; one does not come to know any one of them particularly well. Neither Junger (who also wrote a book about this same experience, aptly entitled *War*, published in 2010) nor Hetherington (who was killed several months after the film's US release while covering the Libyan rebellion against Moammar Gadhafi in 2011) imposes himself onto the film, preferring instead to let the men of the 503rd tell the story. Unlike the Iraq War deep-immersion documentaries, however, *Restrepo* finds a way to center its narrative on a single climactic event, known as Operation Rock Avalanche. During this mission, in which members of the 503rd attempt to engage the Taliban in the difficult mountain terrain near Outpost Restrepo, their remote base of operations, unseen Taliban fighters ambush the soldiers, and the Americans suffer severe casualties.

While *Restrepo* explores many aspects of the soldiers' experiences in the Korengal Valley, the effects of Operation Rock Avalanche—even before its proper introduction into the narrative, which occurs approximately two-thirds of the way through the film—hang over the film like the ghost of Juan Restrepo himself, the first soldier of the platoon killed during this particular rotation to Afghanistan and the man for whom the platoon has named its outpost. Seen in footage taken by the soldiers while en route to the war, Restrepo jokes with his army companions and smiles broadly into the camera. Excited and "pumped" about their deployment, all of the young men posture for the camera. The fact that Junger and Hetherington bookend their film with this footage of masculine bravado, as displayed by a soldier whose absence is felt for the rest of the narrative, adds even greater poignancy and emotional weight to this story.

Janus Metz's *Armadillo* feels remarkably similar—at least in terms of structure and approach—to *Restrepo*. The film focuses on a Danish infantry unit, which is deployed to conduct counterinsurgency operations in Afghanistan's Helmand Province in much the same way as the unit in *Restrepo*. Unlike the latter film, however, *Armadillo* never posits a central event to serve as a touching point for an emotional core of the narrative. The viewer does gain a greater understanding of the daily lives of these soldiers, including the struggles they face during operations and combat and the relationships they form with one another. The film also does much for Americans to reveal how coalition forces, like those deployed by the Danes, contribute to the ISAF mission; at the same time, the film explores effectively the reactions in Denmark to these soldiers' alleged wartime transgressions (the Danish unit featured in *Armadillo* is accused of murdering wounded Taliban soldiers). Ultimately, however, viewers feel not far removed from the microscopic view of small-unit operations as featured in *Gunner Palace* and *Occupation: Dreamland*.

Carol Dysinger's *Camp Victory, Afghanistan* stands as the most unusual—and perhaps the most emotionally powerful—film discussed in this essay. Like *The War Tapes*, Dysinger's film finds a potent mixture of logos and pathos that communicates the importance of the ISAF's efforts and, at the same time, renders them undeniably personal. More specifically, the film tells the story of Afghan general Fazil Ahmad Sayar, the chief of staff and brigadier general of the 207th Corps in

Herāt, Afghanistan, and his adviser, US Army National Guard colonel Michael Shute, the commander of the 207th Regional Security Advisory Command, as they battle side-by-side to overcome cultural differences during a multinational effort to create and train an Afghan army.

Viewers come to understand these two men deeply over the course of the film, and their relationship—which Dysinger portrays as growing in both affection and trust over the course of Shute's year-long deployment to Afghanistan—serves as a both a microcosm and exemplar for ideal US–Afghan relations. Sayar, a wearied, battle-hardened veteran of the Soviet-Afghan war, sees a possibility for real change in his country while working with Shute. Likewise, Shute, the consummate professional army man with a can-do attitude and a quick smile, comes to admire Sayar's sincerity, experience, and earnest desires for reform and change. When, near the end of the film, Colonel Shute has returned to the United States and has discovered that General Sayar has died in a plane crash, viewers may feel compelled to share Shute's tears, for even as a door of hope has opened amid the chaos, it has partially closed. In *Camp Victory, Afghanistan*, viewers can relate to the bonds formed by people at war and as expressed by men from vastly different cultures and languages. Although tragic on its face, Dysinger's film stands as the most optimistic and (to use Basinger's term) "ennobling" of any deep-immersion documentary to come out of either war.

Like the Iraq War films, *Restrepo, Armadillo*, and *Camp Victory, Afghanistan* do meet many of Basinger's generic criteria. As with those previous films, however, these Afghanistan deep-immersion documentaries also necessitate some revisions to Basinger's original fiction(alized) film model. Basinger's fourteenth criterion, for example—the call for a climactic battle that results in learning or growth—finds much more purchase in *Restrepo* and *Armadillo*, each of which features a major battle that serves as a life-changing event for all involved. In *Camp Victory, Afghanistan,* however, the major battle takes place offscreen during an extended period when the filmmaker is not in country. She must later rely on photographs from the event to reconstruct its horrors. For this reason, Basinger would probably not place *Camp Victory, Afghanistan*, under the rubric of the "combat film"; indeed, the difficulty in classifying this film as either a combat film or a film about diplomacy may account for the unfortunate troubles it has encountered in securing distribution.[1] Still, Dysinger's film successfully chronicles a climactic battle of a different sort—namely, the aforementioned battle by Shute and Sayar to forge ahead as a team to create an indigenous army to protect Afghanistan's future—and, in this regard, stays more than true to the model's call for "learning or growth."[2] Dysinger states as much in the film's press kit:

> For three years, I filmed the peculiar dance of Afghan soldiers trying to get what they needed from the Americans, and the Americans trying to teach the Afghans what they were told they needed to know. In the beginning it was a struggle at best, but then began the profound and moving friendship that grew between General Sayar and Colonel Shute of the New Jersey National Guard. Against all odds, these two men worked their way across the great divide of language, religion and radically different military cultures to discover their kindred spirits.[3]

For this reason, *Camp Victory, Afghanistan* may well emerge as one of the most representative examples of the ISAF's efforts in Afghanistan and, indeed, as one of the best examples of the modern combat film. This assertion may seem bold or even misguided given that the film lacks an on-screen battle, that titular "must have" for the combat film genre. However, *Camp Victory, Afghanistan* distinguishes itself in how it holds to its genre roots while eschewing their traditional interpretation. The fact, too, that *Camp Victory, Afghanistan*, has yet to secure distribution reveals much about the extent to which distributors make broad assumptions about the genre expectations of their audiences. Assuming that filmgoers will sooner pay to see combat rather than diplomacy, distributors seem to have overlooked the potential of

Camp Victory, Afghanistan, a film that portrays the ISAF mission in a different—and relatively positive—light.

In conclusion, then, the generic definitions for combat films must be broadened to account for the myriad ways in which wars are "fought." Also, how both fictional and documentary forms demonstrate traits inherent to genre demands careful consideration. Film scholars need to reevaluate the way in which useful models such as Basinger's can be reworked and retooled to account for how combat is portrayed in documentaries, in particular, those from the wars in Iraq and Afghanistan. Reworking such genre models will help scholars to recognize the value that these new kinds of combat films bring to the genre at large, thereby generating the kind of exposure films like *Camp Victory, Afghanistan* need in order to tell their stories of successful combat through acts of nonviolence.

Disclaimer: This essay reflects the opinions of the author and does not necessarily reflect the opinions or the endorsements of the US government, the Department of Defense, or the US Air Force.

Notes

1. I am indebted to Alex Vernon for this insight.
2. Again, I am indebted to Vernon for this idea.
3. Carol Dysinger, "Director's Statement," Camp Victory, Afghanistan Press Kit.

Works Cited

Air Force. Dir. Howard Hawks. Perf. John Garfield, Arthur Kennedy, and John Ridgley. Warner Bros., 1943. Film.
Apocalypse Now. Dir. Francis Ford Coppola. Perf. Marlon Brando, Martin Sheen, and Dennis Hopper. Paramount, 1979. Film.
Armadillo. Dir. Janus Metz. Fridthjof Film, 2010. Film.
Basinger, Jeanine. *The World War II Combat Film: Anatomy of a Genre*. Middletown: Wesleyan UP, 2003.
The Battle of San Pietro. Dir. John Huston. US Army Signal Corps, 1945. Film.

The Best Years of Our Lives. Dir. William Wyler. Perf. Frederic March, Dana Andrews, and Theresa Wright. Samuel Goldwyn Company, 1946. Film.

Brothers at War. Dir. Jake Rademacher. Perf. Jake Rademacher, Isaac Rademacher, and Joe Rademacher. Summit Entertainment, 2009. Film.

Camp Victory, Afghanistan. Dir. Carol Dysinger. Perf. Michael Shute and Fazil Ahmad Sayar. Bolo Productions, 2010. Film.

Destination Tokyo. Dir. Delmer Daves. Perf. Cary Grant, John Garfield, and Alan Hale. Warner Bros., 1943. Film.

The Fighting Lady. Dir. Edward Steichen. Perf. Charles Boyer, J. Joseph Clark, and Dixie Kiefer. US Navy, 1944. Film.

Gunner Palace. Dir. Petra Epperlein and Michael Tucker. Perf. Bryant Davis, Devon Dixon, and Javorn Drummond. Nomados, 2004. Film.

The Lady from Shanghai. Dir. Orson Welles. Perf. Orson Welles and Rita Hayworth. Columbia, 1947. Film.

Memphis Belle: A Story of a Flying Fortress. Dir. William Wyler. Perf. Robert Morgan and James Verinis. US Army Air Forces, 1944. Film.

Objective Burma! Dir. Raoul Walsh. Perf. Errol Flynn, James Brown, and William Prince. Warner Bros., 1945. Film.

Occupation: Dreamland. Dir. Ian Olds and Garrett Scott. Perf. Matthew Bacik, Chris Corcione, and Eric Forbes. Greenhouse Pictures, 2006. Film.

Restrepo. Dir. Tim Hetherington and Sebastian Junger. Outpost Films, 2010. Film.

Ricks, Thomas E. *Fiasco: The American Military Adventure in Iraq*. New York: Penguin, 2006.

Star Wars. Dir. George Lucas. Perf. Mark Hamill, Carrie Fisher, and Harrison Ford. Lucasfilm, 1977. Film.

The War Tapes. Dir. Deborah Scranton. Perf. Zach Bazzi, Duncan Domey, and Ben Flanders. SenArt Films, 2006. Film.

The Veterans' Tale: Causes and Consequences_____
Pat C. Hoy II

For the combat veteran, war is a lifelong companion; the aftermath of war is but an extension of war itself. Ask any veteran willing to talk, and he or she will say, directly or indirectly, that the war has not ended. That war-in-the-head (and often in the body), the one that persists beyond the combat zone, is a complicated story about misfits that needs to be told with the same searing clarity soldiers and novelists have brought to the more exciting story of combat. At the heart of stories about war and its aftermath lies a profound mystery about why people and nations persist in the war game and why homecoming is such a troubling and silencing experience.

The definitive history of the combat story is Samuel Hynes's *The Soldiers' Tale* (1997). The book's supreme accomplishment lies in the multiplicity of soldiers' voices that Hynes permits readers to hear, which are accompanied by the deft, analytical voice of Hynes, the soldier-scholar, weaving the many tales about how it feels to be caught in the throes of war.

As comprehensive as *The Soldiers' Tale* is, however, it may leave one without a satisfying sense of the other war story, the longer tale of adjustment and accommodation. No one has written a definitive historical account of this longer story—perhaps because it never ends (perhaps, too, because both language and audience fail the teller). To tell the tale is to bare the soul, to reveal unspeakable secrets, and to betray the lessons of the battlefield about subordinating self, harnessing the ego, and looking out for the welfare of others. Telling is less worthy of the combat veteran than silent self-abnegation. The other story is almost perfectly suited to the novel, a story that can also be enhanced and clarified by the power of images, both moving and still. Fictional accounts, both suggestive and comprehensive, sometimes turn out to be more powerful than witnessing.

Given a choice between learning from psychiatrist Jonathan Shay's account of combat trauma—gleaned from veterans undergoing therapy—and the final terse scenes of *The Hurt Locker* (2008), I will always choose the film. Much that can be learned from Shay's *Achilles in Vietnam* (2003) can also be experienced viscerally and visually in *The Hurt Locker*'s concisely rendered closing scenes. Instead of understanding combat trauma in one's head only, one can experience it in both mind and body.

Consider the movie's final sequence: Sergeant William James returns to his family after a combat tour in Iraq, where each day he faced imminent death as a member of a bomb disposal team. Back home with his wife and son, roaming the aisles of a supermarket, James is as lost as any civilian would be in Iraq defusing bombs. In the cereal aisle, he is overwhelmed by choice, stupefied and unable to function.

At home on a ladder, cleaning leaves from the gutter in the pouring rain, James is equally inept and unhappy. Inside the house with his wife in their small kitchen, he tells her about a moment from the war when a truck pulled up in the marketplace, children rushed to get candy, and the truck exploded, killing fifty-nine people. He also tells her that they need more "bomb techs" in Iraq, but she directs his attention to the mushrooms floating in the sink and asks him to chop them. Each avoids issues central to the other's life.

The last of the home-front scenes isolates father and son. The baby bounces in his crib, fascinated by his music box, as a somber father talks to him about love:

As you get older, some of the things that you love might not seem so special anymore, you know. Like your jack in the box." [Pause, against sounds of child's laughter.] "Maybe you realize it's just a piece of tin and a stuffed animal. As you get older, there are fewer things you really love. And by the time you get to my age, there are only one or two things. . . . With me I think it's one.

The sound of helicopters rises in the background, and the image of James with his son is replaced by an image of helicopters landing side by side in Iraq. Sergeant James steps off the plane to begin another 365-day combat tour.

Love of war (and addiction to the intoxicating thrill of danger) replaces love of family, and one feels what Shay explains about posttraumatic stress disorder (PTSD)—a feeling of dislocation and frustration in the civilian world, a sense of invincibility in the combat zone, and the reality of an ever-increasing feeling of isolation, whether at home or in the war zone. The addictive disorder narrows the circle of trusted friends and closes the veteran off from the larger world.

Not every veteran comes home addicted, but most experience the shock of reentry: dislocation and some form of social isolation. Most do it quietly; a few violently. At the end of *In Pharaoh's Army* (1994), Tobias Wolff recounts his homecoming after a year in Vietnam. Joining the US Army had been essential to Wolff's "idea of legitimacy" because the men he had respected as he was growing up, and most of the writers he looked up to, had all served. Serving was the "indisputable certificate of citizenship and probity" (46).

However, when Wolff came back from Vietnam, he spent a week alone in a "seedy" San Francisco hotel room feeling not "freedom and pleasure" as he had expected but "aimlessness and solitude" (193). It was not the US Army he missed; there was a more troubling condition that he saw reflected in his own "gaunt hollow-eyed" image. "Broodingly alone," he knew that he could not reenter the "circle" of his family: "I did not feel equal to it. I felt morally embarrassed" (194–95). "Lonesome as I was," Wolff writes, "I made damn sure I stayed that way" (195).

In her novel *Jacob's Room* (1922), Virginia Woolf amplifies the readers' sense of what drives young men to war, identifying something in the very seethe of things that works quietly and insidiously. The novel moves across the landscape of Jacob Flanders's life, but instead of a typical linear narrative moving across time, Woolf develops

Flanders indirectly through the observations of other characters who react to him in short, cryptically rendered moments from his life. As readers inhabit these scenes, they overhear snippets of conversation, listen to gossip, and occasionally hear directly from the narrator about ideas related to Jacob and his circle.

Against this character sketching, Woolf reveals a larger purpose. She wants readers to know not only Jacob but also how he is (and, by extension, how everyone is) susceptible to unseen forces that operate in his life. She wants readers to learn something about life in general that a single life can only suggest.

Woven into the novel's strange fabric, a mysterious force accompanies Jacob across the landscape of his life. Readers learn of it bit by bit, sensing over time its power to commandeer crowds as well as young men like Jacob, who even as a boy is marked by the scent of death and an inclination to be heroic. As he plays along the seashore, climbing the rocks, readers are reminded that "a small boy has to stretch his legs far apart, and indeed to feel rather heroic, before he gets to the top" (5). Down from his vantage post, Jacob is startled by an "enormous" man and woman spread out on the sand, and, as he scampers away to find his nanny, he finds what is "perhaps a cow's skull" (5). In this initial scene, Jacob is too young to know anything at all about death and heroism, or life itself, but Woolf plants the seeds for his demise and outlines the internal and external forces that will govern his life.

When Jacob attends Cambridge, readers learn that it is a hierarchical place, that young men discover there a sense of their place in its ordered world, and that they leave with a confidence about their place in the larger world, a place already guaranteed by a well-established line of succession.

> They say the sky is the same everywhere. . . . But above Cambridge—anyhow above the roof of King's College Chapel—there is a difference: Out at sea a great city will cast a brightness into the night. Is it fanciful to suppose

the sky, washed into the crevices of King's College Chapel, lighter, thinner, more sparkling than the sky elsewhere? . . .

Look, as they pass into service, how airily the gowns blow out, as though nothing dense and corporeal were within. . . . In what orderly procession they advance. Thick wax candles stand upright; young men rise in white gowns; while the subservient eagle bears up for inspection the great white book. (24–25)

"An inclined plane of light comes accurately through each window," casting its rays of illumination, signifying that "inside the Chapel all was orderly" (25). Later, readers enter Jacob's room and find "cards from societies with little raised crescents, coats of arms, and initials; notes and pipes; on the table lay paper ruled with a red margin—an essay, no doubt—'Does History Consist of the Biographies of Great Men?'"(31).

Woolf is identifying an enclave of the privileged, an exclusive male society grounded in notions discussed by Thomas Carlyle in *On Heroes, Hero-Worship and the Heroic in History* (1841), an attempt on his part to restore respect for the accomplishments across time and cultures of "Great Men." Carlyle extols the virtues of these men, using those light images that later informed Woolf's own portrait of Cambridge:

We cannot look, however imperfectly, upon a great man, without gaining something by him. He is the living light-fountain, which it is good and pleasant to be near. The light which enlightens, which has enlightened the darkness of the world: and this not as a kindled lamp only, but rather as a natural luminary shining by the gift of Heaven; a flowing light-fountain, as I say, of native original insight, of manhood and heroic nobleness. . . . Could we see *them* well, we should get some glimpses into the very marrow of the world's history. (159)

Playing with allusions, Woolf calls readers both to recognize Carlyle and his images of light-bearing transcendence in her own text and to see that at the heart of her playfulness, she is dead serious. At Cambridge, the mysterious force takes shape in readers' minds, just as it begins to shape the lives and attitudes of Jacob and his friends. Spiritual and ephemeral, this force created an intimacy that "rose softly and washed over everything, mollifying, kindling, and coating the mind with the lustre of pearl, so that if you talk of a light, of Cambridge burning, it's not languages only" (37). The camaraderie, the cohesiveness, drew these young men into a vortex of complicity, without their realizing they were being prepared for sacrifice. That Woolf is not of Carlyle's persuasion must be remembered.

Later, in London, as Jacob entertains and consorts with a spectrum of women, he continues his studies, extends his social relationships, and remains characteristically elusive. As Jacob sits reading in the British Museum, Woolf indicates that an "enormous mind" inhabits this space where people come to read and participate in the workings of all those minds: Plato, Aristotle, Sophocles, William Shakespeare, and Christopher Marlowe. "Names stretched in unbroken file round the dome of the British Museum" (90). This mind, "this great mind is hoarded beyond the power of any single mind to possess it" (93). Nonetheless, Jacob, the individual, is there to get his fill of Marlowe. He cannot help himself. His youth, "something savage—something pedantic," and an inherited sense that the "flesh and blood of the future depends entirely" on him and his friends compel him to take his place among the great (92).

Back in Jacob's room, as Jacob tries to come to terms with the argument in Plato's *Phaedrus*, the narrator states that "when one reads straight ahead, falling into step, marching on, becoming (so it seems) momentarily part of this rolling, imperturbable energy, which has driven darkness before it since Plato walked the Acropolis, it is impossible to see the fire" (95). However, as Jacob finishes his reading, "Plato's argument is stowed away in [his] mind, and for five minutes, Jacob's mind continues alone, onwards, into the darkness" (95). The mysterious force has now become palpable and militaristic, compelling one to march in step with others who are driving the darkness away—even though they cannot see the fire. Like Aristotle before him, Jacob eventually mounts the Acropolis as part of his own longer journey through life, climbs up to the vantage post that commands a sweep of history, and discovers, perhaps, "the emergence through the earth of some spiritual energy" (130).

As World War I works itself into the novel with explicit references to battleships, guns, and the movement of armies, the text explains, "These actions, together with the incessant commerce of banks, laboratories, chancelleries, and houses of business, are the strokes which oar the world forward" (136). Later, the narrator states more clearly, more emphatically, "It is thus that we live, they say, driven by an unseizable force. They say that the novelists never catch it; that it goes hurtling through their nets and leaves them torn to ribbons" (137).

However, Woolf does catch the force, and she indicates that this force affects everyone. She likens it to the music of "trumpets and drums" and reveals that it reaches down to propel the masses every day to cross Waterloo Bridge as they move back and forth to London. "One might think that reason impelled them" (97). However, it has something to do with the "ecstasy and hubbub of the soul" (98). People respond to it unconsciously and submit to it. "This, they say, is what we live by—this unseizable force" that shapes Jacob, that sweeps him into war and, at novel's end, leaves readers with an empty room and pair of old shoes (137). His mother, Betty Flanders, who imagined that she could hear the guns of war back in Scarborough—"her sons fighting for their country"—is there in London in Jacob's room, holding out a pair of his old shoes while asking of his friend, "What am I to do with these, Mr. Bonamy?" (154–55).

Discernible is Woolf's unwillingness, or even her inability, to explain fully the powerful, nullifying force. In these passages, she attributes the knowledge of this ubiquitous force to "the men in clubs and Cabinets" (136). "They say" what the force does, how it moves us around. Finally, readers are left to imagine that in its many guises, it is both a product of culture and a manifestation of something deeply personal, even archetypal. On one hand the force exists independently of time and individuals; however, individuals are moved around by it, inspired to follow certain pathways of self-discovery by it, but are also duped by its invisibility and impersonal savagery, duped too by the legacy of "Great Men." The force also unites men and women erotically, creates a fatal intimacy among aspiring young men, inspires a certain fealty to the sovereign, and excludes women on the one hand but leads them into strange alliances with fate on the other. In Woolf's mind this force is not just a casus belli, but the fundamental cause; it is different in kind, but akin to all that Wolff explains as his reasons for going to Vietnam. Woolf is calling attention to something deeper and more mysterious: an ever-present force that sweeps mankind into war.

In *A Terrible Love of War* (2004), James Hillman sheds light on Woolf's wisdom and brings war across the ocean to the United States, even as he offers an explanation that transcends time and particular cultures. Hillman asks readers to move past causal analysis and the science of logic into the mind's poetic, mythic layer to understand "the underlying patterns that move human affairs" (8). People have to "recognize that war is a mythical happening, that those in the midst of it are removed to a mythical state of being, that their return from it seems rationally inexplicable, and that the love of war tells of a love of the gods, the gods of war" (9). In the "strange coupling of love with war," Hillman argues, humanity "find [it]self transported to a mythical condition and the gods most real" (9). This love of war "unlike any other and which veterans report they found only in the midst of war's terror . . . creates a potency of one's self that is at the same time a sacrifice of one's self" (158). Within that paradox, Hillman finds what other writers, from the Greeks to Tim O'Brien, have revealed: something decidedly sublime.

That sublimity, that sense of self-worth, comes to naught, however, when veterans return home and find no understanding and no one to hear their tales. Their war experiences are nullified when they confront a culture that operates on moral and ethical principles that silence conversation and understanding about the difference between killing on the battlefield and killing elsewhere. At home, bearing the burden of sacrifice and silence becomes increasingly difficult.

In *Mrs Dalloway* (1925), Woolf presents a penetrating look into the madness that war can produce and the ways it affects a nation and cripples its veterans. The unseizable force plays its part, but Woolf's deeper concern is with life itself—life informed by death. On the surface, Woolf plunges into the scintillating activity of a June day in London, in the heart of a bustling, postwar city that is in the midst of an industrial revolution. The novel also rubs up against royalty and order. World War I, just terminated in the world of the novel, has not really ended.

Against the "divine vitality" of that morning in June, the "leaden circles" from Big Ben propagating across the city join with the brief, reverberating reminders of war scattered across the novel: "Mrs. Foxcroft at the Embassy last night eating her heart out because that nice boy was killed . . . or Lady Bexborough who opened a bazaar, they said, with the telegram in her hand, John, her favourite, killed" (7, 4–5). Also, as Clarissa Dalloway scurried about town preparing for the party she would give that evening, "she had a perpetual sense, as she watched the taxi cabs, of being out, out, far out at sea and alone; she always had the feeling that it was very, very dangerous to live even one day" (8). The persistence of death and loneliness troubles her. "Did it matter then, she asked herself . . . that she must inevitably cease completely; all this must go on without her; did she resent it; or did it not become consoling to believe that death ended absolutely?" (9).

While musing, Clarissa makes her way back home from shopping and imagines a strange kind of immortality:

Or did it not become consoling to believe that death ended absolutely? but that somehow in the streets of London, on the ebb and flow of things, here, there, she survived, Peter [her friend] survived, lived in each other, she being part, she was positive, of the trees at home; of the house there, ugly, rambling all to bits and pieces as it was; part of people she had never met; being laid out like a mist between the people she knew best, who lifted her on their branches as she had seen the trees lift the mist, but it spread ever so far, her life, herself. (9)

Then the narrator gives a wider, transhistorical view that calls back into question the here and now rather than the forever: "This late age of the world's experience had bred in them all, all men and women, a well of tears. Tears and sorrows; courage and endurance; a perfectly upright and stoical bearing" (13).

Everywhere in the novel are signs of the "perfectly upright and stoical bearing," a stay against the ebb and flow of life and the turmoil of war. Almost everyone lives constrained lives; throughout the novel are signs of personal denial and of superficial relationships more social than fulfilling. Clarissa is not living the life she might have lived elsewhere in a different time, and she knows the difference between what is and what might be. She persists, nonetheless. She will give her party, bring people together, and insist that something important will come of it.

Clarissa persists in the aftermath of war and against the other cultural and social forces that could easily cause one to forget life's promises. She persists, also, by virtue of a quirk in the novel's design, a surprise that comes almost unbidden during its final pages. To understand, one must return to the moment when Septimus Warren Smith enters the fictional world.

Woolf could have had Clarissa encounter Septimus during her morning walk as she prepared for her party. He was there in the scene when the automobile bearing royalty appeared. However, Septimus is in one place watching; Clarissa is in another, and the narrator, seeing everything from above the scene, knows what others cannot know:

And there the motor car stood, with drawn blinds, and upon them a curious pattern like a tree, Septimus thought, and this gradual drawing together of everything to one centre before his eyes, as if some horror had come almost to the surface and was about to burst into flames, terrified him. The world wavered and quivered and threatened to burst into flames. It is I who am blocking the way, he thought. (14–15)

However, Septimus is not blocking the way. This first glimpse of him, at thirty, gives readers a sense that he is perhaps on the verge of madness. At this moment, when he and Clarissa are in the same place at the same time, Woolf chooses to keep them apart (except in the minds of readers and through the language of trees they both share). These trees bear strange signs of life, always.

Despite not wanting Clarissa and Septimus to meet at this moment, Woolf wants readers to see them in close proximity and wants to call attention to the force that attends the movement of the motor car—"the enduring symbol of the state"—as it "left a slight ripple" in its wake, causing strangers to think "of the dead; of the flag; of Empire" (17). As the car moves closer to Buckingham Palace, the people "stood even straighter, and removed their hands, and seemed ready to attend their Sovereign, if need be, to the cannon's mouth, as their ancestors had done before them," as Jacob had done, as Septimus has done (18). In the aftermath of war, there is living proof of the "savagery" that attends any sovereign's power. Woolf presents evidence of the chilling aftermath of war.

Septimus "left home, a mere boy" and went to "London leaving an absurd note behind him, such as great men have written, and the world has read later when the story of their struggles has become famous" (82). Nourished by the beauty and presumed wisdom of Miss Isabel Pole, who taught him Shakespeare, Septimus "flowered from vanity, ambition, idealism, passion, loneliness, courage, laziness, the usual seeds," and, eventually, "was one of the first to volunteer" (83–84). In the trenches, "he developed manliness, he was promoted"; developed friendships; and by war's end was unable to feel (84–85). Burdened by the fear of not being able to feel, he became engaged one evening in Italy when the "panic was on him" (85). Back in London with his Italian wife, he finds himself unfit to live in the culture that had sent him to die—a culture that knew little about how to care for him on his return. His war-induced madness is beyond the comprehension of his wife and the doctors who attempt to minister to his psychological needs.

Nevertheless, there is a strain of sanity in Septimus's madness, a knowledge, acquired perhaps indirectly from his war experiences, that eludes his wife, Rezia, and the doctors. One doctor, Holmes, insists that Septimus need only put the war out of his mind; the other, Bradshaw, insists on a simple regimen of "Proportion" as a cure (97). To Septimus these doctors represent the worst of "human nature," what he characterizes as the "repulsive brute, with the blood-red nostrils" (90). There is no doubt that Septimus is a victim of what was then called shell shock and what is now known as PTSD. He seems to be sometimes "straying on the edge of the world" (90). Sometimes he speaks out loud to his dead friend Evans, with whom he fought in the war, and he is given to habitual pronouncements and exhortations that seem to Septimus sent from either God or dead: "Do not cut down the trees; tell the Prime Minister. Universal love: the meaning of the world. Burn them! He cried" (144). When he felt that Rezia was truly on his side, "she was a flowering tree; and through her branches looked out the face of a lawgiver, who had reached a sanctuary where she feared no one; not Holmes; not Bradshaw; a miracle, a triumph, the last and greatest" (144).

Thus, Septimus sometimes seems to be the sanest person in the novel. The narrator's language and the novel's imagery put him in league with Clarissa, on the side of a life force with which almost all others have lost touch:

To watch a leaf quivering in the rush of air was an exquisite joy [for Septimus]. Up in the sky swallows swooping, swerving, flinging themselves in and out, round and round, yet always with perfect control as if elastics held them; and the flies rising and falling; and the sun spotting now this leaf, now that, in mockery, dazzling it with soft gold in pure good temper; and now and again some chime (it might be a motor horn) tinkling divinely on the grass stalks—all of this, calm and reasonable at it was, made out of ordinary things as it was, was the truth now; beauty, that was the truth now. Beauty was everywhere. (68)

For Septimus, toiling against the forces of humanity, there is no stay against loneliness and the "brute with the red nostrils" (144). When Holmes finally comes upon Septimus with his own imperatives, "there remained only the window, the large Bloomsbury-lodging house window, the tiresome, the troublesome, and rather melodramatic business of opening the window and throwing himself out" (145–46). Thus, with Holmes at his door, Septimus cried out that he would give him his life, "and flung himself vigorously, violently down on Mrs. Filmer's area railings" to his death (146). Strangely and surprisingly, however, death is not the end of Septimus.

Clarissa's daily life swings from tumescence to emptiness, from moments of ecstasy to moments of self-doubting deflation. At times, she senses a powerful life force operating in the nature of things; it is a counterforce to the masculine one that sweeps men and women into destructive ways of life, leads young men into war, and pushes the crowds back and forth across Waterloo Bridge. It is a counterforce that rides "on waves of that divine vitality which Clarissa loved" (7). There are times in Clarissa's life when she can with "some effort, some call on her to be her self, [draw] the parts together." She can sit in her drawing room and create "a meeting-point, a radiancy no doubt in some dull lives, a refuge for the lonely to come to, perhaps" (36). She can give her party, standing at the head of the stairs, radiant.

Without the presence of Septimus, the particular party toward which this novel moves might have been hollow, a manifestation of Clarissa's self-delusion. Even in the midst of the lords and ladies in attendance, Clarissa "was not enjoying it. . . . She had this feeling of not being herself, and that everyone was unreal in one way; much more real in another" (166). Then the prime minister arrives, and "her severity, her prudery, her woodenness were all warmed through" (170). Walking about the rooms with the prime minister, "she had felt that intoxication of the moment, that dilatation of the nerves of the heart itself till it seemed to quiver, steeped, upright . . . [but] still these semblances, these triumphs . . . had a hollowness; at arm's length they were, not in the heart" (170). As she vacillates, it remains difficult to accept the importance of her soiree, difficult to imagine that what Clarissa is doing matters, and even more difficult, to believe in Clarissa herself.

When the Bradshaws arrive late and bring "death" into the party, the trajectory of the novel becomes more visible. The whispered word of a young man's suicide captures Clarissa; Septimus's death is relived in more gruesome detail than at the moment of his leap. Clarissa understands almost immediately that in flinging his life away, Septimus has "preserved" something. "Death was defiance. Death was an attempt to communicate" (180). She realizes that she and her friends will go on living, that they "would grow old." However, Septimus's death redeems her: "A thing there was that mattered; a thing, wreathed about with chatter, defaced, obscured in her own life, let drop every day in corruption, lies, chatter. This he had preserved" (180). This deeper life force at the heart of the ordinary, he had preserved.

Clarissa goes into a little room to be alone for a few moments and, gaining her composure, comes finally to see her own relationship with Septimus: "She felt somehow very like him—the young man who had killed himself. She felt glad that he had done it; thrown it away. The clock was striking. The leaden circles dissolved in the air. He made her feel the beauty; made her feel the fun. But she must go back. She must assemble. She must find Sally and Peter" (182). Clarissa's logic and her resolve are understandable in the context of the sense of beauty that she and Septimus shared in the language of the trees, and in their sure sense that beneath what Woolf elsewhere called the "cotton wool" of daily life, "there is a hidden pattern; that we—I mean all human beings—are connected with this; that the whole world is a work of art; that we are parts of the work of art. . . . We are the words; we are the music; we are the thing itself" ("Sketch" 72). The mystery of *Mrs Dalloway* (and the mystery of the relationship between Septimus and Clarissa) is the hidden pattern that connects everyone.

Septimus's act of defiance can be meaningful only when it is understood that the other forces working against him are so powerfully repressive that flinging one's life away is indeed an act of preservation. Doing so constitutes a cri de coeur on par with that of Mrs. Flanders's own question at the end of *Jacob's Room*. Woolf and the others have presented a clear sense of the causes and consequences of mankind's never-ending fascination with destruction. Both she and Hillman remind that destruction and beauty have magnetic powers that fascinate and motivate humanity.

All too often, war trails off into stories of tears and sorrows, into lives of isolation and, sometimes, despair. War silences the warriors who secretly bear its burden. Even though fiction breaks into that silence, revealing the wages of war, humanity continues to respond instinctively to the sound of the guns.

Kurt Vonnegut's *Slaughterhouse-Five* (a novel grounded in World War II but published in 1969) offers a sane and funny way to round out this investigation. *Slaughterhouse-Five* is vehemently antiwar, but it is a boldly funny novel that harbors a deep streak of resentment and an even deeper concern for the never-ending parade of young people who are sent off to die. At its heart lies the senseless firebombing of Dresden, an actual historical event that led to useless destruction. The estimated number of deaths varies from 40,000 to 130,000. Vonnegut was there as a soldier during the bombing and survived to tell his tale.

The novel begins, "Listen: Billy Pilgrim has come unstuck in time" (20). It ends as Billy comes out of war's confinement in Dresden, where he and a small group of prisoners have been working the "corpse mines," recovering bodies of those killed during the bombing. The soldiers wander out onto the shady street to find that "the trees were leafing out" (186). All is quiet, except: "Birds were talking. One bird said to Billy Pilgrim, *Poo-tee-weet?*" The moment is one of sweet release, a moment, in terms of this novel's logic, that lasts a lifetime.

During the war, Billy comes unstuck in time, often moving back and forth across his life in defiance of time and space. After the war, he is abducted to a planet called Tralfamadore where he sometimes lives under a geodesic dome with Montana Wildhack, another earthling. They are abducted to satisfy the Tralfamadorians' curiosity about the bodies and reproductive activities of earthlings. Tralfamadorians, "two feet high, and green, and shaped like plumber's friends," have sticklike bodies topped by "a little hand with a green eye in its palm" (22–23). They see in four dimensions, are friendly with Billy and Montana, speak telepathically, and are gleeful as they observe the consorting earthlings.

Billy learns from the Tralfamadorians that "when a person dies he only *appears* to die. He is very much alive in the past. . . . All moments, past, present, and future, always have existed, always will exist" (23). So life consists of a series of moments, none more consequential than others, and the Tralfamadorians counsel Billy to concentrate on the more pleasant ones. Thus, when he is back on Earth, Billy devotes a great deal of time to telling stories about what he has learned elsewhere.

On Earth, Billy is a competent optometrist. Like Septimus, however, he continues to experience things that other earthlings cannot imagine. As with Septimus, a streak of sanity informs Billy's craziness. He imagines himself attracted "to a much higher calling than mere business." By telling his unusual stories, "he was doing nothing less . . . he thought, than prescribing corrective lenses for Earthling souls" (25). However, no one listens, no one's vision is improved by Billy's efforts.

Left with a hoard of fictive knowledge, readers must ask how much smarter they are than Billy and Septimus, men who return from war crazed misfits, burdened by its secrets yet gifted with strange sight. In their fictive worlds, what they know and try to tell others falls on deaf ears. What hope there is for readers may (as the Tralfamadorians would suggest) lie outside the realm of readers' jurisdiction. However, as earthlings, people can still imagine that they have the power to swim against the tide of such logic. Should they choose to do so, they might summon the necessary power to fashion their own survival. The evidence of the fiction suggests that countering the powerful and mysterious forces that sweep mankind unwittingly into war may not be possible.

Works Cited

Carlyle, Thomas. "The Hero as Divinity." *Victorian Literature: Prose.* Eds. G. B. Tennyson and Donald J. Gray. New York: McMillan, 1976. 159–75.
Hillman, James. *A Terrible Love of War.* New York: Penguin, 2004.
The Hurt Locker. Dir. Kathryn Bigelow. Summit Entertainment, 2008. Film.
Hynes, Samuel. *The Soldiers' Tale: Bearing Witness to Modern War.* New York: Viking, 1997.
Shay, Jonathan. *Achilles in Vietnam: Combat Trauma and the Undoing of Character.* New York: Scribner, 2003.
Wolff, Tobias. *In Pharaoh's Army: Memories of the Lost War.* New York: Knopf, 1994.
Woolf, Virginia. *Jacob's Room.* 1922. New York: Penguin, 1992.
_____. *Mrs Dalloway.* 1925. Orlando: Harcourt, 2005.
_____. "A Sketch of the Past." *Moments of Being.* Orlando: Harcourt, 1985. 61–160.
Vonnegut, Kurt. *Slaughterhouse-Five or The Children's Crusade.* New York: Dell, 1969.

From Brooke's "The Soldier" to Owen's "Dulce et Decorum Est": The Demise of "Beautiful Death" in the New Poetics of World War I_____

Tom McGuire

Wilfred Owen's "Dulce et Decorum Est" and Rupert Brooke's "The Soldier" stand as two of the most compelling and influential poems of remembrance to come out of World War I, a horrific four-year war of attrition (1914–18) that squandered some 8.5 million combatant lives and left upward of 6 million civilians dead from starvation, disease, and genocide. If "The Soldier" embodies a highly stylized, traditional approach to commemorating the sacrifice of fallen soldiers, the revolutionary rage of "Dulce et Decorum Est" stands in the starkest imaginable contrast to Brooke's soothing pastoral elegy. In his acerbic assault on hyperpatriotic remembrances of the war dead, Owen conjures a kind of antielegy through his no-holds-barred rejection of attempts to idealize the ultimate sacrifice. In this regard, "The Soldier" and "Dulce et Decorum Est" not only serve as important benchmarks in the development of twentieth-century war poetry but also register some of the major aesthetic transformations that swept through modernist poetics during and after World War I.

As writers of their distinctive brands of war remembrance, in "The Soldier" and "Dulce et Decorum Est" Brooke and Owen were, in a sense, doing the work war poets have always done—finding "a way of remembering that which it would impoverish us to forget" (to borrow Robert Frost's phrase). From Homer's time onward, the war poet has been vital to society, playing the role of memory-keeper. With the advent of mechanized, mass slaughter in World War I, however, poets like Brooke and Owen were presented with a new and, in some respects, unprecedented set of aesthetic and ethical challenges as they sought to memorialize the war dead. The respective solutions to such challenges that Brooke and Owen developed in "The Soldier" and "Dulce et Decorum Est" could not have been more radically opposed, but one characteristic these poems share in common has been their ability to stir both opprobrium and approbation. Since the publication of these poems in 1915 and 1917, respectively, critics have both celebrated and pilloried "The Soldier" and "Dulce et Decorum Est" for a variety of reasons; the reasons often fold back on the following interrogations and challenges to the poems: "Does this poem respectfully and adequately commemorate a soldier's sacrifice?" and "What does this war poem say about the causes and consequences of patriotism that favors, at all costs, the good of the state over the individual?" While Brooke and Owen offer two of the most memorable answers to these questions in their respective poems, they were not alone among World War I poets in taking up of the problem of war remembrance.

A less familiar but no less compelling World War I poem that raises similar questions about memorializing the war dead is Siegfried Sassoon's "On Passing the New Menin Gate." An ardent, early proponent of the war, Sassoon eventually evolved into one of the conflict's most outspoken critics after intermittently serving in the trenches for nearly four years. Sassoon, who became a friend and mentor to Owen during the war, began writing "On Passing the New Menin Gate" in late July 1927, shortly after the dedication of a massive monument commemorating the names of soldiers who fell fighting at the Ypres Salient in Belgium. When Sassoon completed the poem in January 1928, he had penned one of the war's most embittered sonnets. Sassoon's poem begins by posing an incriminating question: "Who will remember, passing through this Gate, / The unheroic Dead who fed the guns?" (1–2). This master of irony knows the answer is that few, if any, passersby will remember the 54,896 "intolerably nameless names" inscribed on the monument.

The scale of the war's carnage (twenty thousand men died on average in every four-day period of the war), the monument's own massive scale, the high placement of the inscriptions, and their minuscule size combine to obscure the individual names and lives lost. Sassoon also knew that only a decade after its cessation, the war had become a distant memory, a nightmare many people preferred to forget. In its attempt to memorialize the war and those who perished in it, however, the Menin Gate ironically fosters its own brand of amnesia, a forgetfulness of the actual conditions and cost of the war:

> Who shall absolve the foulness of their fate,—
> Those doomed, conscripted, unvictorious ones?
> Crudely renewed, the Salient holds its own.
> Paid are its dim defenders by this pomp. (3–6)

Instead of honestly and adequately remembering the fallen soldiers by providing some sense of their terrible suffering in the muddy, "sullen swamp" of the Salient's trenches, the monument obscures their identity and sacrifice by commemorating their deaths en masse in a clean and polished memorial. The tidiness and "pomp" of it all stands in sharp contrast to the actual Ypres Salient campaigns, which took place in fly- and rat-infested trenches where troops wallowed knee-deep in mud, mire that swallowed and drowned thousands of troops. The sestet completes Sassoon's sardonic assessment of the monument by punctuating further incriminating questions with an indictment of a cliché phrase meant to assuage grief:

> Here was the world's worst wound. And here with pride
> "Their name liveth forever," The Gateway claims.
> Was ever an immolation so belied
> As these intolerably nameless names?
> Well might the Dead who struggled in the slime
> Rise and deride this sepulchre of crime. (9–14)

The conclusion of the ending couplet ("sepulchre of crime") refers, on one level, to the object of the tomb's commemoration, a war Sassoon deemed criminal, but Sassoon also seems to suggest the gate itself is criminal because the elegant memorial fails to reveal any sense of the gruesome wartime realities that transpired on the site. In Sassoon's view, derision of this war memorial is necessary because such remembrance of the war dead constitutes no meaningful remembrance at all. Building upon his ironic opening question, "Who will remember . . . The unheroic Dead?," Sassoon thus suggests the Menin Gate participates in the same kind of obliteration of individual identity that war does.

War has always staked its existence and efficacy on massively destructive depersonalization. From Homer onward, the greatest war poets have consistently challenged this fact of war, taking upon themselves the responsibility of railing against it by trying to put a face on war. Remembering the war dead in all their concrete humanity and individuality has always been the great challenge and payoff of good war writing. This is a tall order, though, because war so often defaces the human subject and erases personality, that mercurial thing called the self. As Simone Weil puts it, "When exercised to the full, the Force of war makes a thing of the human person literally, for it makes him a corpse" (Weil 5). Ravenous war has always gorged itself, fed its insatiable appetite for souls, on the annihilation of the individual. In modern times, however, with the rise of nation-states and their wars of attrition either for or against cancers such as rabid nationalism and totalitarianism, the ante has been upped in the assault on the individual. Georg Wilhelm Friedrich Hegel, in his apotheosis of the German nation, explains the tension between the state and individual: "The moment the State calls, 'Myself and my existence are at stake!' . . . The individual must forget his own ego and feel himself a member of the whole . . . the loftiness of war—that the small man disappears entirely before the great thought of the State" (qtd. in Ehrenreich 214).

Keeping in mind Sassoon's sonnet and its central question, it is useful to think of war poems, especially remembrances for fallen soldiers, as miniature war monuments. A soldier's elegy has typically served as a kind of memorial, one that seeks to embody and enshrine the honorable qualities distinguishing the warrior's life and death. While many critics have read "The Soldier" as a locus classicus of pastoral elegy, a traditional poetic form used to commemorate the dead, relatively few studies have examined "Dulce et Decorum Est" in terms of its ironic relation to the elegy tradition, pastoral or otherwise. However, Owen crafts a decidedly sardonic poem of remembrance, using a subtle code of antipastoral reference to reinforce his sense of outrage at the war. Since "The Soldier" and "Dulce et Decorum Est" offer such divergent and unique perspectives on the question of memorializing a soldier's death, it is helpful to examine the "The Soldier" and "Dulce et Decorum Est" not only in terms of traditional elegies for fallen warriors but also under the umbrella of the *beautiful death* trope, a time-honored way of memorializing fallen warriors.

Although one may tend to think of elegy as a purely literary mode of expression, elegy is best understood when considered in terms of its social, religious, and political significance. Traditionally, poets in the ancient Greek and Roman contexts composed elegies for use in religious ceremonies. Elegies ritualistically prepared and launched the deceased into the afterlife journey; in the case of fallen soldiers, however, elegies were also intended to raise the dead to a status of immortal honor consistent with the reputation they had earned through combat and excellent death in battle. The memorializing function of elegy places it under the sign of what some classical scholars call the *beautiful death tradition*, a perennial feature not only of war writing, but the whole dynamic of collective memory formation found in Homer's *Iliad* (c. 750 BCE; English translation, 1611) and other sites of oral culture.[1]

In his account of the Peloponnesian War, Thucydides provides a useful description of the beautiful death convention in his discussion of Athenian funeral rites memorializing young warriors who have died honorably in battle. Thucydides records Pericles's commemoration of fallen Athenian patriots to stress the value of the warriors' sacrifices. Because they died in battle defending the polis (city-state), the soldiers receive the distinction of having enjoyed a "beautiful death" (*kalos thanatos*). Thus, Pericles's eulogy constitutes a memorial tribute that honors the war dead not only for their service to the polis but also for the inherent value of their deaths in battle. As the Homeric scholar Jean-Pierre Vernant notes, "For all time to come, [the beautiful death] elevates the fallen warrior to a state of glory . . . this celebrity, this *kleos*, that henceforth surrounds his name and person is the ultimate accolade that represents his greatest accomplishment, the winning of *aretē* (excellence)" (Vernant 312). In short, the "state of glory" is achieved in the name of and bestowed by the polis.

Brooke's elegy seems to reflect Wallace Stevens's statement that "Death is the mother of beauty"; for Owen, however, death only serves to father a nightmarish image of horror. As such, few World War I poets diverge so dramatically in their approach to the beautiful-death tradition as Owen and Brooke do, especially in the two poems in question. Whereas Brooke embraces the beautiful-death trope, Owen explodes it. "The Soldier" features a speaker who suggests the beautifully transcendent terms by which others ought to remember him after his death. In his sonnet, Brooke invokes the pastoral elegy tradition, albeit somewhat unconventionally, as the speaker only imagines his own imminent death, prettifying and therefore transforming the prospect through gorgeous pastoral images. Conversely, in "Dulce et Decorum Est" Owen pens a jolting poem of remembrance, an antipastoral vision of wartime suffering that dispenses with the usual platitudes, niceties, and ceremonial pomp expected of war memorials.

First, note the mellifluousness and dreamy pastoral repose on display in Brooke's "The Soldier":

> If I should die, think only this of me:
> That there's some corner of a foreign field
> That is forever England. There shall be
> In that rich earth a richer dust concealed;
> A dust whom England bore, shaped, made aware,
> Gave, once, her flowers to love, her ways to roam;
> A body of England's, breathing English air,
> Washed by the rivers, blest by suns of home. (1–8)

Next, consider the final twelve lines of Owen's poem in which the speaker incriminates his audience, challenging readers to look squarely at the effects wrought by a lethal poison-gas attack on a nameless soldier, whose anonymity marks him as a kind of Everyman representing tens of thousands of gas victims:

> If in some smothering dreams you too could pace
> Behind the wagon that we flung him in,
> And watch the white eyes writhing in his face,
> His hanging face, like a devil's sick of sin;
> If you could hear, at every jolt, the blood
> Come gargling from the froth-corrupted lungs,
> Obscene as cancer, bitter as the cud
> Of vile, incurable sores on innocent tongues,—
> My friend, you would not tell with such high zest
> To children ardent for some desperate glory,
> The old Lie: Dulce et decorum est
> Pro patria mori. (17–28)

The speaker's sickening recollection of the soldier's death emboldens him to denounce Horace's patriotic phrase as an outright lie. Significantly, *dulce et decorum est pro patria mori* means "it is sweet and decorous to die for one's fatherland/country," but the final gruesome image plaguing the speaker's shell-shocked memory is far from sweet or decorous.

It is perhaps difficult to imagine that "The Soldier" and "Dulce et Decorum Est" were written during the same war, but they were— roughly two years apart. Brooke wrote his poem in January 1915, and Owen his in October 1917. Significantly, Brooke completed "The Soldier" four months before he died on April 23, 1915, from mosquito-bite-induced septicemia aboard a military ship off the Gallipoli coast. His death denied him combat experience, as it came just days prior to his unit's first combat assignment in the disastrous Allied assault of the

Gallipoli Peninsula, on April 25, 1915.[2] Owen, on the other hand, spent more than a year on the front lines. He wrote "Dulce et Decorum Est" in October 1917, well after both sides had normalized the business of mass slaughter. Given each poet's unique story and experience of war, it is not surprising that Brooke and Owen take vastly different paths to imagining and memorializing a soldier's death.

One aspect of "The Soldier" that renders it so compelling as a war memorial is the artistic and technical skill with which Brooke weaves his laurel of elegiac remembrance. The sonnet is a formal and prosodic gem; but the poem's graceful presentation of the beautiful-death ideal also deserves mention. With its recipe for gaining eternal repute in England's collective memory, Brooke's sonnet stands as perhaps the best known and most frequently quoted statement of the notion that a British soldier's death should not be viewed as futile or final. The speaker imagines his impending death as desirable precisely because of the promise it offers: a peaceful, honorable state of eternal existence. The prospect of death also attracts the speaker because he believes his dying will somehow perfect and expand the idea of England itself in the "eternal mind" (10). By fighting and perishing in "the corner of some foreign field," the soldier hopes not only to plant a bit of England there but also to enrich and fortify the very dust of the foreign land through his blood sacrifice. In this way, the speaker expresses a supreme belief in the power of regeneration through violence, regeneration that will not only secure his honorable reputation but also prompt a revitalization of the very foreign field where he longs to die.

In all of this, there is more than a hint of Hegel's notion that "the small man" must disappear "before the great thought of the State." After all, the "loftiness of war" consists of forgetting "one's own ego" and feeling oneself "a member of the whole." "The Soldier" blithely celebrates the prospect of its speaker's disappearance in the great thought of England. Seeing in this dreamy vision of sanctifying self-immolation a veiled justification for imperialistic violence, Brooke's adversarial critics have long noted the jingoistic tendencies of "The

Soldier." Nonetheless, as Britain strained to complete its mobilization efforts, such high-sounding praise for magnanimous self-sacrifice also earned "The Soldier" immediate accolades.

Though "The Soldier" proves itself ignorant of actual war experience, hawkish British supporters of the war likely cottoned onto the poem for that very reason, seeing in the poem's expression of rapturous patriotism fodder for attracting new recruits to man British cannons. Even the dean of St. Paul's Cathedral quoted "The Soldier" in his Easter Sunday sermon on April 4, 1915. That the head vicar of St Paul's would quote from Brooke's sonnet on the feast of Christ's resurrection and victory over death is not surprising. "The Soldier" stakes its entire claim to legitimacy on the hope that death will give rise, for both the soldier-speaker and the nation, to abundant life. Finally, when Brooke died three weeks after the Easter sermon, Winston Churchill wrote a gushing obituary honoring Brooke, calling "The Soldier" an "incomparable sonnet" and lauding Brooke for his willingness to die for "dear England" (qtd. in Roberts 72–73).

With "Dulce et Decorum Est," Owen seeks to question the desirability, wisdom, and promise of dying for "dear England" in the trenches. Owen rejects virtually every political sentiment and aesthetic value found in "The Soldier." Indeed, much of the poem's power derives from Owen's highly concentrated and sustained attack on the beautiful-death tradition, an attack that introduces a revolutionary way of memorializing wartime suffering and death. In "Dulce et Decorum Est" Owen adopts an attitude toward war memorials akin to Sassoon's in "On Passing the New Menin Gate." Both Owen and Sassoon essentially argue that adequate war memorials must recognize the truth of wartime suffering and death, not gloss over and prettify it with high-sounding clichés and consolatory patriotic phrases.

Unlike the tranquil poetic landscape of "The Soldier," violence shakes "Dulce et Decorum Est" at its core. Violence permeates all the key elements of poetic artifice deployed by Owen (disturbing imagery, rough-grating sounds, unsettling and irregular rhythms, and the palpable outrage in the speaker's tone). The poem immediately thrusts the reader into the actual mess of combat, a scene littered with concrete references to a battlefield where troops "deaf" and "drunk with fatigue" trudge through ubiquitous muck, impervious to the screams of exploding shells behind them.

While not averse to using figures of speech to create meaning, Owen deftly balances the metaphorical with the literal; he seeks to create a tangible sense of the actual conditions of trench warfare by forcing his audience to experience what he and his men have experienced. Owen wants readers to see and hear the weight of the soldiers' burdens, burdens that demean and grind them into a stupor:

> Bent double, like old beggars under sacks,
> Knock-kneed, coughing like hags, we cursed through sludge
> Till on the haunting flares we turned our backs
> And towards our distant rest began to trudge" (1–4).

In the first four lines, Owen is already hard at work aurally documenting the sights and sounds of trench warfare through his deployment of excessive plosives and suggestive vowel sounds. In lines one and two, for example, a violent sound system created by multiple harsh consonants (plosive "Bs," "Ks," and hard "Cs") serves to mimic the sound of exploding 5.9-inch artillery shells. Additional sonic mimesis emerges from a preponderance of the most unpoetic vowel sound in the English language—the short *u* vowel sound ("uh") in "double," "under," "sludge," and "trudge"—as Owen punctuates these lines with an aural approximation of soldiers grunting and sighing under the strain of battle and the weight of their packs.

Owen's experience as a soldier-poet and his sense of his responsibility to act as a kind of embedded soothsayer often led him to use such techniques of realist representation. By bringing together specific images and sounds common to the western front, Owen thus engages in what the Vietnam War poet Dale Ritterbusch aptly calls "documentary realism," a kind of reportage aimed at representing the experience of trench warfare in highly graphic, concrete, and realistic terms. Writing in June 1918, a few months before he died in action, Owen explained his commitment to truth-telling in the following preface drafted for a collection of poems he hoped to publish after the war:

> This book is not about heroes. English poetry is not yet fit to speak of them. Nor is it about deeds, or land, nor anything about glory, honour, might, majesty, dominion, or power, except War. Above all I am not concerned with Poetry. My subject is War, and the pity of War. The Poetry is in the pity. Yet these elegies are to this generation in no sense consolatory. They may be to the next. All a poet can do today is warn. That is why the true Poets must be truthful. (qtd. in Roberts 319)

Owen highlights the aesthetic values that guide his production of war poetry after 1916. Granting no quarter to any of the old abstractions about duty, majesty, and dominion that may have previously guided war poets, Owen rejects the possibility of writing in the beautiful-death tradition when he eliminates "glory" and "honor" from his mix of acceptable subject matter. His primary responsibility is to function as a kind of truth-teller, a prophetic voice that bears the burden of warning readers about the actual cost and consequences of war in real human terms. Finally, truth-telling for Owen demands a commitment to inspiring pity for his fellow comrades.

As a writer of lyric poetry (i.e., poetry concerned with the interior status or subjectivity of an individual consciousness at a particular moment in history and time), Owen had to balance the demands of documentary realism with the lyric poet's responsibility to express truthfully and adequately the complexity of interior, psychological reality. Thus, the dual commitment to truth-telling and the lyric impulse required Owen to portray not only the external material conditions and dangers of trench life but also the psychological, spiritual, and affective pressures that are inevitably brought to bear on human beings struggling for survival in extremis.

The staying power of Owen's work often derives from his profound poetic explorations of the psychological and physiological disruptions and disorientations common to wartime experience. In this respect, Owen uses the first stanza of "Dulce et Decorum Est" to document the troops' utter numbness and loss of affect. Fatigue and ennui give way to a general feeling of indifference to the danger of exploding shells. Frequent shelling, the lack of sleep, physical deprivation, and the psychological effects of routinely witnessing and smelling death have deadened the soldiers' emotions and sensory perceptions:

> Men marched asleep.
> Many had lost their boots.
> But limped on, blood-shod.
> All went lame; all blind;
> Drunk with fatigue; deaf even to the hoots
> Of tired, outstripped Five-Nines that dropped behind" (5–8).

In this passage, the soldiers are too lightning-blasted and calcined by their conditions to care about the threat of incoming mortars. However, when the soldiers detect poisonous vapors in line nine, the tired rhythm of the poem shifts dramatically to provide a sense of panic: "Gas! Gas! Quick, boys—An ecstasy of fumbling" (9). While most of the soldiers successfully don their gas masks, the green fog of poison gas overcomes one hapless soldier. Standing helplessly by, the speaker recounts the effects of chlorine gas by launching into a staccato catalog of the violent progress of the chemical's assault on the victim's respiratory system. Owen heightens the dual weight of panic and sheer violence bearing down on the speaker through a progression of onomatopoeia that aurally mimics the sound of the victim choking on and drowning in his own body fluids: "I saw him drowning. / He plunges at me, guttering, choking, drowning" (15–16).

By graphically documenting the soldier's death throes, Owen recreates one of the most terrifying aspects of life in the trenches, the onslaught and lethal effects of a gas attack. To be caught unprepared in a gas attack typically meant either an agonizing death or a life of horrible disfigurement. During the war, both sides used a combined total of more than 150,000 tons of chemical agents, including various insidious types of gas, such as mustard, phosgene, chloropicrin, and prussic acid (Roberts 259). Each form of poison wrought its own uniquely hideous destruction on its victims, but chlorine (the type of gas attack described in "Dulce et Decorum Est") posed a particularly brutal threat.[3] Lance Sergeant Elmer Cotton described the effects of chlorine gas:

> It produces a flooding the lungs . . . a splitting headache, terrific thirst (to drink water is instant death), a knife edge of pain in the lungs and the coughing up of a greenish froth off the stomach and lungs, ending finally in sensibility and death. The colour of the skin turns a greenish black and yellow, the tongue protrudes and the eyes assume a glassy stare. (qtd. in Roberts 259)

No wonder the shell-shocked speaker reacts in outrage to the fact that he must endure flashbacks of the gruesome scene, while others have the gall to proclaim it is sweet to die for one's country. While it may sometimes be necessary and even just to die for one's country, Owen reminds readers it is wrongheaded, even dangerous, to prettify the stark reality of wartime death with a veneer of elegant language and high-flown sentiment.

The strength of Owen's angry approach to war remembrance largely rests on its rejection of clichéd consolatory statements, pleasant diction and imagery, and a kind of blind patriotism. The ironic mode of remembrance in "Dulce et Decorum Est" also gains power through its rejection of what might be called "soft pastoralism," the predominant tonal feature of "The Soldier." Generally speaking, pastoral refers to a literary mode of expression that emphasizes situations, imagery, and subject matter set in the natural or rural world. Pastoral often interrogates the human longing for peaceful repose, a desire that often seeks peace through a return to a state of prelapsarian bliss in an arcadian or edenic setting. Brooke's "The Soldier" expresses precisely such a desire, but it rates as "soft pastoral" because of its elision of the complications of real life that render such desire problematic or impossible. Because mankind lives in a world tainted by disease, conflict, violence, suffering, and death, the best and most complex pastoral works manage to stress the impossibility of realizing the edenic or arcadian dream. Such works, therefore, incorporate a clash of the arcadian ideal with a startlingly violent counterforce.[4] Annabel Patterson has coined the phrase "hard pastoral" to describe this kind of complex pastoral literature.[5]

"The Soldier" embodies the arcadian dream of "soft pastoral," for it bears virtually no trace or hint of a violent counterforce. When Paul Fussell suggests, "If the opposite of war is peace, the opposite of experiencing moments of war is proposing moments of pastoral" (Fussell 213), he helps explain the logic of Brooke's adoption of the pastoral. Brooke's speaker does not want to consider the truth of war. What interests him is the promise of a noble death enjoyed in a beautiful paradise regained. Only the slightest mention of violence taints Brooke's enameled world of pastoral pleasure when his speaker considers the possibility of his own death, a death rendered beautiful by means of the speaker's use of a rich code of pastoral reference. Soothing pastoral imagery and deep longing for transcendent peace dominate the poem's emotional landscape, a bucolic landscape full of flowers, country ways, and fields dappled by a sun shining in an "English heaven." Brooke combines such pastoral images with nearly perfect metrical control, deft end rhymes, and mellifluous sonic effects, all of which conjures a sense of imperturbable pastoral repose.

Brooke intends his pastoral effects to console by building an image of the generative power of death. In this regard, the pastoral mode serves Brooke well because the pastoral almost invariably concerns itself with fertility and the life-giving power of the natural world. Pastoral often preoccupies itself with peaceful green thoughts in a green land not for recreational purposes alone, but rather for the purpose of re-creation, the purpose of raising a corpse from the dead into new life. Such is the purpose of the famous pastoral elegy "Lycidas," a ritualistic memorial honoring John Milton's dead young friend. Brooke thus situates "The Soldier" in this hallowed line of pastoral elegy when he stresses the curative and generative power of death by casting his image of the afterlife in pastoral terms.

In contrast, "Dulce et Decorum Est" contravenes all such thoughts by turning the pastoral tradition on its head with subtle, yet unmistakable ironic references to pastoral tropes. The poem begins with an image reminiscent of the pastoral: workers laboring in the field. In traditional pastoral such laborers take the form of happy shepherds or farmhands who sing to lift their spirits, easing the burden of work. Owen's laborers, however, are neither happy nor capable of song. His laborers are trench grunts, "bent double" under the weight of rucksacks and the burden of combat. Striking a pose more beastlike than human, the troops display a kind of herd mentality as they trudge through a landscape denuded and devoid of the signs of fertility populating "The Soldier." The phrase "bitter cud" in the final stanza completes the suggestion that these men, especially the victim of the gas attack, are like cattle led to the slaughter.

Also absent from Owen's poem are the tidy English pathways winding through the verdant, flowery fields of "The Soldier." The landscape reproduced by Owen is not edenic, but rather becomes a slaughterhouse. For Owen, truthful antipastoral representations of life and death in the trenches served as a powerful and highly suggestive counterforce for exploding the belief that the pastoral citadel of genteel English politics and life were constructed on a peace-loving arcadian foundation.

Given their radically different approaches to crafting memorials for the war dead, it is not surprising "The Soldier" and "Dulce et Decorum

Est" have inspired both intense controversy and great fanfare. Having already considered the reception of "The Soldier," it is perhaps instructive to close with a brief sampling of responses to "Dulce et Decorum Est." With its disturbing photographic realism and bitingly sardonic protest against blind patriotism, Owen's poem continues to be perhaps the most frequently anthologized poem of World War I. It is a perennial favorite among teachers and critics who wish to highlight the senselessness and brutality of the war.

For all its fans, though, "Dulce et Decorum Est" has never been universally respected or beloved. Many commentators have singled out the poem's defects, noting how its language and prosody often suffer from overwriting and excessiveness. Perhaps most famously, William Butler Yeats dismissed the poem when he excluded Owen from his edition of *The Oxford Book of Modern Verse, 1892–1935.* Explaining his decision to snub Owen, Yeats wrote to a friend:

> My anthology continues to sell & the critics get more & more angry. When I excluded Wilfred Owen, whom I consider unworthy of the poets' corner of a country newspaper, I did not know I was excluding a revered sandwich-board Man of the revolution & that somebody has put his worst & most famous poem in a glass-case in the British Museum—however if I had known it I would have excluded him just the same. He is all blood, dirt & sucked sugar stick (look at the selection in Faber's Anthology—he calls poets "bards," a girl a "maid," & talks about "Titanic wars"). There is every excuse for him but none for those who like him. (Wellesley 113)

Yeats no doubt had his own aesthetic reasons for rejecting "Dulce et Decorum Est." In his own work, Yeats favored gorgeous poetic images and diction and grew wary of direct political statement about war. Fair enough, but calling the poem Owen's worst? If Yeats has no stomach for the blood and mud of Owen's poetry, one wonders if he would have found much to recommend in the flowery beautiful death of "The Soldier."

In the end, perhaps none of this debate really matters. Perhaps all such literary opinions boil down to nothing more than matters of taste, which ultimately cannot be debated. So, why all the fuss? Has a lyric poem ever stopped a tank, as the poet Seamus Heaney asks, or, for that matter, cured a child of leukemia? In other words, does poetry, especially war poetry, matter? This is a difficult and complex question to answer, but the various uses to which advocates and adversaries of war have put "The Soldier" and "Dulce et Decorum Est" over the past century suggest that poetry does, in fact, matter. While on some level W. H. Auden may have been correct when he famously quipped that "poetry makes nothing happen," the reception history of the "The Soldier" and "Dulce et Decorum Est" reveals that each poem has, in its own fashion, done much to inform perceptions about and attitudes toward modern war.

With this in mind, there is yet another way to consider the impact of "Dulce et Decorum Est" and "The Solider." What specifically do these poems invite readers to remember about the World War I? In assessing the legacy of these two poems, another standard for measuring their worth can perhaps be profitably applied—namely, Sassoon's litmus test for adjudicating the appropriateness, adequacy, and efficacy of a war memorial: "Who will remember . . . The unheroic Dead who fed the guns?" Upon reading both Brooke and Owen, it is instructive to ask, "Who will remember, by virtue of this poem, the sacrifice of the 8.5 million men who died during World War I?"

At first glance, "Dulce et Decorum Est" would seem to provide the most honest and accurate portrayal of World War I. Through its graphic representation of death by poison gas and the speaker's raging attack on wrongheaded patriotism, Owen's poem puts a haunting face on war, one in touch with the actual mess of trench warfare. Owen's nightmarish image of a soldier drowning in his own body fluids forces a recognition of the specific and terrible price exacted of the soldiers of World War I. Judged according to Sassoon's standard of remembrance, Owen's war memorial undoubtedly emerges as the most powerful and respectful monument to the war dead because it traffics in harsh truth-telling. After reading "Dulce et Decorum Est," it is hard to forget what *gas attack* really means.

There are, however, elements of truth-telling running through Brooke's "The Soldier" as well, elements that recommend the poem as an important, even necessary, war memorial. Brooke's poem performs its own important work of remembrance by explaining why so many millions of young men felt compelled to enlist for the war effort. Whether one agrees or disagrees with the brand of patriotism espoused by "The Soldier," telling the story of the speaker's reverie of beautiful death completes the commitment to truth-telling.

As some critics argue, Brooke may well have intended an ironic reading of his speaker's attitude toward wartime death, but perhaps the poet's own inexperienced understanding of war places his own view of war much closer to his speaker's naïve views. Whatever the case, human beings have always possessed a deep-seated need to make sense of wartime death. Even as poets like Owen and Sassoon rejected the traditional approach to the beautiful-death ideal in favor of their hard-hitting, "in-your-face" brand of documentary realism, the prospect and promise of a beautiful death was likely as appealing to the young men of Europe in 1914 as it was to Pericles's countrymen during the Peloponnesian War.

In modern times, in the wake of recent wars, the longing and need for consolatory expressions of beautiful death continue to inform many efforts to memorialize the war dead. Something rooted deep in the human animal looks at the beastliness of war and seems to need the repose and consolation offered by the redemptive refuge of pastoral elegy. Reflecting that aspect of the human response to war, then, must be part of the truth-telling endeavor, too.

Finally, there is perhaps one more useful standard by which to measure the value and legacy of these poems. If one finds himself or herself standing before a war memorial on the beaches of Normandy or at the Vietnam Veterans Memorial in Washington, DC, one might ask which poem, Brooke's or Owen's, comes to mind while contemplating the sacrifice and suffering of the war dead. Which poem fires the imagination the most and helps bolster one's understanding of the causes, costs, and consequences of war? Recalling each poem in this way should give readers much to consider while standing before a war monument. Thinking back on these poems will help to generate an opinion on what it means to honor the war dead adequately, respectfully, and truthfully. In this regard, each poem should give pause, but for different reasons.

Notes

1. Homer's *Iliad*, the war poem par excellence and a model of war writing for many of the World War I soldier-poets, can, to some degree, be said to be a series of cameo insets in which Homer explores how the deaths of various warriors either exemplify the qualities of beautiful death or somehow fall short of the standard.

2. The Battle of Gallipoli, which lasted from April 1915 to January 1916, was a joint Allied operation mounted to capture the Ottoman capital of Constantinople and secure a sea route to Russia. The attempt failed, with heavy casualties on both sides. By battle's end, Allied forces suffered 252,000 casualties and 51,000 deaths, while the Turks suffered 300,000 casualties and 86,000 fatalities.

3. One commentator notes that "Dulce et Decorum Est" actually recounts a phosgene gas attack. For maximum effect, phosgene was typically mixed with chlorine. The symptoms described in the poem match those commonly associated with chlorine.

4. Such tension characterizes the most compelling and successful pastorals. Indeed, it is present in Jeremiah's Old Testament depiction of destroyed flocks and wasted pastures; the antipastorals of many World War I poets who, as Paul Fussell notes, use the mode "as a way of invoking a code to hint by antithesis at the indescribable" brutality of trench warfare; and Derek Walcott's brutal satires of the "Great House" tradition and its violent exploitation of slaves and the Jamaican landscape.

5. See Patterson, who makes the useful distinction between soft and hard pastoral.

Works Cited

Brooke, Rupert. "The Soldier." *The Norton Anthology of English Poetry*. 1955. Ed. Stephen Greenblatt. Vol. 2. New York: Norton, 2006.

Ehrenreich, Barbara. *Blood Rites*. New York: Metropolitan Books, 1997.

Fussell, Paul. *The Great War and Modern Memory*. New York: Oxford UP, 1973.

Owen, Wilfred. *Wilfred Owen: War Poems and Others*. Ed. Dominic Hibberd. London: Chatto, 1973.

Patterson, Annabel. *Pastoral and Ideology: Virgil to Valery*. Berkeley: U of California P, 1987.

Roberts, David, ed. *Minds at War*. London: Saxon, 1989.

Sassoon, Siegfried. *The War Poems of Siegfried Sassoon*. Ed. Rupert Hart-Davis. London: Faber, 1983.

Vernant, Jean-Pierre. "A 'Beautiful Death' and the Disfigured Corpse in Homeric Epic." *Oxford Readings in Homer's* Iliad. Ed. Douglas L. Cairns. New York: Oxford UP, 2001. 311–41.

Weil, Simone. "The *Iliad*, or the Poem of Force." *Chicago Review* 18.2 (1965): 5–31.

Wellesley, Dorothy. *Letters on Poetry from W. B. Yeats to Dorothy Wellesley*. New York: Oxford UP, 2007.

Strangers in Strange Lands: Distorted Landscape in the Modern American Military Memoir_____

John Nelson

> In war you lose your sense of the definite, hence your sense of truth itself, and therefore it's safe to say that in a true war story nothing much is ever very true.
>
> Tim O'Brien, "How to Tell a True War Story"

Early in his Korean War account *The Coldest War: A Memoir of Korea* (1990), James Brady observes the alien surroundings: "Outside the hut there was again the cold and behind it the wind. Korea looked like what I expected and then it didn't. Maybe I didn't know what to expect. The smell was new, for one, I liked to catalogue things, and the smell didn't fit anywhere. Neither did the quiet. There should have been activity but there wasn't" (4). Brady's unsettling observations, coming on the first morning after his arrival in the combat zone, reveal the disorienting sense of displacement characteristic of many contemporary American war memoirs. Soldiers hold a long tradition of sharing their personal experiences in a foreign land in the form of the military autobiography, a personalized account of war-fighting. In so doing, they capture the unfamiliar geography—both human and physical—during their time deployed abroad. The military memoir often serves, then, as a variant of the travel-writing genre, in which the author is displaced—at times abruptly and involuntarily—into unfamiliar terrain, while threatened by the pending violence of combat. These dynamics dramatically alter the soldiers' perspectives on the landscape and the people they encounter, resulting in characterizations that expose far more about their own psychological state than the subjects they strive to represent.

To a degree, this essay builds upon the insights of Samuel Hynes's *The Soldiers' Tale: Bearing Witness to Modern War* (1997), which explores the patterns with which soldier-authors characterize their wartime experiences during both world wars and during the Vietnam War.

This study limits it scope, however, to post–World War II memoirs composed by American fighting men, both army and marine, an admittedly problematic yet necessary restriction. Brady's *The Coldest War* provides a glimpse inside a marine platoon during the Korean War, as Lieutenant Brady fights against the Chinese and North Koreans in the Taebaek Mountains. Tim O'Brien's acclaimed narrative *If I Die in a Combat Zone, Box Me Up and Ship Me Home* (1973) recounts his experience fighting the Vietcong during the Vietnam conflict. Anthony Swofford's *Jarhead: A Marine's Chronicle of the Gulf War* (2003) tells of the author's 1991 deployment as a marine scout sniper in the Arabian Desert in support of Operation Desert Shield and Operation Desert Storm. Lastly, Craig Mullaney recounts his wartime experience as an infantry-platoon leader fighting the Taliban and al-Qaeda along the Afghanistan-Pakistan border in his work *The Unforgiving Minute: A Soldier's Education* (2009).

Though restricted by time frame, gender, and nationality, this chapter reflects on the military memoir's literary traditions and considers the way in which these specific authors embrace, complicate, or challenge firmly entrenched conventions of travel writing. Moreover, these wartime accounts are representative of the personal reflections of their respective conflicts and capture the prevailing anxiety of soldiers from different generations who are displaced into exotic and dangerous places. Whether their battlefield is atop the frozen mountains of Korea, the jungles and hamlets of Vietnam, the sandy expanses of the Arabian Peninsula, or the vertiginous peaks of Afghanistan, these military writers envision their surroundings in a manner that reveals an anxiety unique to a soldier deployed on foreign soil. The usual exoticism of foreign terrain and culture found in travel literature is further complicated by a very real and seemingly omnipresent existential threat. The physical surroundings—both immediate and distant—serve, in a sense, as screens upon which these soldier-authors project their anxieties.

While not entirely dissimilar to the traditional modes of representation found in travel writing, the military memoir postures the soldier-traveler in a way that is at once both empowering and extremely limiting. The soldier usually possesses the strength in numbers, the unit camaraderie, the training, and the firepower, while military necessity severely restricts his movement and his interaction with the local people through rules of engagement, topography, unit sectors, linguistic barriers, and cultural divides. The soldier most obviously lacks the nomadic freedom and wanderlust of the itinerant traveler—the luxury of hither and thither exploration—but he nonetheless experiences the exotic in unique and potentially revealing ways. However, the resulting textual representations—though penned from the relative comfort of redeployment and often recollected in stateside tranquility—are often profoundly distorted and provide the reader with a skewed glimpse of the unfamiliar.

The deployed soldier also physically alters the foreign landscape by creating and seeking refuge in the familiar—the trench, the foxhole, the firebase, the forward operating base (FOB)—small, transient sanctuaries from the enemy outside the perimeter, adorned with trappings reminiscent of hometown America: boom boxes, video games, letters and photographs from loved ones, chain restaurants, and portable toilets. The jarring disjuncture between the sanctuary and the real—an increasingly common phenomenon—disorients the reader and profoundly magnifies the strangeness of the world beyond the wire. A common trope in these memoirs, then, is the clash between the comforting interiority of the defensive position and the threatening exteriority of the aptly named "no-man's-land."

Lastly, while a soldier's initial entry into the combat zone reveals a self-alienation from both the indigenous people and their terrain, the return home—that much anticipated journey stateside—makes clear the profound psychological changes that take place while deployed onto strange lands. As British writer G. K. Chesterton asserts, "The whole object of travel is not to set foot on foreign land; it is at last to set foot on one's own country as a foreign land" (98). This radical disassociation of the familiar becomes another common trope in the narrative of homecoming. Indeed, a quick survey of American military memoirs highlights an all-too-common disconcerting return to the normal. Through the journey abroad, the soldier-traveler finds himself changed in ways that few authors can clearly articulate, hinting at a deep psychological alteration.

James Brady's *The Coldest War: A Memoir of Korea*

Brady published *The Coldest War* nearly forty years after his return from the Korean Peninsula, yet the grittiness and the brutality of his account make clear that his memories from "The Forgotten War" have not tempered with time. Commissioned into the US Marine Corps in 1951 and then quickly deployed, Brady arrived in Korea during Thanksgiving weekend of the same year. The unique nature of the conflict emerges in the memoir's opening page. "Korea was a strange war in a strange land," Brady tells his reader, "a war the generals warned we should never fight, a ground war on the Asian mainland against the Chinese" (1). Indeed, *The Coldest War* makes tangible the sense of displacement and the sentiments of futility and frustration felt by many servicemen and -women who, with fresh memories of World War II, find themselves fighting a protracted conflict in a far distant and radically different land. Brady manifests his own anxiety early in his memoir, for his initial trepidation is fueled by returning veterans' war stories, *Life* magazine photographs of uninhabitable Korean terrain, and uncertainties about leading troops in combat.

As his troop-transport plane approaches the Korean landing strip, the twenty-three-year-old lieutenant observes the mountainous terrain below him in a trope characteristic of the contemporary war memoir, an ironic twist to what Mary Louise Pratt calls the "monarch-of-all-I-survey" scene:

From the starboard windows you could see real mountains in the north, hunched like white Dominicans at prayer. I didn't like the look of them. Here near the coast the hills were only hills, no Gothic menace about them, but even on the low hills there was snow. Only in the flat of the valley where the plane would come down was there bare earth, brown and frozen hard. We banked and came in low over the hills. A sort of landing field was marked out, flanked by agricultural terraces reaching gently for the hills, the terraces lined with dull ice in the furrows and the wind chasing little whorls of brown dust. Up and down the valley you could see huts and tents and a few unsuccessful fires giving no apparent heat and little light in the gray morning. (3)

This unwelcoming panorama of the war zone serves as a common theme in the contemporary wartime memoir. The panoptic view allows the author to convey his initial trepidations about the terrain immediately below the plane as well as across the horizon, while also previewing for the reader the contended landscape from a commanding, aerial perspective previously unimaginable until the advent of the troop transport plane. While traditional travel writers often describe their entry into the exotic with a blend of excitement and uncertain promise, Brady's wartime arrival appears sinister and foreboding.

Thus begins Brady's yearlong participation in the Korean conflict and his account that captures the brutality, the horrific intimacy, and the frustrating stagnation of a conflict marked by stalemate and firmly held hilltop fortifications. Told from a platoon leader's perspective, but with the subtleness of a longtime journalist's eye for ironic detail, *The Coldest War* reveals the frustrations of an impasse of haphazard lines dividing NATO forces from the North Korean–Chinese alliance. However, geopolitics are not Brady's focus; rather, he concentrates on the daily challenges a marine lieutenant and his troops face together.

Through Brady's words, Korea appears a barren and depopulated land. "Except for a few native hangers-on at the airfield no one had seen any civilians," he reflects as he surveys the area surrounding his initial base camp. "We didn't know it yet but we wouldn't be seeing any for a long while. They'd been rooted from their homes and packed south out of the zone of battle" (12). Brady's interaction with the

Korean people is extremely limited during his tour, a curiosity, considering his repeated reference to the offensively named "gook train," the dehumanized line of Korean nationals shuttling gear and rations to the front line. In fact, *The Coldest War* characterizes the Korean people and the opposing forces from a pronounced distance, their strangeness magnified by the absence of individuality or defining characteristic. Tellingly, Brady's personal sense of isolation appears profound despite the evident camaraderie within his unit: "It was strange being here instead of home, among people who loved me. Here were only strangers in a strange land, and up ahead, worse than strangers" (20). Brady also comments on the way his fellow marines reductively homogenize the indigenous people through racial epithet: "'The other side.' They called them that, or 'gooks,' or 'people.' They also called our Koreans 'gooks.' The Chinese were 'chinks'" (29). The marines' self-distancing from the indigenous is one of Brady's most startling revelations.

Similar to his portrayal of the Koreans, Brady characterizes the landscape as barren and ominous, littered with what he calls the "flotsam of war" (20). He spends much of his narrative reflecting on the menacing expanse beyond the American defenses: "In front of us was no man's land and, beyond that, the enemy" (22). Brady's enemy—the Chinese and North Korean forces entrenched just within eyeshot of the marine lines—remains a faceless threat, very real yet distant and looming just on the horizon, their presence made knowable through sporadic bursts of machine-gun fire and the occasional artillery barrage. As he surveys this no-man's-land separating his marines from these enemy lines, he reads the landscape before him. "For the first time I was looking at ground that matched my notion of what it would be like. There were three untidy fences of barbed wire a few yards to the front and some rusty concertina wire looped farther out," he observes. "Beyond that were a field of snow pocked by shell holes, a few scrub pines badly chewed, and, about a football field away, a long, dirty mound of snow" (25). This unnatural, dystopic terrain, scarred by previous skirmishes, would become Brady's home for much of his Korean tour, his connection to his fellow marines and the immediate terrain growing with a surreal intimacy. The no-man's-land to Brady's front serves, in a sense, as a distorted cultural landscape, or what Hynes calls "anti-landscape," land marked by wartime destruction that serves as a tangible reminder of the dangers beyond the fortifications (Hynes 7). Brady employs words such as "untidy," "rusty," "pocked," "chewed," and "dirty" to convey a sense of depravity, of war being waged against the earth itself, an objective correlative that illuminates the text's themes of alienation and isolation.

This psychological projection continues as Brady, much later in his tour, looks to the horizon beyond the myopic immediacy forced on him by combat necessity and soldierly discipline:

Amid the evergreens were other trees, and I wondered if they bloomed and grew leafy when the snow melted, sprouted lush green foliage and buds and flowers and maybe even fruit. Would we still be able to see that terrible 2,000-meter mountain that loomed so frighteningly just a few miles to our north? Or would the death that waited there be veiled by blossoms? I hoped I would live until spring to see. (114)

Brady's use of words that sing of life—"evergreens," "bloomed," "grew," "lush," "buds and flowers"—contrasts strikingly with the theme of death informing his previous discussion. His springtime imaginings seem oddly out of place in the frigid war zone, yet he still maps his own existential uncertainty upon the landscape before him.

The lieutenant then reflects on the abrupt and profound personal changes he has experienced, observing that, until recently, he had been living with his brother in "a small row house in Sheepshead Bay, going to work on the subway and writing furniture and household appliance ads for Macy's," a rather tranquil existence compared to "living on a mountaintop in Asia with a hundred other men," fighting a protracted war against a faceless enemy (116). A common theme among these military memoirs is the profound distance between premilitary life and combat. Brady, like many other military memoirists, intersperses his linear narrative with flashbacks to use his quotidian New York life as a foil by which to highlight the strangeness of his wartime experience in North Korea's Taebaek Mountains. The soldier-author, akin to the travel writer, makes the abstract knowable, at least to a degree, through contrast and difference.

As Brady's tour comes to an end, he hopes for a protracted return home, "a leisured transition from one life to another" to recuperate psychologically from his experiences abroad; he returns home by sea, in stark contrast to his airborne arrival, a chance to "lay in the berth, enjoying the novelty of electric light and the sheets and the pillow and the shiny white paint of the ceiling" (239). The sterile sanctuary of the ship's stateroom replaces the rustic trenches that sheltered the lieutenant during his deployment.

Unlike some veterans who embark on "organized tours" of their battlefields of yesteryear, Brady knows he "would never go back to Korea, never sign up for an old soldiers' tour" (240). "I didn't want to see the hills again or feel the cold or hear the wind out of Siberia," he confesses to his readers. "I didn't want to disturb the dead" (241). Inverting the norms of travel tradition, Brady, with four decades of hindsight, rejects the thought of a future visit to the Korean Peninsula, of experiencing it anew when freed from war's immediate burdens. He shuns the thought of healing the alienation of his yearlong deployment by returning; from Brady's perspective, a former war zone is an unsuitable travel destination indeed.

Tim O'Brien's *If I Die in a Combat Zone, Box Me Up and Ship Me Home*

Like the Korean conflict (1950–53), the Vietnam War (1955–75) brought young, inexperienced draftees into a morally ambiguous conflict fought on a radically unfamiliar landscape. Like Brady's *The Coldest War*, O'Brien's *If I Die in a Combat Zone, Box Me Up and Ship Me Home* unveils the anxiety of a young soldier uprooted from his middle-American hometown and transplanted into a foreign war; unlike Brady, however, O'Brien is drafted into wartime service. He chronicles his experiences as young soldier fighting the North Vietnamese and Vietcong in the area around My Lai from 1969 to 1970. Also unlike Brady's account, O'Brien clearly voices his moral uncertainty about the war in which he is involved, so much so, in fact, that he nearly deserts to Canada during his initial training after seeking counsel from the unit chaplain and battalion commander, who tells him that "the Korean war and the Vietnam war aren't much different. One country divided by an artificial line. People of the same race killing themselves. Communist aid, American aid. Communist troops, American troops" (58). The colonel's reductive analogy does little to ease O'Brien's burdened conscience. Thus, he enters his war zone with the usual combat anxiety but is also troubled by a profound moral dilemma.

Eschewing the linear narrative form, O'Brien's memoir opens in medias res, abruptly placing his reader directly into the line of fire alongside a combat patrol. The author thereby establishes an unsettling tone from the memoir's start and allows the reader an intimate perspective into the soldier's experience. "Ever think you'd be humping along some crazy-ass trail like this one, jumping up and down out of the dirt, jumping like a goddamn bullfrog, dodging bullets all day," a soldier abruptly remarks. "Don't know about you, but I sure as hell never thought I'd ever be going on all day like this. Back in Cleveland, I'd still be asleep" (1). This opening exclamation by Barney, O'Brien's fellow infantryman, immediately juxtaposes the comfort and stability of hometown America against the utter foreignness of the soldiers' predicament and provides a parallel to Brady's comparison of his Sheepshead Bay's apartment to sleeping atop the fortified Korean mountaintop.

The opening passage captures, in an abrupt way, the profound sense of dislocation felt by many combat veterans. The specificity of the Cleveland reference is soon countered by the anonymity of their current locale. Barney asks, "What's the name of this goddamn place?"

(4), to which O'Brien sullenly replies, "I don't know. I never thought of that. Nobody thinks of the names for these places" (4). The act of appellation—of bestowing a name on a place or a thing—is a critical step in establishing familiarity, a sense of belonging, yet O'Brien emphasizes the exact opposite: a denial of the locale's importance and a sound rejection of any sense of the familiar. This deliberate self-alienation from place informs the remainder of the narrative of *If I Die in a Combat Zone.* Barney's exchange with O'Brien suggests a distinct lack of interest, bordering, in fact, on contempt for the indigenous surroundings, a divergence from travel writing's usual geographic sensibilities and place-name litanies.

After the abrupt opening chapter, O'Brien returns to a standard linear narrative, devoting nearly the first third of his memoir to his all-American childhood in Minnesota and his initial military training at Fort Lewis. This framework enables the reader to comprehend the vast chasm between the United States and the Vietnam of the opening dialogue. O'Brien's hometown appears as idyllic Americana, yet one informed by a fevered patriotism bordering on militarism in the wake of World War II and Korea: "Sparklers and the forbidden cherry bomb were for the Fourth of July: a baseball game, a picnic, a day in the city park, listening to the high school band playing 'Anchors Aweigh,' a speech, watching a parade of American Legionnaires. At night, sometimes after nine o'clock, fireworks erupted over the lake, reflections" (12). This Rockwellian image magnifies the differences after O'Brien arrives in combat, for as he relates, "To understand what happens to the GI among the mine fields of My Lai, you must know something about what happens in America" (31).

After his initial army training in Washington, where O'Brien vows "to remain a stranger," he enters the war zone already self-marginalized (34). When his plane first approaches Vietnam, O'Brien observes the landscape below in a move reminiscent of Brady's earlier aerial survey:

First there is some mist. Then, when the plane begins its descent, there are pale grey mountains. The plane slides down, and the mountains darken and take on a sinister cragginess. You see the outline of crevices, and you consider whether, of all the places opening up below, you might walk to that spot and die. In the far distance are green patches, the sea is below, a stretch of sand winds along the coast. Two hundred men draw their breath. No one looks at the others. You feel dread. (66)

In a rhetorical move similar to Brady's, O'Brien's use of the second-person pronoun "you" places his reader alongside the inbound soldiers, whose anxiety is palpable as they watch the alien geography unfold below. This fear hardly fades with time, however, as the soldiers continue to project their anxieties onto and even into the landscape, from the panoramic aerial view to the combat patrol's myopic intensity: "when you step about these pieces of ground, you do some thinking. You hallucinate. You look ahead a few paces and wonder what your legs will resemble if there is more to the earth in that spot than silicates and nitrogen. Will the pain be unbearable? Will you scream or fall silent" (120). As *If I Die in a Combat Zone* progresses, the reader witnesses this collective anxiety among the troops, an anxiety fueled by the alien landscape.

Like the danger lurking just below the jungle's surface, the faceless enemy O'Brien and his fellow soldiers hunt is also fleeting, blending into the pacified villages and even into the terrain itself (127). O'Brien conveys this overwhelming uncertainty:

He is hidden among the mass of civilians or in tunnels or jungles. . . . And each piece of ground left behind is his from the moment we are gone on our next hunt. It is not a war fought for territory, not for pieces of land that will be won and held. It is not a war fought to win the hearts of the Vietnamese nationals, not in the wake of contempt drawn on our faces and theirs, not in the wake of a burning village, a trampled rice paddy, a battered detainee. (124)

Despite his commander's earlier reductive analogy, Korea and Vietnam are manifestly distinct, particularly in the way in which physical and cultural geography factor in the soldiers' collective psyche. Indeed, O'Brien captures the frustrating physical and psychological disconnect between the American soldier and the Vietnamese people whom, ideally, he strives to protect. The contempt on both sides of the cultural divide suggests an unbridgeable gap, a divide all the more understandable when O'Brien reveals that the shameful My Lai Massacre occurred in this same location only one year before. In her study "Art in the Contact Zone," Pratt defines the "contact zone" as the "social spaces where cultures meet, clash, and grapple with each other, often in contexts of highly asymmetrical relations of power" (33). Her term takes on a sinister significance in light of O'Brien's revelation.

As O'Brien's wartime experience comes to a close and he prepares for redeployment, readers note a growing tension, an awareness, perhaps, that unavoidable changes have occurred in the author and his fellow travelers. O'Brien calls his last chapter "Don't I Know You?"—a title with telling ambiguity, the pronoun referents left doubly uncertain. Who is O'Brien's "I" and "you"? Whose identity has Vietnam left uncertain? Indeed, the memoir's final pages unfold a disconcerting stateside return characterized by an unsettling estrangement. O'Brien's rather abrupt shift from combat patrol to freedom plane arrives jarringly in the narrative despite his continuous thoughts of home. Both the smell and the feel of the freedom plane are "artificial," he writes; he finds the "stewardess" enraging because of her casual disinterest and willful ignorance of the soldiers' collective ordeal (196). O'Brien describes an odd disinfecting ritual of departure as the flight attendant sprays "a mist of invisible sterility into the pressurized, scrubbed, filtered, temperature-controlled air, killing mosquitoes and unknown diseases, protecting herself and America from Asian evils, cleansing us all forever" (196). The ritual purification amplifies the growing estrangement of the returning soldiers, a collective desire to forget, to erase the war from America's cultural memory.

As he departs the war zone, however, O'Brien pines for a "last look at the earth," a need to "say good-bye" to that foreboding terrain that he ironically learned to embrace (197). It is the earth that deserts the soldier, he suggests, rather than the other way around. He confesses to never comprehending the Vietnamese people, but knowing the land "like a farmer knows his own earth and his neighbor's" (198). O'Brien claims no wide-ranging familiarity with Vietnam as one might expect after a yearlong journey; instead, his is an intimacy with Vietnamese earth, one offset by a professed ignorance of both the people who populate it and their culture. Adding to this disconnect is O'Brien's disillusioned portrayal of middle America: "an empty, unknowing, uncaring, purified, permanent stillness," a land "arrogantly unchanged" during his year abroad (199). O'Brien returns home a stranger in a strange land.

Anthony Swofford's *Jarhead: A Marine's Chronicle of the Gulf War and Other Battles*

Iraq's invasion of its southern neighbor Kuwait in August 1990 caught most of the world off guard. Thus, marine sniper Anthony Swofford's journey to the Saudi desert could not be informed by war stories, oral or written, of veterans who had fought on the same sandy expanses he would soon encounter. Instead, his combat deployment comes abruptly; nonetheless, his characterization of the desert war zone shares many of the same themes as the other memoirs, partly because of a tradition of intertextuality in war representation. Swofford's *Jarhead: A Marine's Chronicle of the Gulf War and Other Battles* is rife with contradictions, at times vulgar and self-deprecating, yet the author still projects the familiar sense of alienation and fear onto a distorted landscape.

Like *If I Die in a Combat Zone, Jarhead* opens in medias res with a recently repatriated Swofford opening his deployment rucksack in the sanctuary of his Iowan home. He observes that his "desert cammies" are "ratty and bleached by sand and sun and blemished with the petroleum rain that fell from the oil-well fires in Kuwait" (1). He opens his well-weathered map of Kuwait, and Arabian "sand falls from between the folds" (2). Traces of the terrain that haunt Swofford during his Middle Eastern deployment have followed him home to his basement, a tangible manifestation of his wartime memories. Indeed, as *Jarhead* progresses, readers witness the author's antipathy toward the desert landscape; the vast sandy expanse parallels the frozen Korean hilltops of Brady's memoir and the jungle of O'Brien's.

Like O'Brien's memoir, *Jarhead*'s narrative quickly shifts to predeployment activities to contextualize Swofford's participation in Operation Desert Shield and Operation Desert Storm. When his unit learns of the pending deployment, the marines "send a few guys downtown to rent all of the war movies they can get their hands on" (5). It is curious and revealing that the films they find most inspirational are the antiwar movies portraying the Vietnam era. Swofford recalls the excitement these movies instill in his fellow marines as they vicariously bear witness to last major American conflict:

> We concentrate on the Vietnam films because it's the most recent war, and the successes and failures of that war helped write our training manuals. We rewind and review famous scenes, such as Robert Duvall and his helicopter gunships during *Apocalypse Now*, and in the same film Martin Sheen floating up the fake Vietnamese Congo; we watch Willem Dafoe get shot by a friendly and left on the battlefield in *Platoon*; and we listen closely as Matthew Modine talks trash to a streetwalker in *Full Metal Jacket*. We watch again the ragged, tired, burnt-out fighters walking through the villes and the pretty native girls smiling because if they don't smile, the fighters might kill their pigs or burn their cache of rice. (6)

The passage shows not only how popular media informs, and misinforms, contemporary perceptions of warfare but also the growing intertextuality of war's representation as the result of the popularity of cinema. Swofford imagines how these same, decidedly antiwar, films were being viewed at military bases across the country as units prepared for the next American conflict. Soldiers, marines, and sailors, he argues, "are excited by them, because the magic brutality of the films celebrates the terrible and despicable beauty of their fighting skills. Fight, rape, war, pillage, burn" (6–7). A prominent theme of these films is the alienation of the individual soldier when facing hostilities in a strange land. That these marines would turn to them to contextualize their pending deployment makes sense in a disturbing way, as evident by Swofford's distasteful yet revealing exultation: "Now is my time to step into the newest combat zone. And as a young man raised on the films of the Vietnam War, I wanted ammunition and alcohol and dope, I want to screw some whores and kill some Iraqi motherfuckers" (7). Fueled by these thoughts, Swofford and his fellow marines deploy to the Arabian Peninsula. Much as a traveler might view a travel documentary to gain familiarity with a new destination, the war-bound troops of *Jarhead* turn to cinematic representations of a foreign war that, in part, defined their parents' generation.

As Swofford deplanes in the Saudi desert, he immediately faces his initial aggressor: "the oven heat of the Arabian desert grips" his throat, thus beginning a growing and obsessive conflict between soldier and terrain (10). His fixation with the desert environ grows unabated, and, after weeks of training and waiting under a scorching sun for the war to begin, he despairs at the landscape's sublime infiniteness:

I look at the sky, blue like no blue I've known before, and at the desert that will not stop. This is the pain of the landscape, worse than the heat, worse than the flies—there is no getting out of the land. No stopping. After only six weeks of deployment, the desert is in us, one particle at a time—our boots and belts and trousers and gas masks and weapons are covered and filled with sand. Sand has invaded my body: ears, and eyes and nose and mouth, ass crack and pisshole. The desert is everywhere. The mirage is everywhere. Awake, asleep, high heat of the afternoon or the few soft, sunless hours of early morning, I am still in the desert. (15)

Much as Korea's no-man's-land serves as an objective correlative for *The Coldest War*'s refrain of alienation of soldier from environment, the Arabian Desert's vast expanse and infiltrating sand diminish Swofford and his fellow marines to insignificance. As they anticipate their inevitable confrontation with the Iraqi forces massed along the border, they are assaulted ceaselessly by the very landscape they have been sent to protect. The interminable wait in the desert's heat for the war's first shot magnifies this collective anxiety.

While the Arabian Desert is omnipresent, the Arabs themselves are peculiarly absent from the narrative. Swofford's first encounter with the indigenous population, the seminomadic Bedouins, initially shocks him, as they emerge jinni-like from the desert haze, "their robes [warped] in the mirage," seemingly manifestations of the desert itself. The encounter, which centers on camels allegedly shot by US troops, illuminates Swofford's empathy rather the expected rejection of the unfamiliar: "The Bedouins are not our enemy, the Bedouins will not try to kill us whenever the Coalition decides to act. I've just experienced a human moment with the Bedouin, free of profanity and anger and hate" (136, 139). His earlier antipathy quickly fades as he recognizes the Bedouins' shared humanity. His fellow marines, according to Swofford, lack his self-proclaimed refinement: "Because they are ignorant and young and have been well trained by the Corps, [they] are afraid of the humanity of the Bedouin, unable to see through their desert garb into the human" (139). The marines' occasional glimpse of Saudi men driving *abaya*-clad women confined to the backseat reinforces this separation: "These brief, high-speed glances are our only exposure to the citizens of the country we're protecting" (140). The author wryly comments on this vast cultural gap and the sequestering of the American forces from the Saudi public, "We are the ghost protectors" (140). The same self-distancing from the indigenous population witnessed in Brady's and O'Brien's text informs *Jarhead*; the Saudis, when they do emerge in the narrative, appear as alien as the landscape from which they emerge, the only human connectedness resulting from this brief encounter with the Bedouin tribesmen and a later encounter on the Kuwaiti streets.

As the US ultimatum to Iraq passes, the unremitting wait in the desert sun causes Swofford, once again, to contemplate the land before him: "I return to the disturbing nature of the terrain, the lack of variation, the dead repetition, and constantly, the ominous feeling that one is always in the open" (135). Much as O'Brien felt claustrophobic and threatened by the intricate jungle foliage, assuming that the "phantom-like" enemy and the much-feared land mines lay hidden within, the Arabian Desert's openness exacerbates the marines' sense of vulnerability, made all the more real by Swofford's sniper-trained sensibilities. This obsession with the desert landscape increases exponentially with the oil-well fires set by the Iraqi troops as they retreat from the Kuwaiti desert to the sanctuary of Iraq. The sky that earlier was colored a sublime blue turns a dark black, as day morphs into night, and billowing oil clouds mar the distant horizon. "Iraqi troops have lit fire to hundreds of oil wells in southern Kuwait, and we're told that they're also spilling crude onto the desert floor," he explains while gazing with a growing horror at the horizon. "The oil fields burn in the distance, the sky a smoke-filled landscape, a new dimension really, thick and billowing. A burning, fiery oil hell awaits us" (200). Swofford, like Brady before him, maps his fate onto the horizon. The awe-inspiring expanses of the open desert turn hellishly surreal as war is waged directly against the landscape, adding to Swofford's and his fellow marines' sense of alienation and angst.

After the brief, violent ground war expelling the Iraqi forces from the emirate, Swofford witnesses from a distance the celebrations on the streets of Kuwait City. He notes the Kuwaitis celebrating their homeland's liberation by holding American flags and cheering the passing war-weary troops. In a move uncharacteristic of the earlier narratives, he empathizes with the newly liberated crowd, much as he did with the wandering Bedouins: "These flag-waving women are just like us, these mothers are our mothers, and those children dirty at the mouth with skinned and bloody knees, they are us and our sisters and our neighborhood friends" (240). Swofford's ability to project his own familial connections upon the alien faces of the Kuwaiti citizens shows a profound humanity, more often than not missing from wartime narratives.

As hostilities come to a violent and quick conclusion, Swofford reflects on how his unit rummages through the destroyed Iraqi bunkers, much like tourists collecting trinkets from a local bazaar before departing an exotic locale:

> The treasures in the bunker—correspondence, a bayonet, a beret, a helmet, homemade Iraqi dog tags with the information scrawled by hand with an awl—worthless treasures call. The platoon continues collecting relics . . . in order to own a part of the Desert, to further scar this landscape already littered with despair and death, and to claim and define themselves, define their histories, to confirm that they are marines, combatants, jarheads, to infuse the last seven months of their young lives with value, and to steal history from the dead Iraqi soldiers who now have nothing to remember. (242–43)

The passage's ironic tone captures the author's disappointment with himself and his fellow marines, a clear recognition that the gathering of war trophies, however trivial the items may be, diminishes the enemy's humanity in a futile effort to make sense, through tangible evidence, of their seven-month deployment. Again, the author reads the damaged, postwar landscape as "littered with despair and death," echoing the "flotsam of war" that pollutes Brady's no-man's-land. Those inconsequential war trophies, physical proof of the marines' participation in history's latest footnote, will accompany the homeward-bound troops much like the Arabian sand that spills on Swofford's basement floor.

Jarhead employs many of the same tropes as Brady's and O'Brien's texts, particularly in its exoticization of the physical and cultural geography of the Arabian Peninsula. Swofford intersperses his nonlinear narrative with recollections of childhood memories, marine training, friendships, family, and camaraderie, all serving to illuminate the unsettling otherness of his desert ordeal. His combat tour was shorter and less brutal than Brady's and O'Brien's experiences in Korea and Vietnam, yet the same alienation emerges from his text. It is the landscape, however, the immense openness of the Arabian Desert, that disquiets the author and remains with him in his Iowan home's basement (1–2).

Craig Mullaney's *The Unforgiving Minute: A Soldier's Education*

As with the earlier accounts, Craig Mullaney's *The Unforgiving Minute: A Soldier's Education* devotes much of its space to acquainting readers with the author's personal and professional formation before his eventual arrival in Afghanistan in 2003 in support of Operation Enduring Freedom. Mullaney details his journey through West Point, his struggles in US Army Ranger School, and his exploits as a globetrotting Rhodes scholar, before his arrival at his first unit at Fort Drum, New York, as an infantry platoon leader. In fact, his entrance into the combat zone does not occur until midway through the text, but his characterization of the foreignness of the landscape and of the Afghan people rings similar to the representations found in the already examined texts. *The Unforgiving Minute* creates a sense of suspense for the reader, as Mullaney's narrative slowly builds to his account's climax along the Afghanistan-Pakistan border.

Mullaney equates his deployment to "Dante's descent into the Inferno," a "slow immersion" rather than the rushed entry into the war zone that readers witness in Swofford's quick mobilization for Desert Storm (217). During his unit's initial intelligence briefing, the author reflects on futility of the required classes:

We knew more about Afghanistan's flora and fauna than the tribes inhabiting the districts we patrolled. We could identify the Hindu Kush Mountains and the Helmand River on a map of Afghanistan, but knew little about the dry riverbeds surrounding our bases. We knew politics at a

---

national level, but not at the local level where it mattered. We had Arabic phrase books that were useless in Pashto-speaking provinces. (218)

This noteworthy attempt at geopolitical familiarization for the deploying soldiers misses its mark, strategic awareness in lieu of tactical practicalities. After a seven-thousand-mile journey and predeployment training, Mullaney and his soldiers disembark from the rear of their cargo plane. His description of this entry is remarkably similar to Swofford's initial view of the Arabian Desert: "The heat nearly knocked us over, sucking the oxygen out of the air and leaving us breathless. It was like walking into a furnace. My boots felt as though they were melting into the black tarmac. The sky was a red canvas of dust obscuring the setting sun" (219). Basking in the nearly 130-degree heat, the unfamiliar terrain looms in the distance: "soldiers standing guard at posts scattered around the airfield scanned the horizon. Beyond them, barely visible through the choking haze, a ring of barren mountains stuck up out of the flat plain like shards of glass embedded in concrete" (219). Like the Taebaek Mountains of North Korea that haunted Brady more than a half century before, the Afghan mountain range towered over the valley below, reminding the newly arrived soldiers of the hardships ahead: It is to those mountains that Mullaney and his soldiers would soon deploy.

The mysterious world beyond the barrier, pronounced by the magnificence of the Hindu Kush Mountains, was oddly offset by a comforting familiarity within the FOB: "industrial air-conditioning units," electrical wires powering "video-games and DVD players," Porta-Johns, volleyball and basketball courts dotted the Kandahar airbase (216–17). The mess hall strikes Mullaney as "more Ponderosa than Beetle Bailey," with "ice cold Cokes, Snapples, and Gatorades" and "a spread of unimaginable variety" (220). These stateside comforts transplanted into the remote and inhospitable Afghan terrain serve as a startling foil to the rigors that Mullaney and his troops would soon endure as they patrol the contended landscape beyond the perimeter.

In part, what is distinctive about *The Unforgiving Minute* is the juxtaposition of the brutal hardships of the combat soldier's life and the creature comforts found in man-made sanctuaries such as the Kandahār base. Mullaney makes this contrast abundantly clear when his company commander immediately orders him to depart for Gardēz, a village near the Pakistan border, to begin his combat duties. He describes the helicopter trip to the remote village in revealing detail from the familiar and privileged aerial vantage point:

> Our flying flotilla sped just two hundred feet above the highest peaks, emerging on the far side at a dizzying height over broad valleys and steep gorges. The landscape was almost devoid of vegetation. In places, the ground cracked like old parchment. Between infertile plots stood the isolated square shapes of Afghan family compounds with high walls and guard towers. . . . As we flew farther and farther from Kandahar, it seemed as if we were rolling the clock back from the twenty-first century. The view from this height probably hadn't changed much in six hundred years. (221)

The rapidity with which the lieutenant departs the Kandahār base coupled with the dramatic shift from modernity to primitiveness as they travel further into the unknown allows readers to witness a significant aspect of contemporary American warfare: the widening gap between the comforting sanctuary of the FOB and the arduous conditions faced by forward-deployed combat troops. This jarring contrast exacerbates the foreignness of the indigenous physical and human geography and is made more surreal by the helicopter's swiftness, which allows troops to move from one world to the other in little time but without much physical or psychological transition.

Even in the remote backcountry of Afghanistan, Mullaney reflects on the constant reminders of home, comforting surrogates to make the tour pass more quickly: regular mail, tea, trail mix, Bollywood films, hand-drawn birthday cards, beef jerky, brownies, magazines, "mountains of PowerBars and Twizzlers," and, tellingly, "a ten-day-old copy of the Sunday *New York Times*"(244). The airmail arrives regularly from Kandahār, Mullaney informs his reader, thus shortening the psychological distancing of Gardēz from hometown America. Despite these tokens of home, however, the brutality of combat continues across the rugged Afghan terrain for Mullaney and his unit.

Later, after an arduous tour patrolling the Afghan-Pakistan border, Mullaney returns to Kandahār, which "was just as strange to [him] after nine months on the frontier as it had been when [they] first arrived" (338). He observes a "boardwalk surrounding two beach volleyball courts straight out of a pro tournament in San Diego" and describes the "Green Beans café, which was selling iced chai soy lattes" (339). The base store even carries flat-screen televisions for those soldiers fortunate enough to reside within the HESCO bastion perimeter walls. According to Mullaney, for every combat soldier patrolling the frontier, at least five soldiers are sustaining him from the confines of the support base. For the author and his troops, "waking up in Kandahar was like a prisoner's first day out of jail" (338). The Kandahār base serves, then, as a transitional phase from the hardships they faced on the battlefield to their stateside return.

Even with the transition provided by the pseudo-Americana of the FOB, the alienation of homecoming hits Mullaney strongly upon his arrival at Fort Drum. "The normalcy was disconcerting," he confesses. His civilian clothes "fit loosely" on his combat-slimmed body, "as if they belonged to someone else" (345). Indeed, much as O'Brien's final chapter title—"Don't I Know You?"—unveils his disquieting repatriation, Mullaney's redeployment title—"Dislocated"—exposes his own sense of estrangement, leaving the reader to ask the question: From where is the author dislocated? "I felt like Rip Van Winkle," the author tells us, "as if I were waking up from a nine-month sleep to find that the world had continued to turn on its axis while I had stood still" (346).

Conclusion

French Algerian writer Albert Camus claims that travel's true psychological benefit comes from its sense of displacement, of moving outside our zone of familiarity and into the unknown:

> For what gives value to travel is fear. It breaks down a kind of inner decor in us. We can't cheat any more—hide ourselves away behind the hours in the office or at the plant. . . . Travel takes this refuge from us. Far from our own people, our own language, wrenched away from all support, deprived of our masks. . . . We are completely on the surface of ourselves. (46)

From an existentialist perspective, these soldier-authors do reap the benefits of the world traveler, for they do indeed depart their zone of comfort and become "completely on the surface" of themselves. Their journey is an inward one, more a sense of self-discovery, of learning limitations and potentialities, of confronting the unknown while facing the dangers of combat, rather than a journey outward to explore exotic places and cultures. The soldier-authors discussed in this essay penned their wartime accounts for varied reasons: to educate an uninformed audience about the physical and psychological effects of combat, to entertain their readership, to make sense of the time spent away from family and loved ones, and to purge their personal demons. Nonetheless, each narrative captures the utter foreignness of these soldiers' wartime experiences: the uprooting of their lives from the safety and comfort of home into a foreign land to fight an often faceless and nameless enemy, and doing so often lacking the moral certitude that earlier generations of soldiers used to justify their sacrifices and their actions. The texts represent a multigenerational perspective on the American war experience and show how soldiers have struggled with the strain of combat anxiety in wildly unfamiliar settings. Each of these authors varies significantly in the way he characterizes the exotic, yet the accounts employ similar tropes to convey a sense of disjuncture, disruption, and alienation across generations of soldiers.

Works Cited

Brady, James. *The Coldest War: A Memoir of Korea*. New York: Orion, 1990.

Chesterton, G. K. *Tremendous Trifles*. Fairford, Eng.: Echo, 2006.

Hughes, Edward J., ed. *The Cambridge Companion to Camus*. Cambridge: Cambridge UP, 2007.

Hynes, Samuel. *The Soldiers' Tale: Bearing Witness to Modern War*. New York: Penguin Books, 1997.

Mullaney, Craig. *The Unforgiving Minute: A Soldier's Education*. New York: Penguin, 2009.

O'Brien, Tim. "How to Tell a True War Story." *Postmodern American Fiction: A Norton Anthology*. Eds. Paula Geyh, et al. New York: Norton, 1998. 174–83.

___. *If I Die in a Combat Zone, Box Me Up and Ship Me Home*. New York: Dell, 1973.

Pratt, Mary Louise. "Arts of the Contact Zone." *Profession* 91 (1991): 33–40.

___. *Imperial Eyes: Travel Writing and Transculturation*. New York: Routledge, 1992.

Swofford, Anthony. *Jarhead: A Marine's Chronicle of the Gulf War and Other Battles*. New York: Scribner, 2003.

The Captivity Narrative: An American Genre _____

Robert C. Doyle

Anthropologist Clifford Geertz struck a chord when he stated in *The Interpretation of Cultures* (1973) that scholars should consider approaching culture in terms of organization of social activity, institutional forms, and systems of ideas in order to define and describe the world (362). These three organizational terms can be applied to better understand the experience Admiral Jeremiah Denton summed up briefly in his captivity memoir *When Hell Was in Session* (1982) as "difficult circumstances."[1]

American narrators like Denton and numerous other former wartime prisoners have shown through the development and use of a consistently repeated structure that the literature of captivity has maintained a remarkably rich, extended vitality. Each captivity narrative is individually styled because each prisoner's experience is unique. However, after one examines a large number of these works, one can see that prisoners from the American colonies to those held during the Vietnam War and beyond have styled their narratives within a set of recognized and understandable temporal, contextual, sequential, and categorical boundaries. The contents and flow of events within these boundaries constitute the *narrative contour,* a concept based on the experience itself. Characteristically, the narrative contour is expressed through variables within four major patterned contexts, seven descriptive domains, and seven major event-scenarios. Thoroughly integrated, these ingredients have enabled former-prisoners-turned-narrators to make readers come to understand what happened to them, what they did, and why they did it.

How do narrators translate the experience not only for themselves but also for a public that has little or no firsthand knowledge of captivity? The first step involves the creation of qualitative domains of "prisonerness"; the second step redefines time, from chronological to narrative-event time; and the third step requires the narrator to follow the natural flow of major events that took place "behind the wire" or in a prison. By completing this process, narrators create a string of sequentially ordered event-scenarios that contain enough detail to make sense of the experience. In order to sort out meanings in the captivity experience, one can categorize seven distinct interpretive domains that appear most frequently in the narratives: the different kinds of prisoners (their status), polemic intent, descriptions of actions taken in captivity, kinds of heroics, types of cultural idyllic myths that regulate individual and group responses, corresponding fears, and different kinds of faith the prisoners hold.

Status, Time, and the Natural Flow

The first level of interpretive distinction prominently clarified in a captivity narrative is the status of the narrator. The term captive implies that a person has no legal status, and the treatment of the prisoner is based solely on the whim of the captor. The captive loses any and all rights, has nothing on which to base any legal actions whatsoever, and is virtually a slave of the captor. If a captive is kept alive, it is because, as a prisoner, the person may have some intrinsic value. If a captive is wealthy, a ransom might be negotiated. If a captive has political significance, some kind of cartel or exchange might be created. A modern application of the status of captive is "hostage." Prisoner, on the other hand, as well as other associated terms such as *internee, evader*, or even *renegade* (the latter a prisoner who assimilates into the captor's culture to a point that the former prisoner joins the captor's armed forces), implies that there exists a recognized legal status. In that case, there exist rights and responsibilities between captors and POWs. A recognized process of hostility (war) creates status captivity in which there are international rules for the treatment of POWs and other prisoners. These rules are not mere utopian suggestions or guidelines for voluntary action; they are, like the 1949 Geneva Convention and other associated documents, international laws that must be obeyed by all the signatories. It should be clear from the experiences of American

POWs, in particular, that many captor nations have disregarded the laws in favor of punitive captivity.

The second level of interpretive distinction defines five specific polemic intents: jeremiad, apology, propaganda, complaint, and romance. The jeremiad, or sermon, narrative focuses on the captivity experience as a curse or a trial imposed on an individual, or even on a people, by an angry God. Whether one examines the biblical books of Chronicles or Lamentation, the Puritan narratives, or the seventy-three volumes of Jesuit narratives in *The Jesuit Relations* (the first volume of which was published in 1632), the captivity experience translates into a formula of spiritual redemption. The narrative apology functions as a statement of defense: why the narrator acted the way he or she did, or why a community of prisoners acted the way they did. The apologies focus on both the exigencies of the experience and the means for physical survival in general, with or without a deity acting as the central cause-and-effect figure. Most military or soldier narratives fall into this broad category. Apologies defend survival, resistance, vengeance, forgiveness, condemnation, assimilation, and escape. Some narrators explain how and why a prisoner or a community of prisoners survived through active or passive resistance; others describe the motivations that determined the unalterable need for escape. Some tell why a prisoner joined the captors and assimilated into the captor's culture. The narrative of propaganda rails against the captors' behavior and ideology; more important, one finds implicit political, ideological, or military calls to action. Some narrators are vengeful; others are forgiving; and most are inquisitive in varying degrees about discovering the mysteries of their captors' culture.

The third level of interpretive distinction defines the narrative from a position of action. This tends to include "playing it cool" to survive the captivity, resisting the captor's efforts to convert or assimilate POWs, planning and executing escapes from the prison camp, deciding to assimilate into the captor's culture partially or totally, deciding or being forced to collaborate with the captor's demands for cooperation, and, in the case of evaders and raiders, committing some form of sabotage against enemy forces.

War has a steady appetite for heroics, and the fourth level of interpretive distinction answers that need by describing six kinds of heroic actions directly or, in some cases, indirectly related to the captivity experience. The first archetype is the defeated hero: for example, Marine Corps major James P. S. Devereux, who had to surrender Wake Island in 1941, or American general Jonathan Wainwright, who surrendered Corregidor Island in 1942. Next are the stoic heroes who continue to perform their duty in the face of varying levels of adversity, up to, and including, possible execution. Also included are the different types of escapers who decide to risk their lives to liberate themselves, the assimilators who make decisions of conscience to join the captors, the passive survivors who force themselves to withstand captivity in order to tell their stories, and the raiders who attempt to free prisoners from their camp during hostilities.

In captivity, heroism translates into a force that generates a will to live. Resisting prisoners withstand enormous physical strains in interrogation and torture; others break down at the mere thought of physical abuse and collaborate to avoid pain. Stoic prisoners withstand what they have to withstand with a quiet sense of duty; others defy the odds and escape, while some die trying. Some prisoners reflect on the situation and decide that joining the captors takes more courage than remaining in captivity. The currency of prison-camp heroism is resistance; the end result is not only survival but also the sense that life in the prison camp was not wasted.

Prisoners bring their major belief systems with them into a prison camp. In the American experience, those beliefs include a passionate demand for success, a sense of material abundance, a reliance on the fruits of technology, a sense of the power of community over the desires of the individual, a sense of military duty to a war's just cause, a sense of individual fairness, loyalty to a POW community, and a dependence on the strength of international and military law. The American ideals of success, abundance, technology, and community shatter upon entry into a prison camp. In time, however, the narratives reveal that prisoners rebuild values one by one until a community of POWs resembles, in many ways, the essence of the American small town.

The prisoner's enemies include chronological time, bad luck, lawlessness, torture, collaborators and renegades, and circumstances over which they exercise little or no control. Their fears, as they have expressed them in their respective narratives, include failure, starvation, atrocities, solitude, personal weakness, and rejection from the POW community. The narratives show abundant evidence that POWs have adapted to insufficient food, sickness, and the constant presence of unnecessary suffering and death. Technology, no matter how primitive, is owned by the captor. In captivity, high-tech pilots become thieves who learn the ways of the criminal. A soldier who may have been self-reliant before capture may become community-reliant in captivity.

In everyday life, many Americans tend to keep their religious faith to themselves. The American tradition dictates that religious faith is a private matter. Americans interact with one another based on a long continuity of accepted secular values and ideals. From the colonial wars with the Native American tribes to the modern era, prisoners have displayed six major categories of faith: in one's God; in the idea and integrity of country; in the military and civil institutions they represent in captivity and in the strength of the community of prisoners behind the wire; in international laws and conventions that protect prisoners and limit what the captors can do; and in the family at home and in the individual prisoner to survive the experience. The second step in the process is the deliberate restructuring of time. French novelist and former POW Pierre Boulle commented: "The memoir of a prisoner can scarcely be set down as a continuous narrative corresponding to the dreary procession of each hour, each day, or even each month. To follow this procedure would amount to imposing on the reader a boredom as unbearable as that suffered by the captive himself" (170). As a result, Boulle, the narrator of *Aux sources de la rivière Kwaï* (1966; *My*

Own River Kwai, 1967), converted long periods of chronological time into synchronic, narrative time that gave some order to long periods of uncertainty, boredom, hunger, danger, and fear. Like narrators before and after him, he expresses his experience as a series of patterned events that compress the chaos in captivity into understandable, expressive units of time. Chronological time becomes encased into distinct narrative event-scenarios, and from capture to lament they contain examples of what narrators sequentially pattern as their personal drama. Embedded deep within the context of the captivity experience, each event-scenario relates the culture-bound meanings of individual and community survival.

Natural flow is the third step in creating a captivity narrative; this consists of constructing event-scenarios. From the earliest Indian wars to the Iraq War, captivity literature has shown relatively consistent, highly repetitive narrative contours that have been derived from the experience. Structurally, such patterns take shape as seven important repeated event-scenarios that must be in place in varying degrees so that the narrative contour makes sense within the complex relationships of captor to prisoner, prisoner to prisoner, and prisoner community to both prisoners and captors. Beginning with a precapture autobiography, the captivity narrator shapes the story according to the seven major events of the actual captivity experience: precapture autobiography, capture, remove, prison landscape, resistance, and release. The narrative ends with deep reflections that form a prisoner's lament. Whether former prisoners were resisters, survivors, escapers, or assimilators, their narratives show brevity, clarity, drama, precision, and the condensation of time, all of which culminates in the experience-structure-idea relationship found in the event-scenarios.

The Seven Event-Scenarios

Autobiographical Precapture. Captives or POWs tell the audience about themselves. Military prisoners may explain what their concept of duty was and why they were placed in harm's way. They describe and contextualize the frame of reference and initial point of view before going into captivity, including idyllic remembrances of home, family, happiness, freedom, and normalcy.

Capture. The capture phase describes how, where, and when a free man, soldier, or even passerby is taken into captivity by an aggressive enemy. The victim can be an individual soldier or sailor or an entire military garrison forced to surrender as a unit. With the advent of airplanes as combat weapons, a new word was invented, *shoot down*, which describes individual capture after aerial combat or loss of the aircraft to a surface-to-air missile or concentrated ground fire. What is vital in this event-scenario is that the narrators have lost the battle they were in and, in the space of a moment, also lost their freedom. Comrades or, in the case of the tribal captivities, family may be dead at the hands of the captors. Whether in the air, on land, or at sea, the prisoner has to admit that the surrender has become a reality. No longer does a person have anything more than the moment at hand. Death is close, and life hangs on a new captive's every move. A radical transition, perhaps the first real transformation in the captivity experience, has been accomplished. In spite of the laws of war, international conventions, or military traditions that may be in force, the prisoner loses everything at the moment of capture. Life itself depends on luck; fate rests on the whim and will of the captor.

The act of being captured represents the beginning of the prisoner's descent into a type of hell, there to survive or die at the whim of the captor. Capture itself is, perhaps, the dimmest, most frightful moment in the spectrum of the captivity experience. For the person involved, it involves radical, catastrophic shifts in status: from freedom to captivity, from relative independence to total dependence, from institutional protection to personal vulnerability, and from the assumption of the rule of law to the hope that some laws might be obeyed by the captors. Ultimately, capture means a shift from community to chaos, from civilization as the prisoner knows it to a world of savagery controlled by unpredictable captors whose aims symbolize that value system to which the prisoner is opposed.

Mary Rowlandson set the tone for the captivity narrative and established the polemic intent during King Philip's War in New England. Rowlandson was captured by Native Americans on February 20, 1676, and her description of capture characterizes the hundreds of similarly detailed accounts that followed. The attack comes without warning; the fighting takes place in her home. Her relatives die before her eyes, and she cries to God for help in her hour of sorrow, "Lord, what shall we do?"[2] Mary has little to do but try to escape the holocaust unfolding before her eyes. She takes her children and leaves the house, but the attacking Native Americans continue firing bullets. With no escape possible and a fire increasing inside the house, Mary and those with her dart for freedom. Her brother-in-law falls dead, and the Native Americans kill her nephew with a tomahawk. According to Mary, her own capture followed the butchery. Her captors tell her to go with them. Mary responds that she believes they will kill her, but they tell her that if she goes along, they will not hurt her. Reflecting for a moment, Rowlandson repeats Psalm 8, "Come behold the works of the Lord, what desolations He has made in the Earth."

Death March/Remove. This event-scenario describes when and where the prisoner was taken from the place of capture to the place of permanent captivity. *Remove,* a term found in Rowlandson's and other colonial captivity narratives, gives way to *long march* or *death march* in the twentieth century. Usually in this stage of captivity, the first outer layers of the captive's cultural veneer are peeled away by the captors. This dreadful event-scenario first reveals what the existence of true danger is and what can happen to the captive or prisoner. Comrades may be killed by the captors for trifles, such as wanting water, walking too slowly, falling down, being hungry, or, in extreme cases, showing physical resistance. Next to capture itself, it is the most dangerous event of captivity because the prisoner suffers the first seriously dangerous encounter with the captor's value system.

In the Puritan wars against their Native American neighbors, captivity acted as a ritual of redemption. For the Puritan prisoners, removes/marches represented the second phase of redemptive suffering in the captivity experience. Assuming that captivity was imposed by God as a test, trial, or ordeal of faith, some prisoners believed that the remove was a punishment for sins; others believed it signified steps in the gathering of tangible evidence of Divine providence and God's wisdom (VanDeerBeets, *The Indian Captivity Narrative* ix).

During the American Revolution, and later in the War of 1812, American soldiers captured by British, Hessian, or Loyalist forces on land were removed from the battlefield and interned in dungeons, churches, or local jails. No military prison facilities were set aside for them. About three hundred soldiers surrendered to the British at Quebec in 1776, including Ethan Allen. Allen described his six-week remove in irons aboard the British ship *Gaspee*. First condemning his captors, Allen commented that, "All the ship's crew behaved toward the prisoners with that spirit of bitterness which is the peculiar characteristic of Tories, when they have the friends of America in their power, measuring their loyalty to the English King by the barbarity, fraud, and deceit which they exercise toward the Whigs" (qtd. in Dorson 47). Allen described his irons:

The handcuff was of the common size and form, but my leg irons I should imagine would weigh thirty pounds; the bar was eight feet long, and very substantial; the shackles which encompassed my ankles were very tight. The irons were so close upon my ankles that I could not lay down in any other manner than on my back. I was put into the lowest and most wretched part of the vessel, where I got the favor of a chest to sit on; the same answered for my bed at night. I procured some little blocks off the guard, who day and night with fixed bayonets watched over me, to lie under each end of the large bar of my leg irons, to preserve my ankles from galling when I sat on the chest, or lay back on the same, though most of the time, night and day, I sat on it. (qtd. in Dorson 46)

After General William Howe's first offensive in the American colonies, more than four thousand Americans surrendered. By 1780, the British held more than three thousand soldiers, if not more, as prisoners after the big captures of Continental troops at the American defeats at Fort Washington, Camden, and Charleston, South Carolina.³

If one fast-forwards to the Vietnam War, similarities abound. Colonel Fred V. Cherry, an air-force fighter pilot and the first African American prisoner of war in North Vietnam, was shot down in May 1965. Shuffled between various prison camps near Hanoi until his release on February 12, 1973, Colonel Cherry suffered considerably at the hands of the North Vietnamese. In Wallace Terry's *Bloods* (1984), Cherry narrates his remove and reflected on the length of time he would have to spend in captivity. He had little notion that it would last eight years:

> Now they got me dressed the way they want me, and they are going to walk me three miles to this village. I didn't know my ankle was broken, too. I was dusty, hot, sweaty, and naturally, pissed off 'cause I was shot down. Didn't wanna be there. I'm thinkin' about two, three, four months. I'm not thinkin' 'bout years. I'm not even thinkin' six months. (qtd. in Terry)

Cherry was brought into the village and encountered violently angry civilians: "And this guy jumps on me, straddling my back. And he puts his automatic weapon right behind my ear with my nose pretty much in the dirt. And I said to myself, you know, this man might even shoot me" (qtd. in Terry). Then Cherry began to resist his captors: "When we got to the vehicle, they had a cameraman there. And he wanted to take pictures of me walkin' toward him. I wouldn't do it. I'd frown up and fall on my knees and turn my back. Finally, they quit. They never took any pictures. And they got me in the jeep" (qtd. in Terry). Finally, Cherry was interrogated for the first time: "The first place they tried to interrogate me appeared to be a secondary school. And they put me in this hut. I did what I was supposed to do. Name, rank, serial number, date of birth. And I started talking about the Geneva Convention. And they said forget it. 'You a criminal.'"[4]

Whether the remove is acted out on an individual basis or it is undertaken as community events such as the death marches in World War II and Korea, prisoner accounts and testimonies reveal that it is during this phase that they begin to accept that they are prisoners and, thus, gain a clearer vision of the meaning of captivity. Prisoners begin to square off against their captors and may meet members of the civilian population. They feel the wrath of and learn to understand the enemy's fears and resentments. Once the march is complete, the subsequent event-scenarios describe how prisoners solidify sets of traditional survival values that surface when they live in community and how prisoners come to decisions to escape or how captors offer political and social values to assimilators and collaborators that attack and destroy the old ones.

Prison Landscape. If prisoners survive the remove or death march, they will ultimately arrive at a permanent prison facility. During the American Revolutionary War, it may have been an Indian village or, perhaps, one of the British prison hulks; during the Civil War, it may have been Andersonville, Libby, Elmira, or Fort Delaware prisons; during World War II, a German stalag, Changi Prison in Singapore, or Karenko Camp in Formosa; in North Korea, the numbered camps; and during the Vietnam War, the Hoa Lo (the Oven) Prison, the "Hanoi Hilton," built by the French in downtown Hanoi and later used to house Americans during the Vietnam War.

Camp Sumter (located in the Sumter County, Georgia, near the town of Americus) was better known in the North as Andersonville. The Confederate government leased the land from two farmers. In December 1863, Captain Richard B. Winder of the Confederate army received orders to proceed to Andersonville and supervise construction of both a stockade for confinement of six thousand men and facilities for a large number of guards.

As happens in war, what may have originated as a good idea turned into a catastrophe for the inmates. Andersonville was an innovation gone sour. It was supposed to be a large, centralized military-prison facility established to relieve the field commanders of some of their burdens and a place to keep thousands of prisoners in one place at one time. John Urban, a member of Company D of the First Pennsylvania Regiment, offers a clear and detailed portrait of the landscape of Andersonville in *Battle Field and Prison Pen, or Through the War, and Thrice a Prisoner in Rebel Dungeons* (1882):

The general appearance of the place . . . is wild and desolate. It is very thinly settled, and was well calculated for the purpose it was intended for. The extent of ground enclosed by the stockade has been a subject of considerable difference of opinion, as it was somewhat difficult to form an opinion, owing to the crowded state of the prison; but I suppose after the enlargement of the pen in July, it contained about twenty-five acres. Of this, four or five acres were swampy, and could not be occupied. A small stream of water, about five or six inches deep, and several feet wide, entered the east side of the prison, and ran through it. This stream had its origin in a swamp a short distance from the stockade, and the water was warm and impure. To add to its natural filthiness, the rebels had built their cookhouse directly across the stream on the side where it entered the prison, and the water was often covered with filth and grease. The rebels also washed their dirty, lousy clothes in the stream. On almost every clear day we could see dozens of them sitting along its banks for that purpose; and thirsty as the poor prisoners were, they could hardly make use of the water. The entire prison was enclosed with a high stockade made of pine logs. These logs were about sixteen feet long, and were put into the ground about four feet, thus making a fence twelve feet high. Sentinel boxes were built on top of the stockade; these were about fifty feet apart, and were reached by steps from the ground on the outside. On the inside, about thirty or thirty-five feet from the stockade, was a small railing, fastened on stakes about two feet high. This was called the "Dead Line," and woe to the poor prisoner, whether ignorant of its terrible meaning or not, who crossed, or even reached under it, for instant death was sure. . . . One of my comrades, with a groan of despair, exclaimed, "My God, can this be hell?" (Urban 254–65)

Regardless of the war or the century, memories of the prison camp or the prison cells are branded into prisoners' consciousness; it is no wonder, then, that prisoners take great pains to describe each enemy prison facility in remarkably rich detail. Prisoners, especially bored ones, become expert ethnologists in this respect. In capture, the individual separates from his own culture and begins the journey into a world of chaos. The prison landscape is the body of that chaos; it represents a place of evil, a place so horrible that narrators are compelled to describe it in the most graphic terms. However, there is a hidden agenda beneath descriptions of individual prison landscapes: the individual and collective recognition of the "we-ness" of the captivity experience. Forming the beginnings of a captive community during removes, prisoners find themselves locked into individual cells or cages and collective prison camps, ones in which they have to work together first to resist, then to destroy, or take the risk of being swallowed up, discarded, and forgotten.

Resistance, Survival, or Assimilation. Resisters narrate their experiences soon after repatriation. They have a story to tell. Survivors often wait years, sometimes decades, before they take up the pen, often because specific incidents are too painful to confess or to remember. Many passive resisters have yet to narrate their experiences. Many hard resisters, including escapers, are executed outright by their captors or, in some cases, tortured into passivity. In any case, the choices of resisting and surviving are hard to make, and narrators have shown conclusively that decisions to resist incur high prices both in captivity and after it. The experience of captivity creates a spiritual transformation in the individual through great physical and psychological pain. This event-scenario of the captivity narrative describes how, where, and when captors apply physical torture and/or psychological pressure on prisoners in order to change their ways of thinking, or at least change their overt behavior. Major Devereux sums up the resistance predicament of the American POWs in Japanese hands. The fight was not only one for life but also to maintain self-respect:

> Hidden behind the routine, under the surface of life in the prison camp, was fought a war of wills for moral supremacy—an endless struggle, as bitter as it was unspoken, between the captors and the captives. The stakes seemed to me simply this: the main objective of the whole Japanese prison program was to break our spirit, and on our side was the stubborn determination to keep our self-respect whatever else they took from us. It seems to me that struggle was almost as much a part of the war as the battle we fought on Wake Island. (qtd. in Bailey 25)[5]

In this event-scenario, prisoners understand their captors better. Faceless, stereotypical captors become real people with names. Captives understand what the captors want and what the enemy's expectations and weaknesses are. How captives feel about captivity begins to surface as they continue to undergo deep psychological transformations. Prisoners are confronted with some basic decision making. In this event-scenario they examine the nature of their fundamental cultural values as they surface as weapons against the captor. Either these values lend support to or destroy the prisoner's sense of self and community.

Release and Repatriation. This event-scenario of the captivity narrative describes the happy and sad repatriation and return (or attempted return) of captives to the worlds from which they came. Release may come if advancing friendly forces overrun the enemy and liberate the prison camp. Liberation may also take place if friendly forces raid the prison camp in a secret operation during hostilities or as a result of formal exchanges.

In the Civil War, The primary issue in regard to the release of prisoners was not so much the existence of parole or exchange, but the condition of each side's prisoners upon release. The United States Sanitary Commission, the forerunner of the American Red Cross, sent representatives to tend to soldiers as they returned north from Southern prison camps. One member of the commission, Anna Holstein, was present in Annapolis for a prisoner exchange in 1864. She was horrified by what she saw:

> In one arrival of 460, only 60 were able to walk ashore; the 400 were carried; half of these died within a few days; one third of the whole number imbecile. They appeared like a wretched bundle of bones, covered with a few filthy rags. Though coming from different prisons, all agree in this one fact: they were starved, without shelter, and wearing only the scantiest clothing—the rags which remained from the time they were captured—when their coats, blankets and valuables were all taken from them. Many, after conversing about it, will say: "You never could imagine such horrors." (qtd. in Dannet 322)

In some cases, parole or the payment of a ransom results in liberation. More commonly, however, liberation and repatriation take place after a truce or as the result of a treaty of peace. Toward the end of World War II, liberation brought the war to American POWs' doorsteps the hard way. Liberating Stalag VII A at Moosberg on April 28, 1945, General George S. Patton led a charge of tanks that broke through the barbed wire and barriers surrounding the camp. For the prisoners inside, all hell broke loose when the American tanks ripped through the German defenses. Angered, General Patton went on to say, in his gruff manner, "These German bastards are going to pay for this. The sons-of-bitches will suffer, and don't you ever forget it" (Simmons 240). According to Kenneth Simmons, who was present in Stalag VII A at the time:

Tears from my eyes blurred the picture. The Stars and Stripes waved and rippled as they moved slowly toward heaven. Soldiers from General Patton's Army snapped to attention and saluted. Those of us who were able joined in with them. When the flag climbed to its full height, salutes were concluded, but eyes remained on the Stars and Stripes. Men about me were kneeling. I knelt too. While kneeling, I prayed and thanked God. I wiped my eyes, but the tears would not stop. (Simmons 242–43)

Escaping, perhaps the most naturally heroic event in captivity, belongs to this event scenario too. A small number of prisoners escape, but most escapers suffer recapture and severe punishment for their efforts.[6] Most important, in this event-scenario prisoners take the time to consider the intensifying social, ethical, and moral conflicts about the efficacy of escaping, especially when the well-being of the prison community is at stake.

Lament. In the lament, former prisoners express a sense of loss. The lament gives them the opportunity to grieve for the time wasted in captivity, for the material opportunities that were lost over time, and for their dead comrades. Some former prisoners lament their captivity experience through poetry, song, written narrative, and prayer, others through alcoholism and suicide. Former prisoners of war insist that a permanent cultural transformation of values, insights, ethics, and morality takes place in captivity. People, places, institutions, and even daily circumstances are compared to those in captivity. Every day in freedom means a day not being a captive. The act of writing about their experiences of captivity serves as a catharsis and a forum to tell the world what happened to them; writing also functions as an ethical forum for former POWs to express individual and collective outrage against willful, often illegal, acts of inhumanity.

Conclusion

The seven-point structure forms a step-by-step chronology of captivity told in patterns of significance derived from direct experience. Some examples are bitter condemnations of the captors; others have been rationales for American prisoners joining their captors' cause. Time, the bitter enemy of the prisoner, is replaced by a series of events in which time stands still. Relying on a relatively formalistic sequential synchronic structure as a replacement for chronological time, event-scenarios contain the general thematic, dramatic, and interpretive elements needed to describe the captivity experience. Dramatic structure in the captivity narrative is determined by two conditions: the human need to express the realities of the experience and the structural need to collapse chronological time into consistently patterned, synchronic event-scenarios, the essence of which consists of a dynamic synthesis of description, explanation, clarification, and evaluation of what happened in captivity.

As a category of wartime literature, captivity narratives describe individual transformations of life based on pragmatic, lifesaving value systems. Failures transform into successes. Acts of defiance, torture, resistance, escape, evasion, and liberation constitute the framing devices for individual heroism and come together to act as the captive's defense against seemingly improbable actions. War is rarely, if ever, glorified or romanticized in captivity narratives.

As a storytelling device, the captivity narrative reflects meanings not only in an author's belief system but also in the social, community, and institutional groups to which the narrator belongs.[7] Organizing principles have differed considerably from one kind of captivity memoir to another, and from one country to another, but the degree of structural and thematic consistency outweighs the differences. Reflecting on systems of conventions and levels of expectations that become part of an individual's experience, narrators often reveal what people make of captivity and how they fit their captivity experiences into conceptual frames of reference within their culture. With origins reaching into both secular and biblical lore, the themes, motifs, ideals, and beliefs expressed in captivity narratives connect various generations of men and women with a common Western literary and folk tradition, one that describes and defines traditional ideas about religion, heroism, adventure, soldiering, and even fictional romance.

Although captivity literature is created as an individual act, as a class of literature, it functions as a means by which narrators reflect not only on personal belief systems but also on the doctrine of social, community, and institutional groups to which they belong. By alternating between personal encounters and group experiences, narrators use each event-scenario to examine their principles with unprecedented scrutiny: "Did I bring adequate sets of values to the captivity environment or not?"

After each war, some American soldiers returning from the enemy's dungeons and prison camps have described their experiences for the public. Whether the descriptions appeared in the form of published diaries or full prose narratives, military prison memoirs became part of a captivity literature that resembled the original colonial narratives in structure but had distinct observational context, feelings, and modes of expressing fundamental values and ideals. Tested by capture, solidified in confrontation, and confirmed in resistance, escape, or rescue, the captives, through their narratives, affirm ideals of stoic heroism, sacrifice, humility, resistance, success, and victory.

There is virtually no narrative of captivity, from the colonial wars through the twentieth century, that does not contain descriptions and reflections of release, exchange, liberation, repatriation, and lament. Regardless of the individual's pathway to freedom, bringing the unnatural life behind the wire toward closure is a necessity. Closure acts as an opportunity to lash out against a captor's excess and to damn the captors and the experience categorically and completely; in some cases, however, it allows captives to forgive transgressions by the captors. The three concluding event-scenarios (release, repatriation, and the prisoner's lament) act in consort to form a continuing contest of opposites: euphoric happiness against timeless grief, personal freedom against individual lowliness, a pursuit of life against the imminent threat of death, and the perception of success against the self-accusation of failure. It is no wonder that so many former civilian and military prisoners insist that what happens in captivity causes permanent cultural transformations of values, insights, ethics, and morality. The degree of transformation remains individual and personal; the act of transformation seems to be universal.

Notes

1. See Voices from *Captivity: Interpreting the American POW Narrative* (Doyle) for a full treatment of the narrative contour.
2. For an analog to Mary Rowlandson's approach to the captivity experience, see Peter Williamson, qtd. in *Held Captive by Indians: Selected Narratives 1642–1836* (VanDerBeets), 216–27.
3. See Burrows for an outstanding study of Americans in British hands.
4. Cherry, qtd. in *Bloods* 266-91. See also Hirsch.
5. See also Devereux. Interview is held by the USMC Historical Center, Washington Navy Yard.
6. For a full treatment of American escapers, see *A Prisoner's Duty* (Doyle).
7. See Jones for a full treatment of the American war novel as genre.

Works Cited

Bailey, Ronald H. *Prisoners of War.* Alexandria, VA: Time-Life, 1981.

Boulle, Pierre. *My Own River Kwai.* Trans. Xan Fielding. New York: Vanguard, 1967.

Burrows, Edwin G. *Forgotten Patriots: The Untold Story of American Prisoners during the Revolutionary War.* New York: Basic, 2008.

Dannet, Sylvia G. L., ed. *Noble Women of the North.* New York: Yoseloff, 1959.

Denton, Jeremiah A. *When Hell Was in Session.* Mobile, AL: Traditional, 1982.

Devereux, Colonel James P. S. *The Story of Wake Island.* Philadelphia: Lippincott, 1947.

Dorson, Richard M., ed. *America Rebels: Narratives of the Patriots.* New York: Pantheon, 1953.

Doyle, Robert C. *A Prisoner's Duty: Great Escapes in U.S. Military History.* Annapolis, MD: Naval Institute, 1997.

___. *Voices from Captivity: Interpreting the American POW Narrative.* Lawrence: U of Kansas P, 1994.

Geertz, Clifford. *The Interpretation of Culture.* New York: Basic, 1973.

Hirsch, James S. *Two Souls Indivisible: The Friendship That Saved Two POWs in Vietnam.* New York: Houghton, 2004.

Jones, Peter G. *War and the Novelist: Appraising the American War Novel*. Columbia: U of Missouri P, 1976.

Rowlandson, Mary. *Puritans among the Indians, Accounts of Captivity and Redemption, 1676–1724*. Eds. Alden T. Vaughan and Edward W. Clark. Cambridge, MA: Belknap, 1981.

Simmons, Kenneth. *Kriegie*. New York: Nelson, 1960.

Terry, Wallace. *Bloods: An Oral History of the Vietnam War by Black Veterans*. New York: Ballantine, 1984.

Urban, John W. *Battle Field and Prison Pen, or Through the War, and Thrice a Prisoner in Rebel Dungeons*. Philadelphia: Hubbard, 1882.

VanDerBeets, Richard. *The Indian Captivity Narrative: An American Genre*. New York: UP of America, 1984.

VanDerBeets, Richard, ed. *Held Captive by Indians: Selected Narratives 1642–1836*. Knoxville: U of Tennessee P, 1973.

War and Witnessing

Elisabeth Piedmont-Marton

Phillip Knightley's revised and updated history of war journalism, *The First Casualty: The War Correspondent as Hero and Mythmaker from the Crimea to Iraq* (2004), draws a stunning and, for most American readers, a counterintuitive conclusion: War reporting since the 1960s has become not better, but worse. Technologies and practices such as satellite phone transmissions and digital media have provided the public not with better information but with "wave after wave of images that add up to nothing" (504). In addition, the relatively recent US policy of embedding reporters with military units actually enlisted the press in the effort to censor dispatches from war, a "comprehensive and cleverly devised plan but one in which—although not many realized it until it was too late—the traditional war correspondent had been bypassed" (500). The Gulf War of 1991, Knightley concludes, "marks an important turning point in the history of war correspondents. Not only was it a war in which the military succeeded in changing people's perceptions of what battle was really like, one in which the 'surgical' precision of new high-tech weapons meant few if any civilian casualties, but one in which the way the war was communicated was as important as the conduct of the war itself" (500).

Knightley quotes Barry Zorthian, chief Pentagon public-affairs spokesman during the Vietnam War, speaking to the National Press Club in March 1991: "'The Gulf War is over and the press lost'" (500). For Americans, accustomed to thinking of the US press corps as the flag bearer for freedom of information in the world, this account can be baffling. This essay contextualizes American assumptions about war reporting since its heyday during the Vietnam War by examining three book-length accounts of late-twentieth-century wars by non-US writers. The transnational perspective helps in the critical analysis of the way contemporary narratives of war are shaped not only by individuals and emerging technologies but also by state-controlled institutions and deeply held cultural assumptions.

Represented in this essay are three firsthand nonfiction narratives of war and revolution, representing authors of three nationalities, conflicts that stretch across five continents and dozens of countries, and countless lives lost and ruined. Together Ryszard Kapuściński's *Wojna futbolowa* (1986; *The Soccer War*, 1991), Vladislav Tamarov's *Afghanistan: A Russian Soldier's Story* (1992), and Anthony Loyd's *My War Gone By, I Miss It So* (1999) take readers through a harrowing tour of late-twentieth-century war, much of it forgotten, discounted, or overshadowed in the United States by conflicts more directly involving American interests.

A Polish national who worked as a journalist under the state-controlled press of the Soviet-style socialist regime, Kapuściński writes about Africa, Latin America, and the Middle East from 1958 to 1976. Tamarov was a nineteen-year-old draftee from Leningrad (now Saint Petersburg) when he was sent to Afghanistan to fight for 621 days, the experience he records in his photo-essay. A British veteran and journalist, Loyd reports closely on the Yugoslavian wars of 1990–95 and the First Chechen War with Russia, beginning in 1994. While many American readers tend to regard US coverage of the Vietnam War as the starting point of a tradition of "new" journalism, often represented by Michael Herr's iconic *Dispatches* (1977), the works of writers such as Loyd, Kapuściński, and Tamarov suggest that, while each of them owes a debt to Herr and others, the recent history of war reporting follows a different trajectory.

In the preface to the 2004 edition of his book first published in 1975, Knightley acknowledges how his view of war reporting has changed: "When I first wrote this book . . . I wanted to record how war had been reported through the ages and to highlight the unforgiving verdict of history on those reports. In most cases journalism, meant to be the first draft of history, had to be substantially redrafted as hindsight revealed that important parts of the story had been omitted or twisted." In recent decades, however, Knightley sees the need for journalists to be more self-reflexive and aware of the ways in which their own identities and voices are constructed and presented: "As I added new chapters for new wars I found that I had another aim. I wanted to challenge journalists to examine their own role in the promotion of war and urge them to consider the burden they bear—every time they write a story they have an immeasurable but definite responsibility for what happens next" (xiii).

All three of the books examined in this essay wrestle with the difficulties Knightley gestures toward; and, moreover, these struggles reveal themselves as intertwined problems of genre and subjectivity. In other words, the complicated question of what kind of a book it is—soldier memoir, reporter memoir, or straight reportage—is inextricable from the problems of subjectivity (how the writer presents himself both in the action and to the reader). Late-twentieth-century and early-twenty-first-century war writing demands that both writer and reader be willing to cross porous boundaries between genres and to be reflective and critical about the ways in which stories constitute and represent selves.

Loyd's *My War Gone By* chronicles the writer-photographer's experiences in the series of conflicts often referred to as the Yugoslav or Bosnian wars and in the Russian suppression of the Chechen rebellion. Loyd relishes in, and takes full advantage of, his freelance status, moving relatively unimpeded among various groups of fighters and reporters as alliances shift in the baffling series of conflicts that make up the war. Clearly indebted to (and enamored of) Herr, Loyd weaves autobiographical narrative with war reporting, foregrounding the individual experience in and attraction to war. Employing a nonlinear narrative structure (and a somewhat tedious use of italics), Loyd zigzags back and forth between the always-shifting front lines in the wars in Bosnia and Chechnya, his current life in London, and his childhood, including the author's troubled relationship with his father and his struggle with addiction.

One of the remarkable (and frustrating) qualities of Loyd's work is how insistently it fails to illuminate the murky corners of both the war and the author's psyche. Born into a distinguished military family in the United Kingdom, Loyd served in the British army during the Persian Gulf War. His experience in that unbalanced and short-lived war left him disappointed, however, and he returned to England and struggled with depression and alcohol addiction. Readers seeking to understand the war will come away frustrated, as will a reader invested in learning more about the causes of and the treatments for Loyd's depression and addiction. In fact, *My War Gone By* stretches the genre boundaries of the war memoir by foregrounding the memoirist instead of the war. In many ways, the book dramatizes the problem of war memoir and reporting in an age when most do not believe in "objectivity," in the capacity of the observer to stand apart from what he observes: One can only see the war as it is refracted through the prism of the writer.

In *My War Gone By,* the war swims in and out of focus, always eluding readers' ability both to resolve the details on its surface and to parse its underlying structures. To be fair, however, the series of conflicts that tore apart the former Yugoslavia are so complicated that no one even seems to be able to agree what to call them. Known variously as the Balkan, Bosnian, or Yugoslav wars, the violent eruptions that lasted from 1991 to 1999 were fueled by nationalism, religious difference, and ancient history; pitted village against village and family against family; challenged the US and NATO's peacekeeping capacities; and killed and dislocated tens of thousands of people. It is far beyond the scope of this essay to explain the sequence and causes of the events of the wars; instead, this essay looks more closely at the subject position that Loyd carves out for himself as a correspondent.

Beginning in medias res, Loyd drops readers into Srebrenica in 1996 and defers the explanation of how and why he got there. Later, he discloses that he went to war because, like so many before him, he wanted to; also, he found civilian options unsatisfying in England after he finished his uneventful service in the army. Calling the Gulf War "one of the greatest anticlimaxes of my life," Loyd reenlisted with the hope he would find another war against which to test himself (131). Adrift and depressed without the structure and purpose of military life, he prescribes himself equal doses of alcohol, psychotherapy, and running, and eventually hatches the idea to enter the latest war in Yugoslavia after enrolling in a postgraduate course in photojournalism to acquire "enough knowledge to pass myself off as a freelancer once I got to the war" (135). Loyd explains his motivation: "I wanted to throw myself into a war, hoping for either a metamorphosis or an exit. I wanted to reach a human extreme in order to cleanse myself of my sense of fear, and saw war as the ultimate frontier of human experience. Hindsight gives you strange wisdom. In some ways we all get what we want" (136). What follows, however, are almost two hundred pages of stories of people who did not "throw themselves into war," but had war thrust upon them, of people dragged not so much to the ultimate frontier of human experience but to terror and death, of people who most emphatically did not get what they wanted.

Rooted in Western post–Enlightenment ideas about the individual, bolstered by a political system with a deep attachment to the idea of freedom of speech, and further strengthened by his gender, race, and social position, Loyd has unshakable faith in his own agency, and this is the hallmark of *My War Gone By*. Loyd's self-representation dominates the narrative, sometimes relegating the wars to the background. Loyd characterizes everything he does as a function of unfettered personal choice: his desire to make himself into a correspondent with minimal effort and go to war, his shifting allegiances and moral positions on the war, his decision to initiate and then abandon an attempt to mend his relationship with his father, and even his heroin addiction.

Like many writers, Loyd describes war as a remedy for all aspects of his life that are unsatisfying, destructive, or emasculating. In words that are almost comically derivative of Herr and the genre he spawned, Loyd proclaims: "I had come to Bosnia partially as an adventure. But after a while I got into the infinite death trip. I was not unhappy.

Quite the opposite. I was delighted with most of what the war had offered me: chicks, kicks, cash, and chaos; teenage punk dreams turned real and wreathed in gunsmoke" (207). In Chechnya, Loyd decides to return to the fighting one more time, even though "the prospect of squealing around in the snow in Grozny smashed to pieces by a Russian shell, alone, in agony and terror, did not feature too high on my list of preferences" of "places, wars and ways to die" (253). It need hardly be mentioned that he is surrounded by people who do not have lists of preferences of places and ways to die, and even if they did, would be forced to forfeit them to the exigencies of war. Of course, Loyd doesn't die there, so he must have "chosen" not to.

Loyd's narrative of personal choice and autonomy is most interesting (and most troubling to some readers) when it comes to his heroin habit. As discussed in "'I'm Not Trying to Compete with You': Gulf War Fiction and Discursive Space," many post–Vietnam War narratives by US writers, fiction and nonfiction both, feature addiction and recovery stories in which war and the geopolitical theater recede into the background and the individual's triumph over a pernicious disease of addiction occupies center stage. Readers learn of Loyd's heroin use early in the book, and those who expect some kind of resolution are disappointed to finish the book without learning whether he still uses.

Upon returning to London from Chechnya, Loyd describes himself as traumatized by his experiences, "haunted," "furtive," and "fucking shattered" (262). Nonetheless, he describes his return to heroin in almost loving terms, never suggesting that he is operating under some compulsion or disease model of addiction: "I sucked in the smoke greedily, and the cold wash of anaesthesia hit me. It swept over me . . . every sense unwinding, unburdened of the crushing weight of pain I never even knew I had: the rush, the wave, death, heaven, completion. For hours and hours" (263). "It does not take long to get a habit," Loyd concludes, "and I ran in to get mine, hands outstretched, determined, like it was all I had ever wanted. Maybe it was" (264). Like he said earlier, "In some ways we all get what we want." However, readers are left to wonder how much of what is learned of the wars has been shaped by Loyd's unfinished and shifting selves, how the war emerges in his writing as a function of his addiction and depression. If he has a burden and a responsibility to tell the "truth" about war, as Knightley suggests, what truths can readers distill?

As opposed to Loyd, Kapuściński does not come from a political culture that valorizes individual choice and freedom of the press. Born and raised in Communist Poland, Kapuściński (1932–2007) spent "much of his life, happily, in uncomfortable and obscure places, many of them in Africa, trying to convey their essence to a continent far away," according to his obituary in the *Guardian Online*. *Time International* also notes that in the course of his long career, he was "jailed forty times, witnessed twenty-seven coups and revolutions, survived four death sentences, contracted tuberculosis, cerebral malaria and blood poisoning, and was once doused with benzene and nearly set ablaze" (62). A widely decorated writer, Kapuściński often departs from strict notions of journalistic "truth," a practice that earned him the controversial label of magical-realism journalist (in fact, noted magical-realist author Gabriel García Márquez was an admirer).

Magical realism is a fluid literary term used to describe instances in literature and film in which the magical is not only juxtaposed to the real but also is treated as if it were an ordinary part of the real world. In magical realist texts, magical occurrences are treated as though they were ordinary events, thus causing readers and viewers to question the distinctions society maintains between the real and the imaginary. Referring to journalism as magical realism is problematic, since journalists are ostensibly supposed to be concerned only with the real, if not the "true." To say that someone practices magical-realism journalism, however, is not necessarily to question that person's adherence to the facts. Rather, it is to question the authority of the facts themselves, to suggest, as Tim O'Brien does in "How to Tell a True War Story," that the truest stories are not always the ones that actually happened.

Like Loyd, Kapuściński has an inflated sense of his agency in the world, but unlike Loyd, his subjectivity is constrained by an asymmetrical relationship with the state of which he is a citizen. He is required to be much more Polish than Loyd is to be English. Kapuściński must secure permission to travel outside of Poland in order to do his journalistic work and is subject to recall at any time. His work is also subject to substantial editing and censorship. Some critics have argued that his accounts of the fall of dictators in the far corners of the developing world were meant to be read as allegories for the totalitarian Polish government, which he was not allowed to criticize. Jack Schafer, in the online magazine *Slate*, disagrees with some of the notable Kapuściński apologists. The *New York Times*, in its obituary of the legendary globetrotting journalist, Schafer argues, "negotiates its way around the master's unique relationship with the truth diplomatically, stating that his work was 'often tinged with magical realism' and used 'allegory and metaphors to convey what was happening.'"

For Schafer, Kapuściński's credibility comes down to one question: "If Kapuściński regularly mashes up the observed (journalism) with the imagined (fiction), how certain can we be of our abilities to separate the two while reading?" Journalists likes to give themselves credit for having access to the "Truth," but thoughtful readers will recognize that even with the best of intentions, writers' accounts will always be inflected by emotion, trauma, and personal history, as well as practical limitations such as mobility, language barriers, and the reliability of sources. In fact, Kapuściński seems to recognize the fraught nature of claims to truth in the intermittent sections of the book that refer to the book he did not write. These "meta" sections stitch the episodic chapters together and provide a discursive space for Kapuściński to reflect on and complicate (some may argue, obscure) his position in the world he reports on. "What I am writing is not a book, but only the plan (and a plan is even less substantial than an outline or a sketch) of a nonexistent book," he writes about the experience of being imprisoned and tortured in Africa (*Soccer War* 82).

Just a few pages later, having been summoned back to Warsaw; Kapuściński is questioned by Polish authorities, inviting a comparison between the two regimes: "I had to prepare a note on what I had seen in the Congo. I described the battles, the collapse, the defeat. Then I was summoned by a certain comrade from the Ministry of Foreign Affairs, 'What have you been writing, you?' he stormed at me. 'You call the revolution anarchy! You think Gizenga is on the way out and Kobutu is winning! These are pernicious theories'" (83). When Kapuściński gives his bosses the truth, they reject it for not conforming to ideological orthodoxy.

Later, he writes about the impossibility of establishing a stable subject position outside of the flow of events on which he is reporting, the postmodern dilemma in a nutshell:

> Yet I have not written a dictionary or a book because whenever I start, taking a deep breath and crossing myself as if getting ready to jump into deep water, a red light starts blinking on the map—the signal that at some point on this overcrowded, restless, and quarrelsome globe, something is again happening, the earth quivering, staggering, because this relentless current, this stream of events—it is so difficult to step out of it on to a calm shore—keeps rushing and hurtling by, pulling me under. (197)

If Kapuściński is not permitted to pursue the admittedly chimerical truth and objectivity in the Western sense of journalistic ethics, then perhaps the choice to veer closer to the border with fiction is strategic. If this is so, then many of the criticisms of Kapuściński's technique appear ideologically biased. Schafer fails to take into account what it might be like to work for the press arm of a totalitarian government, covering postcolonial nationalist and Marxist uprisings in the contested developing world, and unfairly accuses Kapuściński of simple, fanciful embellishment: "The measure of a journalist, especially a foreign correspondent, is to achieve the effect of Kapuściński without scattering the pixie dust of magical realism."

The more serious critique of Kapuściński's work after his death, however, is more difficult to explain, but seems also to be a function of ideologically and politically biased assumptions about the autonomy of the individual and the economy of information. Kapuściński's fifty-year career and the veracity of his two dozen books were compromised after his death when it emerged that he had worked for the Polish communist intelligence services, gathering information on American companies and citizens as well as on the intelligence agencies of the United States, Israel, and West Germany. Many believe these revelations cost him the Nobel Prize in 2007. This may be unfair: Working in a culture and with a government with no strong tradition of individual rights and a free press, amid the turbulence of the Cold War and postcolonial uprisings in the developing world, what other choices did Kapuściński have? In the same way that Loyd's mobility and autonomy are "purchased" with his (mostly unacknowledged) race, gender, and class privilege, Kapuściński negotiates a deal that allows him to travel the world and report on some of the least understood conflicts of the second half of the twentieth century in a genre that reflects postmodern understandings of truth and objectivity. As history has shown, the self he constructed in his writing was itself something of a fiction as well.

Tamarov, however, has no such negotiating power in the construction of subjectivity. He has published one book to Kapuściński's two dozen, and so far, no one has questioned his veracity or his motives in his account of his 621 days serving in the Soviet army in Afghanistan. However, he shares with Kapuściński one important quality: an unequal relationship to the state. Not only does nineteen-year-old Tamarov have no control over the decision to serve in the Soviet military, but also he has no control over the larger historical narrative within which his service takes place. As a teenager in Leningrad, he hears that Soviet troops were building hospitals and planting trees; after he was drafted in 1984, he trains as a paratrooper but is assigned the even more dangerous job of minesweeper. "He never planted a tree, and was told there was no time to build hospitals," in the words of reviewer Linda Rocawich of *The Progressive.*

Originally published under the title *Afghanistan: Soviet Vietnam,* Tamarov's book makes no lofty claims to professional journalism. In fact, Tamarov did not go on to a career as a writer and journalist, working instead as a professional break-dancer and mime. Although Rocawich (in *The Progressive* in 1992) says that he is a freelance photographer and writer, Google and scholarly searches do not produce any results under his name, and *Afghanistan: A Russian Soldier's Story* appears to be his only book.

One of the most striking aspects of the book is how little the young Tamarov would have known about the world outside of the Soviet Union, let alone the arguments about the reporter's responsibilities to certain ideas of truth and objectivity. Like Kapuściński, Tamarov experiments with genre in his powerful and elliptical account of his experiences serving with the Soviet army in Afghanistan in the early 1980s. Employing both photographs and short, elliptical narrative sections, Tamarov assembles a collage of images from his experiences in Afghanistan, but readers get surprisingly little information about him (and rarely a hint of his inner life) in a text that claims to be autobiographical.

Of the three books discussed in this essay, Tamarov's, paradoxically, may have the most resonance with American readers. As an Englishman, Loyd's narrative persona is closest to American readers, but the wars he writes about are so complex and remote that many readers will have difficulty relating to him. Kapuściński's work is not only translated from the Polish but also covers a mind-boggling array of events over a period of decades; also, his relationship to the government is unfamiliar at best and at least compromising (if not damning). Mediated through translation, about a distant war involving former US enemies, and strangely impersonal in style, Tamarov's text would seem to be the strangest to American readers, but his words and images strike powerful chords, as they both recall the American experience in Vietnam and hauntingly anticipate the American experience in Afghanistan beginning in 2001. Though a stranger to Americans, he seems familiar; and the images of war are haunting and proximal.

Like Kapuściński, Tamarov is a somewhat unwilling subject of his state. Unlike Kapuściński, however, he is thrown into war not as an observer (or intelligence agent), but as a soldier. As a minesweeper, he is literally an instrument of the state. Young, untraveled, relatively uneducated, and without access to the larger political and military objective he serves, Tamarov documents his 621 days in the field with both black-and-white photographs that he processes himself and brief written passages that link the images together and evoke, in the faces of the impossibly young men, universal images from other wars.

According to John Yurechko, reviewing the book for *Library Journal*: "This is more than a photographic essay, this evokes the microcosm of combat: the last image of a young soldier who dies hours later, the dusty, the unshaven, the deadly simplicity of a directional shrapnel mine cradled like some votive offering. Victims, officers, killers, Mujahadeen prisoners: something in all of their eyes that is a frozen visual tragedy." Rocawich writes: "There's something about the juxtaposition of these faces anticipating their first battle with the straightforward acceptance of the nature of war and the inability of the young to change it: It's unsettling, it's unacceptable, and you know he's probably right. And he knows he hasn't discovered something that applies to Soviet veterans alone." Tamarov's naiveté (he had never left Leningrad) produces in him not the xenophobia of the provincial but a profound empathy and a sense of history that belies his youth. He reflects on his encounters with local residents:

> We knew they were telling the truth, and didn't want the deaths of our soldiers any more than they wanted the deaths of their people. Somewhere in our subconscious, we understood that the only thing they wanted was to go home. We also knew if someone invaded our land, we would defend ourselves, just as these Afghans were doing. That's how it was for

Napoleon in Russia, for Hitler in the Soviet Union, for the Americans in Vietnam, and for us in Afghanistan. (117)

What Tamarov's words and images lack in sophistication they more than make up for in empathy, poignancy, and the power of eye-witnessing. Whereas Loyd tells his readers about the terrible lot of the Bosnian, Serb, Croatian, Chechen, and Russian soldiers, he does so as a mildly detached observer; Kapuściński covers so much territory that he barely pauses to show the faces on one set of front lines before jumping to the next set. In fact, the most visceral scene in *The Soccer War* is the one in which Kapuściński is the central figure in the conflict, the famous episode in which he is soaked in benzene and nearly set on fire (beginning on page 129).

One of the most moving documents in *A Soldier's Story* is the photograph of a page in Tamarov's notebook in which he charts each day and hour of his 621 days. In columns he charts days served and days remaining, making calculations in the final column of "how many weeks I had to serve till the next Order, after which I'd have only a half a year left to serve . . . six months . . . twenty-six weeks . . . one hundred eighty-one days . . . four thousand three hundred twenty hours. Each one of these hours could have cost me my life" (96). The chart seems to be a kind of bulwark against the forces against Tamarov and the other young Soviet soldiers, sweeping them up in events over which they have no control. Other than counting days and hours, Tamarov has no control over his destiny, no agency in the disposition of his body in a foreign land. Here is how he describes one day's mission, the photograph accompanying it showing four heavily laden soldiers perched on a steep and rocky ravine, one of them looking at a map:

The helicopter just let us out here. We didn't know exactly where we were; we didn't even know why we were here. We fired at everything that fired at us. But over the radio someone told us where we were supposed to go. We didn't know why we should go there, and therefore we went. All night we climbed to the very top; once we got there, we got the order to go back down immediately. . . . And we came to a place that we didn't know for a reason that we didn't understand. There was something insane about all of this—as if no one knew what we were doing there. (52)

Despite the crushing futility and alienation of the conflict, Tamarov's book helped to improve the lives of the Afghansti (veterans of the war in Afghanistan) after Tamarov became connected to a group of Vietnamsti in the United States and learned about treatments for post-traumatic stress disorder and other problems for returning veterans.

What these three book-length nonfiction accounts of war relay about the nature of war stories at the turn of the twentieth-first century, first of all, is how important these stories are and how citizens have a duty to read, to listen, and to bear witness. Second, these books ask readers to think in new ways about war narrative, genre, and the problems of self-representation. Just as the contours of conflicts shape the contours of genre, the blurring of genre boundaries problematizes the construction of authorial voice and presence in war narratives. In *My War Gone By,* Loyd locates struggles to construct a coherent self against the backdrop of an almost impenetrable tangle of ethnic conflict and genocide, challenging readers' assumptions about the purpose and the ethics of war reporting, while also offering a compelling glimpse of the wars. Kapuściński, in *The Soccer Wars,* invents the new genre of magical-realism journalism as he tries to camouflage his roles as an informant and agent of the Polish state. Finally, Tamarov uses a self-consciously postmodernist collage and mixed-media genre to evoke powerful eyewitness images of a war that seems impossibly remote to American readers, while also essentially writing himself out of the narrative. Together, the works of Loyd, Kapuściński, and Tamarov challenge readers to reconsider assumptions about the nature of war narrative, objectivity, truth, fiction, and the voice and position of the writer at the dawn of the twenty-first century.

Works Cited

Kapuściński, Ryszard. *The Soccer War.* Trans. William Brand. New York: Random, 1986.

Knightley, Phillip. *The First Casualty: The War Correspondent as Hero and Myth-maker.* Baltimore: Johns Hopkins UP, 2004.

Loyd, Anthony. *My War Gone By, I Miss It So.* New York: Doubleday, 1999.

Morrison, Donald. "Fellow Travelers." *Time International* 18 June 2007: 62.

Piedmont-Marton, Elisabeth. "'I'm Not Trying to Compete with You': Gulf War Fiction and Discursive Space." *Thirty Years After: The Vietnam War in Film and Literature.* Ed. Mark Heberle. Newcastle-upon-Tyne: Cambridge Scholars. 2009. 433–43.

Rocawich, Linda. "A War Is a War Is a War." *The Progressive* 56.6 (June 1992): 39.

"Ryszard Kapuściński, Polish Writer of Shimmering Allegories and Nes, Dies at 74." *New York Times* 24 Jan. 2007.

Shafer, Jack. "The Lies of Ryszard Kapuściński." *Slate* 25 (Jan. 2007).

Tamarov, Vladislav. *Afghanistan: A Russian Soldier's Story.* Trans. Naomi Marcus, Marianne Clarke Trangen, and Vladislav Tamarov. Berkeley: Ten Speed, 2001.

Yurechko, John. Rev. of *Afghanistan: A Russian Soldier's Story*, by Vladislav Tamorov. *Library Journal* 117.81 (1 May 1992): 101.

Native American Military Involvement in (De)Colonial Contexts

Lindsey Claire Smith

When considering "war literature" as a genre, springing to mind might be images of young male soldiers hunkering down in trenches in dangerous and desultory faraway locations, where foreign enemies create chaos for those who may never again see home. This imagining of war is complicated by the experiences of Native Americans who, while having participated in high numbers in conflicts between the United States and its enemies, have at times been classified as enemies of the United States, colonized within their own homelands. To bridge this divide between Native Americans' readiness to serve and the colonization of their homelands in the United States, one must understand an essential concept: sovereignty.[1]

The US government formally recognizes indigenous sovereignty in its government-to-government relationship with Native American tribes. David Wilkins explains that the "extension of federal recognition by the United States to a tribal nation is the formal diplomatic acknowledgment by the federal government of a tribe's legal status as a sovereign" (17). Though this act of recognition has been problematic for several reasons, the legal basis for tribal sovereignty, as well as the great diversity among hundreds of tribal nations, makes Native Americans distinct politically, historically, and culturally.

Since sovereignty is a key consideration for the unique cultures of Native Americans, its persistence throughout the history of interactions both among tribes and between tribes and the United States cannot be overstated. These interactions most often involve negotiations over land and natural resources.[2] The correlation between tribal sovereignty and land has also factored strongly into the context of war in early America, as "colonial interests" in the Americas involved military control over Native American land bases. Native Americans' history of wartime service, which includes both warrior traditions that predate colonial encounters and military service within colonial America and beyond, encompasses diverse experiences of war. Tribal communities have warred with other tribes; have aligned with one foreign nation over another, fighting alongside it against other tribal nations; and have allied in resistance to colonialism altogether. Native Americans' encounters with foreign sovereigns have been dynamic, varied, and shifting, making a simplistic narrative of Native American subjugation and disappearance inaccurate.[3]

Though heightened in the twentieth century, the high rate of Native American enlistment in the US military has a long history. In addition to military alliances that were forged via treaties on behalf of tribal communities as a whole, scouting (in which individuals contracted their military service to the United States) was regularized in the aftermath of the Civil War. According to Thomas Britten, in 1866, the US military expanded this program of Indian recruitment with the Army Reorganization Act, which increased the number of both Indian cavalry regiments and scouts, who were recruited from several tribes (10). Britten explains that these options for military service were attractive to indigenous recruits because they afforded a higher standard of living than was possible on reservations (11). At the same time, the United States found value in native recruits' proficiency in language interpretation and tracking skills.

Despite some opposition within the military by those who questioned Native Americans' loyalty and discipline, the United States continued to seek Native Americans to serve in its armed forces. By the 1880s, there was strong support for the incorporation of Indian enlistees as regular soldiers rather than as scouts hired on a contractual basis.[4] By 1891, an organized effort was underway to recruit indigenous soldiers from western reservations (19). Ironically, these soldiers, though perceived to be in need of assimilation into white American society, would be segregated from their white counterparts until the turn of the century.

Although they were included in the draft beginning with World War I, Native Americans increasingly enlisted voluntarily in the US military, citing opportunities for employment, for learning new skills, and for demonstrating racial pride and patriotism as key reasons for their volunteerism.[5] This strong record of military service also contributed to later American Indian civil rights movements in the 1960s and 1970s, as those returning from war were empowered by new skills and confident in their abilities to manage their own affairs.[6] Native American enlistees continued to demonstrate pride in their diverse national heritages while also proving their sense of patriotism and readiness for success in large-scale war efforts.

In Native American war literature, sovereignty factors into the motivations, decisions, and challenges that characters face as they navigate military engagement in a US colonial context. Works by three indigenous authors—William Apess (Pequot), John Joseph Mathews (Osage), and Leslie Marmon Silko (Laguna Pueblo)—depict this context in distinct eras. While Apess's writings unfold against the backdrop of early conflicts between tribes and the United States, Mathews's fiction focuses on personal and community crises associated with modernism in the first decades of the twentieth century. Silko's experimental work portrays a rejuvenation of land and culture in the contemporary period of self-determination. These literary and historical episodes emphasize negotiation between roles within and without a US military framework.

Apess's critique of US colonialism and of discrimination against people of color, found in his most well-known works, *A Son of the Forest* (1829) and *Eulogy on King Philip* (1836), occurs in both his account of his own participation in war and his telling of the events of colonial history from a Native American perspective. Apess's asserted attempts to undermine the hypocrisy of non-Indian attitudes and policies toward his people may be construed as a challenge to President Andrew Jackson's eagerness to eliminate the "Indian problem."[7] However, Apess served in the US military and became a Methodist.

His movement among many communities was a key to his rhetorical effectiveness, as he continually employed the rhetoric of patriotism and Christian conversion in order to denounce the damaging effects of colonialism.

His autobiography, *A Son of the Forest,* displays Apess's struggles at the hands of abuse and poverty during his childhood in Connecticut, during his time as an indentured servant, and during his service as a soldier, struggles that lead the way to his conversion to Methodism and his occupation as a minister. According to Barry O'Connell, Apess's attraction to Methodism, which at that time in New England was open to racial mixing, led his masters to forbid him from attending Methodist meetings; thus, Apess ran away to New York City (xiii–iv). Fearing that he was about to be found, Apess hurriedly enlisted as a drummer boy in the War of 1812, and he was later reluctantly made a regular infantryman (xiv). After two years, he deserted. After his service, Apess spent time with First Nations peoples in Canada, during which he "gained some affirmative sense of himself as an Indian" (xiv). However, soon after, he was addicted to alcohol and lacked stable employment, which in his narrative heightens the sense of his urgent need for a change in his life. This change occurred with his baptism in 1818.

Apess's growing confidence in his Indian identity pairs in the narrative with his conversion to a Western religious identity, which may seem paradoxical. In fact, the tale is in the form of a conversion narrative, a testimony of spiritual rebirth that was typical of early American literature by non-Indians. However, the intersection of Apess's religious fervor with his rejection of the subjugation of Native Americans—an important subversive layer to the genre—is clear throughout his autobiography, especially in his description of his military service.[8] He writes that recruitment in the US Army was accompanied by free-flowing alcohol and ready compensation. In his words, "I was pleased with the idea of being a soldier, took some more liquor and some money, had a cockade fastened on my hat, and was off in high spirits for my uniform" (25).

Apess acknowledges that his service is illegal; according to O'Connell, his enlistment records incorrectly listed him as seventeen rather than fifteen. Beyond the enticements of money and rum, he can see little reason to continue to serve: "I could not think why I should risk my life and limbs in fighting for the white man, who had cheated my forefathers out of their land" (25). He refers to soldiers' drinking habits as "wickedness" (25) and feels aggrieved by their negative influence on him, prompting him to discuss with them their disregard for all things sacred, a precursor of his later call to ministry. He states: "I could not bear to hear sacred things spoken of lightly, or the sacred name of God blasphemed; and I often spoke to the soldiers about it, and in general they listened attentively to what I had to say" (25).

During his service, the scale of death he witnesses disturbs Apess, and he even deserts at one point, being recaptured and taunted by fellow soldiers. At the war's end, however, he expresses pride in the success of the United States, which he calls "our country" (30). He immediately obtains his release, remarking on the short shrift he receives in going without the pay and land allotment he was due in return for his service: "I could never think that the government acted right toward the '*Natives*,' not merely in refusing to pay us but in claiming our services in cases of perilous emergency, and still deny us the right of citizenship; and as long as our nation is debarred the privilege of voting for civil officers, I shall believe that the government has no claim on our services" (31).

These comments indicate Apess's disentanglement of his service and religious dedication from the hypocrisies of the US treatment of Native Americans. In his rendering, Christianity, though a Western religion, is the means by which he rejects the "wickedness" of his fellow soldiers and is galvanized to speak out against injustice.

This action of rejecting colonialism from within the colonizer's religious and patriotic rhetoric is even more strongly present in Apess's notable oratorical piece *Eulogy on King Philip*. In this address, Apess furthers his innovative rhetoric in his reframing of a historical event,

King Philip's War, that encapsulates the importance of sovereignty to native peoples. Thus, Apess's eulogy provides an alternative rendering of the implications of this conflict between the Wampanoag and English colonists beginning in 1675.[9] Though the war continued in smaller skirmishes for many years, it waned with Philip's execution and decapitation.

Apess's evaluation of King Philip's legacy begins to point toward an agenda for social justice, especially reform of Christian missions, beyond the author's own individual story of conversion. The text begins with a comparison of Philip to infamous warriors of the Western tradition (Philip II, Alexander the Great, and George Washington) and sets out Apess's purpose: to "vindicate the character of him who yet lives in their hearts and, if possible, melt the prejudice that exists in the hearts of those who are in possession of his soul" (105). Apess also challenges stereotypes of Indians as "savages," pointing out the hypocrisy of those whose hands are likewise stained with blood. He writes:

> If we have common sense and ability to allow the difference between the civilized and the uncivilized, we cannot but see that one mode of warfare is just as the other; for while one is sanctioned by authority of the enlightened and cultivated men, the other is an agreement according to the pure laws of nature, growing out of natural consequences. (106)

Further, Apess emphasizes the kindness at first contact of Wampanoag people with Pilgrims, whom Apess describes as interlopers who immediately took land and continually disregarded treaty agreements. The results of these violations lead Apess to proclaim that December 22, the date he marks as the landing of the Pilgrims at Plymouth, should be a day of mourning, as should July 4.

The bulk of Apess's text rests on exposing the injustice of the treatment of King Philip by his adversaries. Apess carefully deconstructs the crimes with which Philip was charged, highlighting the condescension implied in the colonists' complaints that Philip refused to turn over his weapons, would not submit to summons to English courts, harbored vagabond Indians, and did not behave with civility (120–21).

Apess venerates the leader for the way he responds to these charges: Philip (also known as Metacomet) points out his position of authority in native New England and refuses to make agreements with anyone who is merely a subject of King Charles of England and not a king of similar standing as he. Apess writes, "And never could a prince answer with more dignity in regard to his official authority than he did—disdaining the idea of placing himself upon a par of the minor subjects of a king; letting them know, at the same time, that he felt his independence more than they thought he did" (122). Thus, in his words and actions, Philip, in Apess's assessment, proclaims his personal and political sovereignty.[10]

Having recovered Philip's legacy, Apess critiques his contemporary church leaders and US officials. He obviously takes exception to Jackson's plans to remove Native Americans from their homelands to the West: "[W]e hope we shall not hear it said from ministers and church members that we are so good no other people can live with us, as you know it is a common thing for them to say Indians cannot live among Christian people; no, even the president of the United States tells the Indians they cannot live among civilized people, and we want your lands and must have them and will have them" (134–35). As Lisa Brooks reveals, the shape of Apess's narrative reverses the positions of accuser and accused, as the Pilgrims are the ones now placed on trial (206). Apess's writings then, offering his experience of the War of 1812 and analysis of King Philip's War, provide a counter to usual narratives of indigenous submission and erasure and emphasize the integral role that concerns about sovereignty amid US colonization play in early Native American war literature.

Native American war literature after 1900 places indigenous service within native spaces that are confronted with change in a rapidly industrializing United States. Mathews's *Sundown* (1934)[11] provides a glimpse of the impact of allotment, and the ensuing political and cultural crisis, on the Osage Nation of Oklahoma. As Robert Warrior explains, the difficulties faced by Chal Windzer, the protagonist, mirror the larger political crisis facing the tribe. Chal's service in the military, which takes him away from his community and back again, in turn links him with the troubled homecoming experiences of other characters in modern American war literature.

The political strife that dominated the Osage Nation at the turn of the century involved a power struggle among groups with different agendas, the impact of which touches Chal's own family in the novel.[12] Warrior explains that the US government, undermining the authority of the Osage National Council, was able to achieve the votes necessary from the Osages as a whole to impose allotment in 1904. As part of the agreement, only the surface of the land would be allotted; all mineral rights would be held by original allottees communally. The result was simultaneous loss of land from Osage into non-Osage hands, tremendous wealth for some Osages, and heightened criminality in the Osage Nation as a result of oil revenues from 1916 to 1924.

Mathews's novel begins with an emphasis on land and Chal's connection to it, foregrounding the character's early comfort in his Osage orientation that will be difficult to maintain later in life. Chal's father imbues the child with a sense of standing in the community with his name, so chosen because "He shall be a challenge to the disinheritors of his people" (4). However, as Warrior points out, the tensions between Osages at the trader's store on the day of Chal's birth signify the larger divisions in the tribe, casting an important tone that pervades the novel (46). In fact, the early optimism surrounding Chal's birth and his father's reaction quickly dissipates when John Windzer's trust in the US government is compromised.

A supporter of progressive reform who lobbies within the community for cooperation with the United States, Windzer is disillusioned when the US government undermines Osage council authority, causing him to lose face. Chal observes his father's reaction to this event, and it looms in Chal's own movement inside and outside of Osage contexts.

He witnesses the successes and failures of Osage and white associates along the way, making acquaintances that continually remain only surface relationships. As a youngster, he is sent to private school, where he is not only uncomfortable around white boys but also separate from his Osage counterparts at the government school. He goes to college at the University of Oklahoma (OU) along with two Osage friends but keeps them at a distance so as not to compromise his standing among his white fraternity brothers or with the girl who is the object of his unrequited affection.

Throughout these encounters, Chal is continually at pains to express himself, and even resents his dark skin when he looks in the mirror. While home from university, clearly having no sense of occupational purpose, Chal responds to a suggestion from his mother to join the military now that World War I is imminent. The idea excites him: "A peculiar kind of pride came up in Chal and he felt quite important suddenly. . . . As he stood there, his heart swelled as he visualized the papers with his name among the other heroes of the air" (166). Chal's service displays the sense of pride espoused by Native American enlistees, but also it highlights the complicated dynamics of power relations in which colonial legacies remain.

Soon after his decision to join the military, Chal encounters Mr. Granville, an OU geology professor, fellow pilot, and English eccentric; in an avuncular role, he is intriguing to Chal. Granville and Chal, both armchair naturalists, compare the nuisance of invasive species in their homelands. Granville remarks on a vine that is benign in its American location but threatening in England: "the seed must have come over in a boat from America, and got started in Devonshire. It hadn't got enemies there, and throve like anything. It's really a menace" (190). Chal responds, "Kinda like the English sparrow here" (190). The subtext of first context between "Old" and "New" World is hard to miss in this exchange, where each character expresses a certain fascination with and perhaps even exoticization of his counterpart.

Like Chal's mother, Granville then suggests air service as an appropriate endeavor for Chal, a suggestion he receives warmly.

While in training, Chal feels as if he may be integrating into the white men's world smoothly for the first time. When he sees Sullivan, a cadet who has failed his exams, cry, Chal is surprised and even a little emboldened at this first glimpse of the vulnerability of a white man. When he achieves admission to flying school, he ruminates on the symbol for his squadron:

It was a large sign which carried the picture of a United States bombing plane flying above Potsdam. Potsdam was represented by a round tower, above which could be seen a bomb falling from the ship. As the adjutant called the names, Chal looked intently at this symbol. Instinctively, he felt that it was the usual boast of the white man, then he believed that the white man boasted in everything he did. But he didn't want to think that any more, and he believed that it was pretty clever. But later, he found that he had to keep telling himself that the slogan of his squadron was really clever. (196)

Likewise, Chal enjoys, but sees through, the attention of young women enthusiasts, remarking, "Under the guise of patriotism they called at the field for the cadets" (202). One woman in particular, Lou, is taken with Chal, and when she mistakes him for Spanish, Chal does not correct her. He begins a liaison with her, which surges his confidence and makes him feel less estranged from those around him. After their first date, he feels proud and important: "The University seemed to be far in his past and he felt a little contempt for the people of the University, and certainly for the people in Kihekah. He thought of himself as being separated by a great abyss from Sun-on-His-Wings and Running Elk, and from the village with the people moving among the lodges" (208).

While flying, this feeling is extended. Mathews writes, "He had a feeling of superiority, and he kept thinking of the millions of people below him as white men" (218). This feeling of belonging has its limits, however, as, in a keen likeness to Apess's description of his experience with militiamen, Chal instructs his fellow serviceman. One night, the alcohol flowing, Chal begins to speak about the Osage hills as the other pilots listen intently. The next morning, Lieutenant Stubbs remarks on the discussion: "Gave me an idea about that part of the country I never had before. I thought Indian reservations were full of cactus and rattlesnakes" (234). Though this exchange is subtle, it is worthy of mention, as Chal makes this native space visible to other soldiers.

Chal abruptly leaves the service upon receiving news that his father has been killed, and this event, which takes him home, begins Chal's descent into protracted alcoholism. Chal's mother reminds him that John Windzer, who was killed by white bandits, falsely put his faith in the government; this reminder, along with his inheritance from his father's estate, possibly contributes to Chal's decision not to continue his military service. The swagger that he felt while flying is largely absent from his sensibility as he reengages with his landscape and culture, noting dispiritedly how much has changed as a result of the corruption rampant in local oil and finance activities and to the overwhelming influence of alcohol. He notes the irreverence of younger Osage people but at the same time wishes he were one of them: "He wanted to be identified with that vague something which everybody else seemed to have, and which he believed to be civilization" (281). His strong bond with the animals of his home landscape is now disconnected, emblematized in his running over several nighthawks with his car.

Ultimately, Chal's turning point comes at the end of the novel, in an intimate moment with his mother, who nudges him into recollection of his capacity to be a hero. Noticing that the emblematic English sparrows that he discussed with Granville are becoming more and more of a nuisance, Chal has a memory of a time when he shot the sparrows with arrows. His mother comments, "Many white men are flying across the sea now" (310). Chal is put off by her suggestion, explaining that the service is not enough of a challenge; however, he realizes that his mother sees "into a warrior's heart" (311). At this moment he makes a decision: "I'm going to Harvard law school, and take law—I'm gonna be a great orator" (311). At this moment, which ends the novel, Chal and his mother are united in a sense of calm and hope, and a mother robin, unbothered by the sparrow, is the final image.

As is evident in Apess's early writings, military service inspires pride and newfound confidence for Chal at the same time that it exposes the hypocrisy of the United States, which, in turn, accents his alienation. In *Sundown*, this reality cannot be divorced from the circumstances of Osage allotment that put the colonial role of the United States into stark relief. Ultimately, then, Chal's military service demonstrates both his personal struggles and the larger historical circumstances in which he finds himself; thus, sovereignty is practically threatened on a personal and community basis. Like any soldier returning home, Chal struggles to adjust, but in his case, the additional layer of experience as a Native American adds further dimension to the text as a piece of war literature.

Silko's *Ceremony* (1977) is one of the most well-known and often-studied texts of Native American literature because of its innovative account of a Native American soldier's homecoming.[13] The text's notoriety stems in part from Silko's groundbreaking protagonist; her character moves beyond the types of characters from earlier texts who struggle unsuccessfully to walk between Indian and white worlds. Instead, Tayo's story of healing from his war wounds is facilitated by his careful reconnection with his home community and rejection of destructive colonial influences.

An obvious correlation between Silko's novel and war literature as a whole is the trope of the wounded soldier. Tayo, the Laguna Pueblo protagonist with an absent white father, is suffering from post-traumatic stress disorder and is plagued by nausea and flashbacks. Even the earth itself seems ill, as a drought has the pueblo in its grip. Tayo's dire situation is spurred by his immense grief at the loss of his cousin and fellow serviceman, Rocky, a football star whom Tayo believes he should have been able to protect while overseas fighting in the Philippines.[14]

Tayo not only feels guilty about the loss of Rocky but also feels responsible for the drought, as he prayed against the rain while trying to carry Rocky's stretcher during a downpour in the jungle. Like Apess does in his evaluation of King Philip, Silko challenges readers to consider the humanity of the adversaries within this conflict, indicating her own rejection of war and highlighting indigenous sovereignty as an enduring concern. Still in the midst of trauma and confusion once home from the war, Tayo's nausea remains; he is in urgent need of healing.

Tayo's progression from sickness to healing forms the central journey of the novel. The character receives medical treatment from several different doctors: white doctors at a hospital in Los Angeles, a traditional Laguna Pueblo doctor named Ku'oosh on the reservation, and an unconventional Navajo-Mexican healer named Betonie in Gallup. Mirroring Chal's observation of the corruption of his Osage community, Tayo is in contact with family members and fellow veterans in his pueblo, and each plays either a hopeful or a regressive role in his recovery. Throughout these encounters, Tayo's sickness is physically apparent in his nausea, which is especially pronounced when he abuses alcohol. In a scene that is reminiscent of Chal's loathing of the dark skin he sees in the mirror, Tayo conceptualizes himself while he is in treatment at the hospital in Los Angeles as "white smoke" that "faded into the white world of their bed sheets and walls" (13). His invisibility is indicative of his illness but also connected to his feeling of alienation from the Eurocentric world in which he finds himself.

Once he is back at the pueblo, Tayo's grandmother suggests that Tayo consult a medicine man. Ku'oosh, the local medicine man, attempts to heal Tayo in the best way he knows how, in the way that is as close to tradition as possible. As he leaves him, however, Ku'oosh indicates that he is concerned that Tayo may not recover since the other returning veterans who have received the Scalp Ceremony have not done so. Akin to the substance abuse that Apess and Mathews document, Tayo and his fellow soldiers abuse alcohol continuously through the text,[15] delighting in their abusive and authoritative attitudes toward women. Their bravado is on display in the bars on the towns bordering the reservation, where, as Silko writes, "Liquor was medicine for the anger that made them hurt, for the pain of the loss, medicine for tight bellies and choked-up throats" (37). When it seems that Tayo is consigned to a familiar alcoholic fate, at Ku'oosh's suggestion, he visits Betonie, an unconventional healer, who has a reputation for being crazy. Betonie's philosophy is that it is a mistake to perform ceremonies in the same way because the circumstances of colonization demand new remedies. He explains:

> after the white people came, elements in this world began to shift; and it became necessary to create new ceremonies. I have made changes in the rituals. The people mistrust this greatly, but only this growth keeps the ceremonies strong. . . . Things which don't shift and grow are dead things. They are things the witchery people want. . . . That's what the witchery is counting on: that we will cling to the ceremonies the way they were, and then their power will triumph, and the people will be no more. (117)

Betonie conducts the Scalp Ceremony for Tayo, but at its conclusion, he explains to Tayo, "the ceremony isn't finished yet. . . . Remember these stars . . . I've seen them and I've seen the spotted cattle; I've seen a mountain and I've seen a women" (141). These instructions, subtle markers of the Laguna sunwise cycle, are the pattern for the rest of Tayo's encounters along his journey to healing. Importantly, simple preservation of Laguna tradition as it has always been is not sufficient; Tayo must bring his contemporary experiences to bear on his fulfillment of the cycle and teach Ku'oosh and others what he learns along the way.

In both the content and the narrative structure of *Ceremony,* Silko signifies Tayo's journey from a fragmented psychological and spiritual state to a place of healing. The young soldier's memories of his life before his enlistment are interspersed with traumatic flashbacks to war, creating an interrupted, circular presentation of time. Ancestral Laguna

Pueblo stories are inserted into this unconventional narrative, and, emphasizing the primacy of oral tradition, the novel begins with a story of Thought-Woman, the Laguna *creatrix*, narrated in first person. In the beginning of the text, it is not obvious exactly how these accounts of nonhuman creatures and spirit beings are connected to Tayo's life. However, a closer look reveals that, thematically, the Laguna stories are instructive both for Tayo and for readers, as the accounts describe stories of drought and danger as well as of creation and rebirth. More specifically, the references to stars, spotted cattle, mountain, and woman are contained within both the traditional stories and in Betonie's instructions to Tayo. Further, though the nausea that has interfered with Tayo's well-being has been a signal of his illness, careful readers will observe that the opening Laguna story of the text references the belly: "And in the belly of this story / the rituals and the ceremony / are still growing" (2). In this way, Silko makes clear that Tayo's journey is necessary, is perhaps not entirely new, and is informed by the process of storytelling itself. Grandma echoes this sentiment at the novel's conclusion: "It seems like I already heard these stories before . . . only thing is, the names sound different" (242).

By centering Laguna oral traditions and the value it places on a regenerative connection to indigenous land and culture, Silko's novel demonstrates the author's assertion of sovereignty as a necessary and valuable reality for Native Americans. In the context of military service, Silko's characters are similar to those of Apess's and Mathews's in their realization of complicated colonial dynamics that remain pervasive even in one's contemporary context. Further, Silko's text, like Apess's, can be understood as a sort of conversion narrative. However, while Apess converts to Christianity, Tayo's conversion is toward a Laguna spiritual awareness and away from the Christian one. This contrast reveals the different historical eras in which Silko and Apess were writings, with the late twentieth century typified by a resurgence of indigenous self-determination.

Apess, Mathews, and Silko all create unique contributions to Native American war literature, which, though marked by themes and motifs of war literature generally, is pervaded by ready assertions of the importance of tribal sovereignty. The legal dynamics of tribal alliances and disputes that accompany war, the importance of community to war stories, and the unique personal costs and traumas of service all comprise the rich occurrences that are Native American military experiences. These realities demonstrate that patriotism and self-determination need not be mutually exclusive.

Notes

1. Sovereignty is arguably what sets Native Americans apart from other US "Others," those individuals who are usually lumped together as "minorities" in a multicultural American framework. Though Native Americans share some common ground with these groups, they conceive of themselves as members of distinct tribal nations with the authority to govern themselves.

2. When faced with an increasing number of newcomers (including Spanish, French, and English) to their lands as early as the fifteenth century, Native Americans entered into treaties with foreign powers. These treaties documented agreements regarding land, but also they recorded military alliances between individual tribes and competing foreign powers that were eager to protect their colonial interests.

3. Likewise, a simple characterization of tribal sovereignty is not an agreed-upon goal among academic and tribal scholars. The vexed situation of asserting sovereignty within the parameters of state formations mirrors the apparent contradiction that indigenous service in a military that has at times been dispatched against tribal peoples in their own homelands may entail. As Taiaiake Alfred explains, "In the United States, the common law provides for recognition of the inherent sovereignty of indigenous peoples, but simultaneously allows for its limitation by the United States Congress. The logic of colonization is clearly evident in the creation of 'domestic dependent nation' status, which supposedly accommodates the historical fact of coexisting sovereignties, but does no more than slightly limit the hypocrisy. It accepts the premise of indigenous rights while at the same time legalizing their unjust limitation and potential extinguishment by the state.'" (464–65). This tepid endorsement of indigenous rights within the existing colonial framework perhaps in part explains the disconnect between the integral role that Native Americans have played in US military campaigns and the lamentable conditions that have at times accompanied that service, with voting rights and US citizenship, for example, being unevenly extended to tribal members well into the twentieth century.

4. Among military officers concerned for the welfare of Native Americans there was a sense that standing as regular soldiers rather than in limited scouting roles would afford individuals relief from the poverty of native communities in the aftermath of their relocation onto reservations by the United States. Moreover, fully engaged in the larger project of assimilating Native Americans into Anglo-American society, advocates for making Native Americans soldiers believed that this change would encourage individualization of tribal peoples, weakening their communal orientation and shifting their loyalties away from their tribal nations and toward the United States (Britten 14).

5. This involvement also paved the way for US citizenship for tribal servicemen, a benefit previously denied to them.

6. These veterans were met, however, with the regressive policy of termination, which sought to disperse reservation communities, urbanize Indians, and reduce natives' perceived dependence on the government. Ultimately, the policy was abolished in 1961.This resistance effort laid important groundwork for future movements for self-determination, also galvanized by President Lyndon B. Johnson's War on Poverty, a policy that concentrated on investment in indigenous communities (Edmonds 402–403).

7. Apess's autobiographical and oratorical writings were completed during the Jacksonian era (approximately 1820–50). In the context of Native American studies, Jackson is notorious because of his zeal to open Native American lands to white settlement and his architecture of forced removal of indigenous peoples from their ancestral homelands.

8. According to Joanna Brooks, Apess modifies and transforms the genre in his text and "reveal[s] how religious formulas such as conversion, revival, and resurrection answered the alienating and mortifying effects of slavery, colonialism, and racial oppression" (9).

9. This short but bloody war was a key turning point in America's development from a collection of independent English colonies into its own nation. As Jill Lepore observes, King Philip's War occurred because of growing tensions between increasing numbers of non-Indian entrants into Indian lands and the cultural upheaval and confusion that this caused. In her words, "New England's Algonquians waged war against the English settlers in response to incursions on their cultural, political, and economic autonomy and, at least in part, they fought to maintain their Indianness. Meanwhile, New England colonists waged war to gain Indian lands, to erase Indians from the landscape, and to free themselves of doubts about their own Englishness" (7–8). Lepore also notes that contradictions concerning sovereignty were at the heart of the conflict between King Philip and colonists, with colonists understanding Wampanoag people to be simultaneously sovereigns who were to engage in diplomacy and subjects of the English king (164).

10. Lepore and Brooks contextualize Apess's address within a time when, one hundred years after King Philip's death, the war began to be idealized by non-Indians as a marker of the submission of indigenous New Englanders to colonization.

According to Brooks, Apess resists this erasure of native New England and invites Americans into a native space rather acceding that space to them: Through a persuasive rhetorical strategy, Apess calls on his listeners and readers to participate in communal deliberation, to recognize the shared space and shared history of New England (and America), and to see themselves as agents within it. He challenged Anglo-Americans in particular to acknowledge the legacy of destruction "planted" by their Puritan forebears and to confront the continuing violence that had "grown up" from it (199–200).

11. The events in *Sundown* reflect some of Mathews's own experiences growing up in the Indian Territory (later Oklahoma) of his birth. Like Chal, Mathews studied at the University of Oklahoma and served in the US military, becoming a flight instructor during World War I; unlike Chal, however, he completed his degree and later studied at Oxford University. In Oklahoma in his later years, Mathews founded the Osage Tribal Museum and became involved in the leadership of the tribe, advocating for the tribe's legal and policy interests. Therefore, as with Apess's work, Mathews's novel is firmly connected to concerns regarding continued colonial intrusion on tribal sovereignty on both individual and community levels. For Chal as for Apess, these concerns are present in the context of military service.

12. Warrior lines out these three groups as the "full-blood" group, which was bound strongly to clans and ceremonies; the "mixed-blood" group, which had incorporated non-Indians through intermarriage and was growing in influence; and the group of white newcomers to Osage lands who were attracted to successful rangelands and oil fields (15–16). The struggle among these groups centered on the federal government's intentions to allot Osage lands that had been held communally by the tribe. The full-bloods were against allotment while the mixed-bloods were for it, seeing it as an important step for "progress."

13. Though the protagonist of the text is a veteran of World War II, the novel's publication in 1977 occurred on the heels of both the end of the Vietnam War, which was accompanied by a large antiwar movement, and greater attention to the Native American civil rights movement, which had featured several public protests in the 1960s organized by the American Indian movement. These historical and cultural realities made the novel's appearance timely. Thus, though it is literally about a World War II veteran, the novel can also be understood as a war story about another war, with the problematic reception of returning Vietnam veterans a real-life complement to the narrative. Overall, the text reflects a contemporary era of self-determination in Indian country that was ushered in by victories in courts and through Congress as well as by social movements and activism.

14. Silko's choice of the Philippines as the site of Tayo's military engagement is significant; like the Native American lands, the Philippines were subject to colonization. During his service and in his memory of it once back in the United States, Tayo has a hard time sorting out these shifting standings on the world stage, and he notes that the Japanese soldiers do not look that different from people in his home community.

15. According to Alison Bernstein, alcohol use among some Native American World War II veterans was typical because, during their service, they had been away from the reservation's restrictions on liquor, and consuming alcohol freely was a sign of equal standing with whites (136).

Works Cited

Alfred, Taiaiake. "Sovereignty." *A Companion to American Indian History*. Eds. Philip J. Deloria and Neal Salisbury. Malden, MA: Blackwell, 2002. 460–74.

Apess, William. *A Son of the Forest and Other Writings*. Ed. Barry O'Connell. Amherst: U of Massachusetts P, 1997.

_____. "Eulogy on King Philip." *A Son of the Forest and Other Writings*. Ed. Barry O'Connell. Amherst: U of Massachusetts P, 1997. 105–138.

Bernstein, Alison. *American Indians and World War II: Toward a New Era in Indian Affairs*. Norman: U of Oklahoma P, 1991.

Britten, Thomas. *American Indians in World War I: At Home and at War*. Albuquerque: U of New Mexico P, 1997.

Brooks, Joanna. *American Lazarus*. New York: Oxford UP, 2007.

Brooks, Lisa. *The Common Pot: The Recovery of Native Space in the Northeast*. Minneapolis: U of Minnesota P, 2008.

Edmonds, R. David. "Native Americans and the United States, Canada, and Mexico." *A Companion to American Indian History*. Eds. Philip Deloria and Neal Salisbury. Malden, MA: Blackwell, 2002. 397–421.

Lepore, Jill. *The Name of War: The Origins of King Philip's War and the Origins of American Identity*. New York: Knopf, 1998.

O'Connell, Barry. Introduction. *A Son of the Forest and Other Writings*. By William Apess. Amherst: U of Massachusetts P, 1992. ix–xxii.

Mathews, John Joseph. *Sundown*. Norman: U of Oklahoma P, 1988.

Mathews, Virginia. Introduction. *Sundown*. By John Joseph Mathews. Norman: U of Oklahoma P, 1988.

Silko, Leslie Marmon. *Ceremony*. New York: Penguin, 1977.

Warrior, Robert. *Tribal Secrets: Recovering American Indian Intellectual Traditions*. Minneapolis: U of Minnesota P, 1995.

Wilkins, David. *American Indian Politics and the American Political System*. Lanham, MD: Rowman, 2007.

"Stubborn Experiments": Bearing Witness in Holocaust Literature

Dorian Stuber

> Convinced that this period in history would be judged one day, I knew that
> I must bear witness. (Elie Wiesel)

> Nothing remains of him: he bears witness through these words of mine.
> (Primo Levi)

Two of the most important figures in the field of Holocaust literature
are Elie Wiesel and Primo Levi. Wiesel was fifteen years old and a devout student of Jewish religious texts when he and his family were deported to Auschwitz in 1944 from their home in what is now Romania.
He has written dozens of books on the Holocaust—both fiction and
nonfiction—most famously the memoir *Un di velt hot geshvign* (1956,
in Yiddish; *La nuit*, 1958, in French; *Night*, 1960). He is a prominent
voice on Holocaust matters, especially in the United States, where he
served as a consultant on the design of the United States Holocaust
Memorial Museum in Washington, DC. In 1986, he was awarded the
Nobel Peace Prize.

Levi was twenty-four years old in December 1943 when he was ar-
rested in the mountains near his home in northern Italy, where he had
joined the partisans fighting Benito Mussolini's fascist regime. He was
deported to Auschwitz in February 1944. Like most other members
of Italy's small Jewish population, Levi was secular. He had recently
completed studies in chemistry, which turned out to be instrumental to
his survival in Auschwitz, because he was able to do menial work in a
laboratory rather than physically exhausting work outdoors. After his
return to Italy, he balanced his career as a chemist with his avocation
as a writer. At his death in 1987, he had published numerous books
on the Holocaust—like Wiesel, both fiction and nonfiction. The most

famous of these is the memoir *Se questo è un uomo* (1947; *Survival in Auschwitz: The Nazi Assault on Humanity*, 1961).

Wiesel's and Levi's biographies suggest differences between the two survivors—differences that are even more apparent in their writing. Wiesel and Levi represent two opposed tendencies in Holocaust literature. Each has a different idea about the purpose of that literature. As a result, they stand in for a larger debate about the very idea of Holocaust literature. Should it even exist? If so, who gets to write it, and what should that writing be about?

Levi's and Wiesel's differing responses to these questions are encapsulated in this chapter's epigraphs. Note that each uses the term *bearing witness*. In the preface to *Night*, Wiesel describes his motivation for writing: "Convinced that this period in history would be judged one day, I knew that I must bear witness" (viii). He uses the term to refer to himself—he will bear witness, by describing his own experiences before, during, and after his internment in Auschwitz. The substance of that witnessing, he makes clear earlier in the preface, is the genocidal harm done to the Jewish people by the Nazis.

In a memoir called *La tregua* (1963; *The Reawakening*, 1965), Levi uses the term more peculiarly. He writes, of a prisoner named Hurbinek, "Nothing remains of him: he bears witness through these words of mine" (26). Unlike Wiesel, Levi uses the term to refer to someone else—but someone who bears witness through Levi himself. For Wiesel, bearing witness and writing are synonyms; for Levi, they are differentiated. Levi posits a gap between experience (the one who bears witness) and language (the one who writes or otherwise represents that experience), where Wiesel sees none. This gap can be understood more clearly when considering the context of Levi's statement. The person he is talking about, Hurbinek, is a fellow prisoner, a three-year-old child, whom Levi meets in the ruins of Auschwitz in the weeks after liberation. Levi calls him "a nobody, a child of death, a child of Auschwitz" (25). The child exerts a powerful hold on everyone in the camp—he "emanate[s]," Levi says, a "distressing power" (25)—

not least because he cannot speak. He knows only one word, which nobody understands, even though most of the languages of Europe are represented in the camp. This lack of expressive power (rather than, say, the fact that a three-year-old has been interned) is what so distresses Levi and the other prisoners, especially because Hurbinek so clearly wants to speak. Levi finds this expressive desire in his eyes, which "flashed terribly alive, full of demand, assertion, of the will to break loose, to shatter the tomb of his dumbness" (25). Hurbinek's demand remains unfulfilled; he dies in March 1945, "free but not redeemed" (26); his intransigence in the face of all the wrongs done to him kept alive only in Levi's testimony.

What does it mean for Hurbinek to "bear witness" through Levi's words? Is not the reverse true: does not Levi bear witness to Hurbinek? What is the aim of witnessing, especially if redemption is not, as Levi suggests, possible? It is not quite true that "nothing remains" of Hurbinek: Levi's powerful language has kept something of him alive. However, Hurbinek is indeed gone. Levi's modesty, even ambivalence, about his substantial powers of evocation should be taken seriously. Levi calls Hurbinek's struggles to speak "stubborn experiments" (26); this description applies to Holocaust literature more generally. Wiesel makes a similar claim about his own book: "while I had many things to say, I did not have the words to say them" (ix). However, Wiesel ultimately overcomes this difficulty—he "invent[s] a new language"— thanks to the authenticity of his experience. As a survivor, he believes he can speak, however painfully, of what happened to him. Levi too is a survivor, but he believes even that dubious distinction grants him neither direct access to the truth nor a privileged authenticity.

Levi and Wiesel agree that the events of the Holocaust, like language itself for Hurbinek, resist articulation and comprehension. They disagree, however, about who is able to resist that resistance, how they do so, and what it means when they do. Holocaust literature is arguably a struggle over how directly language represents experience. The overwhelming nature of the events of the Holocaust can be ethically and adequately represented only if the mediated nature of their representation (the fact that they can only be imperfectly captured and understood) is not only acknowledged but also embraced. Holocaust literature shows that there is no transparent or straightforward representation, especially of overwhelming events; instead, representation is invariably hesitant, indirect, and partial—yet no less valid for that.

Holocaust literature, then, is about the difficult relation of representation to experience. The same is true of the term *Holocaust*. Today *Holocaust* is used to refer to the genocidal acts perpetrated by the Nazis against various groups (primarily, but not only, Jews) that they deemed undesirable. The historian Deborah E. Lipstadt usefully distinguishes between groups targeted by the Nazis for complete annihilation (based on race and ideology) and those victimized more haphazardly (based on politics and circumstances). The former group included Jews, Gypsies, Germans citizens with developmental disabilities and mental illnesses, and various ethnic groups in the Soviet Union. The latter included homosexuals and political prisoners, dissidents within Germany, and resistance fighters in occupied territories (8). Some date the Holocaust acts to 1933, when the Nazis assumed power; some to 1935, when the Nuremberg Laws that defined who was Jewish were enacted; and some to 1941, when the first extermination camps were constructed in preparation for the adoption the following year of the "Final Solution," the chilling name given to the decision to exterminate the Jewish people.[1]

The Jews were not the only victims of the Holocaust, but they were its primary ones. Six million of them were murdered. This is the fact that people struggled to name. One of the first texts to enact that struggle is the "Report on the Sanitary and Medical Organization of the Monowitz Concentration Camp for Jews (Auschwitz—Upper Silesia)." It was written at the end of the war in Europe, in the spring of 1945, at the request of Soviet authorities seeking a description of life in the concentration camps they had recently liberated. Its authors are Levi and Leonardo de Benedetti, a fellow Italian Jewish survivor.

(It is Levi's published work.) Interestingly, the term *Holocaust* appears nowhere in the report. Instead, from its opening lines, its authors speak both boldly and coyly about the Nazi genocide:

> The photographic evidence, and the already numerous accounts provided by the ex-internees of the various concentration camps created by the Germans for the annihilation of the European Jews, mean that there is perhaps no longer anyone still unaware of the nature of those places of extermination and of the iniquities that were committed there. (31)

The passage is at once forthright—it acknowledges "the annihilation of the European Jews"—and reticent—it refuses further details on "the nature of those places of extermination and of the iniquities . . . committed there." The authors believe that any reader will know what they are talking about. Even so, soon after the end of the war, "numerous accounts" of the experience of the camp already existed. Nonetheless, readers might not know what the authors mean; the passage does not name some things directly (consider the oblique nouns "those places" and "the iniquities"). Notably, the lengthy concluding noun phrase—"the iniquities that were committed there"—has not yet been condensed into the term *Holocaust*.

Modern discussion of the Holocaust has moved from the hesitancies and omissions of De Benedetti and Levi's claim to the ready use of Holocaust to describe the murder of six million Jews.[2] That readiness is not, however, universal. *Holocaust* did not come into everyday use until the late 1950s, and even in the twenty-first century, its use is debated. After all, the word was not invented to refer to "the annihilation of the European Jews"; it had been a part of the English language for centuries, meaning "burnt offering." Although the word came to mean any destruction by fire, its earliest uses refer to the deaths by burning of Christian martyrs. For this reason, some object to using the word to describe an event whose victims were primarily Jewish. It is not only unfortunate, even grotesque, to refer to those killed in the crematorium with a term meaning "burnt offering," but also it is problematic, even unethical, to use the specifically Christian notion of a redemptive suffering (most canonically expressed in the typology of Jesus, but also in the stories of saints and martyrs) to refer to the nonredemptive suffering of Jews. For that reason, some scholars, such as the philosopher Giorgio Agamben, repudiate the term *Holocaust* in favor of the term *Shoah* (Hebrew for "catastrophe"), finding it a more neutral, less redemptive, and, thus, more appropriate way of describing the Nazi genocide (28–31). Others, such as the historian Dominick LaCapra, suggest that the term *Holocaust* should continue to be used, but should be used critically (that is, conscious of its vexed history). LaCapra finds *Holocaust* more appropriate than other, seemingly neutral choices like "annihilation" or "final solution," which risk replicating and thus validating the language of the Nazis. Still others, like the survivor Elie Cohen, think that "final solution" is in fact the most appropriate term precisely because the perpetrators used it and, as such, is best able to be a reminder of what the Nazis did (qtd. in Clendinnen 9).

Holocaust is the most widely used term to refer to the Jewish suffering at the hands of the Nazis. These disagreements are worth studying, however, because they suggest that names matter. The usual way of thinking about the relation of names to objects is that names are merely attached to the objects that precede them; in this sense, names are neutral descriptions. The example of the Holocaust shows that relationship needs to be rethought. The literary critic James E. Young, one of the most influential scholars of Holocaust literature, argues there is no such thing as a term that comes from nowhere (84–85). (It would be like asking someone to draw an imaginary animal and expecting them to be able to do so without referencing actual ones.) All words are metaphorical, in the sense that they "cross over" (the etymology of the word *metaphor*) and refer to something different than, or preexistent to, them. To say that *Holocaust* echoes earlier events is not to deny the uniqueness of the Holocaust. One can still argue that the Holocaust is unique even as one recognizes that nothing can be understood in isolation.

Young's claim is relevant to the discussion of Holocaust literature because it implies that one's experience of the world is tied to one's ability to describe it. Experience is not the same as language, but it must pass through language. Thus, our experience is "mediated" by the language, the metaphors, used to describe experience. In literature, language is deliberately used figuratively (to compare things that are dissimilar and to distort meanings of words to use them in unaccustomed forms and settings). However, that kind of language play is used in everyday life. What literature does explicitly, all language does implicitly. Literature, then, is not a unique way of using language, but rather an exemplary way of using language, a way that tells the truth about how all language, and, in turn, all experience, works.

In this way, debates about the best term to describe the Nazi genocide are, in disguised form, debates about the proper relation of language to experience. That relation is the central issue of Holocaust literature. People first began to understand Holocaust literature as a coherent entity when they began studying it in the 1960s and, especially, the 1970s. Since then, courses on Holocaust literature have become widespread at colleges and universities across the United States. The first critical studies of Holocaust literature were published in the 1970s; the most notable of these is Lawrence Langer's *The Holocaust and the Literary Imagination* (1975). In the ensuing forty years, hundreds of academic books on the topic have been produced. Two of the most useful ones published relatively recently are Inga Clendinnen's *Reading the Holocaust* (1999) and Ruth Franklin's *A Thousand Darknesses: Lies and Truth in Holocaust Fiction* (2011).

Even these excellent studies, however, spend little time defining Holocaust literature. To do so, one must distinguish between literature *of* the Holocaust and literature *about* the Holocaust. Seemingly, both categories are valid components of Holocaust literature, but they are seldom accepted together as such. Literature of the Holocaust includes various sorts of nonfictional testimony that come from the period: diaries, letters, eyewitness accounts, official documents, and even court statements from postwar trials. Literature about the Holocaust includes texts that acknowledge or foreground their own fictional status—that is, novels, poems, and plays that depict life before, during, and immediately after the Holocaust. The distinction, then, seems to be between nonfictional and fictional texts. This distinction is surprisingly difficult to uphold, however, because it ultimately comes back to the question of whether there is direct, unmediated experience of the Holocaust. Literature of the Holocaust seems to say yes; literature about the Holocaust, no. The most iconic kind of Holocaust literature—testimonial memoirs—proves this distinction to be untenable, however.

By looking at these categories at face value, one gains a brief overview of some of the key names in the field. Literature of the Holocaust includes texts by both writers who experienced its events firsthand and those who did not. Any account of this category would include the bitter, pointed, sometimes shocking stories written by the Pole Tadeusz Borowski in the late 1940s and collected in English in a volume called *This Way for the Gas, Ladies and Gentlemen*. Borowski was a communist, Polish nationalist, and political dissident who was interned first in Mauthausen (in Austria) and later in Auschwitz, where, as a non-Jew, he lived in somewhat better conditions. His most famous story tells a fictionalized version of his own experience working on "the ramp," separating newly arrived cattle-car loads of Jews from their loved ones and belongings. This genre also includes the ironic novels of the Hungarian Imre Kertész, one of which, *Sorstalanság* (1975, *Fatelessness*, 2004), features a naïve adolescent protagonist who finds in Auschwitz his university. (Kertész's works, too, are based loosely on his own experiences.)

An account of literature about the Holocaust includes the British novelist Martin Amis, whose novel *Time's Arrow* (1991) tells the story of a Nazi doctor (based on the real-life Joseph Mengele, who performed hideous medical experiments on prisoners at Auschwitz). In Amis's book, events happen in the opposite way they do in real life—people arrive from death and move inevitably to the effacement of birth. Amis's protagonist arrives at Auschwitz to make and assemble Jews and to unite them with their families. The irony of this narrative structure is at once grotesque and poignant. This category might also include the Serbian Canadian writer David Albahari's novel *Götz and Meyer* (2004), which tells the story of a teacher in Belgrade who becomes obsessed with reconstructing the deaths of almost everyone in his extended family, deaths that he traces to the two SS officers named in the book's title. The character's obsession extends to a disastrous attempt to reenact those historical events with his students.

Texts about the Holocaust, written by people who lived long after the Holocaust and had no personal stake in it, are sometimes criticized twice over: neither "true," because fictional, nor authentic, because written by a nonsurvivor. Some refuse the legitimacy of the very category of literature about the Holocaust. The most outspoken proponent of this view is Wiesel. In an essay called "The Holocaust as Literary Inspiration," he says:

> And now a few words about the literature of the Holocaust or about literary inspiration. There is no such thing, not with Auschwitz in the equation. "The Holocaust as Literary Inspiration" is a contradiction in terms. . . . A novel about Treblinka is either not a novel or not about Treblinka. A novel about Majdanek is about blasphemy. *Is* blasphemy. (7)

These strong words come attached to a claim about authenticity and ownership of Holocaust experience, in which only survivors know the truth: "He or she who did not live through the event will never know it. And he or she who did live through the event will never reveal it. Not entirely. Not really. Between our memory and its reflection there stands a wall that cannot be pierced. . . . We speak in code, we survivors, and this code cannot be broken, cannot be deciphered, not by you no matter how much you try" ("Literary" 7). Wiesel here creates an insider/outsider dichotomy that is accurate, but overstated, even harmful in its aims. (It is even more severe than his claim in the preface to *Night* that he could "invent a new language" to describe his experience.) For what Wiesel champions is a direct access to the events of the past that is given only to a handful and that renders the attempts of others to understand that past hopeless at best and reprehensible at worst.

Wiesel's statement raises two further points. The first is that the Holocaust is simply too vast, too overwhelming, in short, too extreme for anyone to make any sense of it. This first statement is an understandable response, but also one that lends itself to the same dangerous rhetoric of sublimity used by the Nazis on the rare occasions they spoke of their actions. If one suggests that the experience of the Holocaust exceeds people's abilities to make sense of it, people may find themselves unwittingly conceding to this point of view.

The second point is that the very senselessness of the Holocaust is central to its meaning. However, any representation of the Holocaust is bound to make some kind of sense. (Otherwise, how would one know either what it means or that it is a representation?) The result is that any representation of an experience or event, however faithful it seeks to be to it, necessarily distorts the experience, especially if it is senseless to begin with. The objection is that Holocaust literature takes an experience that was fundamentally irrational, even incoherent, and makes it rational or coherent. It takes chaos and orders it, even as it seeks to depict chaos. Even if the work is unconventionally structured, it must be structured in some way, which could be understood as a falsification of the actual events. An example of this dilemma is Levi's story about Hurbinek. In memorializing him, Levi risks misrepresenting him: not only because nobody really knows what Hurbinek wanted to say or how he understood the world but also because the very idea of representing him as something to be understood risks losing sight of one of the essential things about the Holocaust: its destruction of sense or meaning. Thus, readers of Holocaust literature are in a difficult position, not wanting to condemn victims to further silencing but knowing that moving beyond silence is to risk falsifying the horror at the heart of the experience.

There are good reasons to be hesitant about embracing Holocaust literature. Contrary to Wiesel's opinion, it seems these reasons apply to any kind of Holocaust literature, not just its imaginative representation. In other words, literature of the Holocaust does not escape the difficulties of representation. In the essay referred to, Wiesel claims that "our generation invented a new literature, that of testimony" ("Literary" 9). However, his description of where that "new literature" came from and what it is supposed to do is confusing: "We have all been witnesses and we all feel we have to bear testimony for the future. And that became an obsession, the single, most powerful obsession that permeated all the lives, all the dreams, all the work of those people. One minute before they died they thought that was what they had to do" (9). Note that Wiesel switches from "we" to "they" and "those people." Initially, he seems to be talking about everyone; eventually, he is talking about a particular group of people. That confusion, however, does not stop him from concluding that testimony tells the truth of what happened in a way that fiction cannot. Literature, it would seem, has been put in its place.

Wiesel's definition of literature is a narrow one, however. The idea that testimony or literature of the Holocaust offers direct access to the past is naïve. In fact, many of the documents of this genre, most notably the diaries written in secret across Nazi-occupied Europe (be it in the Warsaw ghetto or an attic in Amsterdam), were written with a decided audience in mind, in the hope that the texts would survive to reach the world even if their authors did not. The most famous example of such a text is Anne Frank's *Het achterhuis* (1947; *Diary of a Young Girl*, 1952), which Frank revised heavily with a view to posterity in the weeks before her discovery and deportation. Later, Frank's father edited the diary still further for its initial postwar publication, eliminating, for example, many of Frank's references to her sexuality. In this way, Frank's text, although a valuable document that vividly expresses the constriction placed upon Jews in Nazi-occupied Europe, is as shaped as any novel. Frank wishes to present herself and her family in a particular light (and her father wished to present her in a still different one). She chose to write about certain events and not others, and she made further choices about how to describe those events. That does not mean her diary is fictional; rather, like all diaries, it relies on fictional techniques.

Ironically, Wiesel's claims unwittingly call into question the most representative and compelling form of Holocaust literature, indeed, the one for which he is best known: the memoir. Memoirs are accounts that are autobiographical and factual but that use the conventions and structuring devices of fictional literature more overtly than a letter, memo, or even a diary might. In other words, memoirs bridge the supposed gap between literature about and literature of the Holocaust. There are many remarkable examples of this genre. One of the most famous is Wiesel's *Night*, which has sometimes been classified as a novel and sometimes as an autobiography. (Tellingly, it was crafted over a period of several years and was first published in a Yiddish version many hundreds of pages longer than the French version on which all subsequent editions are based.)

Another memoir is Levi's *Survival in Auschwitz*, which the author characterizes as "fragmentary," governed by two competing tendencies: the desire to "furnish documentation for a quiet study of certain aspects of the human mind" and the need to satisfy "an immediate and violent impulse, to the point of competing with . . . other elementary needs" (9). A third memoir is Art Spiegelman's graphic novel *Maus* (1986, 1991), which wittily tells in visual and written form the story of Spiegelman's own encounter with his parents' experience during the Holocaust. Spiegelman uses the term "comix" to describe his graphic novel because it mixes word and image. The conceit of Spiegelman's two volumes is that the Jews are drawn as mice and the Nazis as cats. This decision makes one think about what it means to classify people (are Jews the natural prey of Nazis, as mice are to cats?); also, one cannot help but think about Spiegelman's choices in light of the Nazis' own mania for classification. Those uncertainties about classification extend to the very genre of the work. What kind of a text is this? The decision to represent people as animals is a clear example of the way fiction is used to tell a true story.

The different tones of these memoirs—Wiesel's mysticism, Levi's liberal humanism, and Spiegelman's caustic irony—do not fail to hide a key similarity: Each questions the distinction between fact and fiction. Memoirs promise the authenticity of experience that Wiesel values but use the narrative, poetic, and rhetorical techniques of the fiction he disdains. In so doing, they show experience to be in need of mediation and structuring. They value the idea of a direct statement of truth but ultimately cannot believe in it. This tendency at work in two examples of testimonial texts, Ruth Kluger's memoir *Weiter leben: Eine Jugen* (1992; *Still Alive: A Holocaust Girlhood Remembered*, 2001) and Vasily Grossman's essay/war reportage "The Hell of Treblinka" (1944). These stylistically and conceptually compelling pieces are less studied than they should be. They were written fifty years apart by people who had little in common other than their Jewishness (which neither finds especially important). Despite the differences in chronology, the texts share what seems to be the central aspect of Holocaust literature: the idea that experience, even of these extreme events, is mediated.

Kluger was deported at age eleven from her childhood home in Vienna, first to the camp at Theresienstadt, Czechoslovakia, and later from Theresienstadt to Auschwitz. Her memoir begins with a scene in the family home in late 1930s Vienna, in which young Ruth eavesdrops on her elders:

Their secret was death, not sex. That's what the grown-ups were talking about, sitting up late around the table. I had pretended that I couldn't fall asleep in my bed and begged them to let me sleep on the sofa in the living room . . . . Of course, I didn't intend to fall asleep. I wanted to get in on the forbidden news, the horror stories, fascinating though incomplete as they always were—or perhaps even more fascinating for their opaqueness, that whiff of fantasy they had about them, though one knew they were true. Some were about strangers, others were about relatives, all were about

Jews. . . . The voices at the table, women's voices, indistinct and barely audible because I kept my head under the blanket, were saying *KZ*. Just the two letters, short for *Konzentrationslager* [concentration camp]. (15)

In this passage, a familiar childhood desire is horribly distorted. Most children, Kluger suggests, want to know the secrets of sex—that is, of life; she wanted to know the secrets of death. Most children want to stay up past their bedtime to pretend they are older than they are; Kluger wanted to stay up so that she could live to be older. Unlike the proverbial ostrich that buries its head in the sand, young Ruth hides herself in order to learn, not hide from, the truth. Nonetheless, she struggles to understand that truth. This anecdote can be read as an allegory for the reading public's own relation to Holocaust literature. Readers struggle to make sense of what is "indistinct and barely audible" or comprehensible and are drawn to "the forbidden news, the horror stories." Readers of Holocaust literature struggle to remind themselves that these fantastical tales are true. Indeed, "the whiff of fantasy" Kluger smells speaks to readers' fascination with these tales, despite (or maybe because) they are incomplete, incomprehensible, and destructive. Most important, like Kluger, readers are on the outside looking in. In Kluger's case, even the survivor has a mediated relation to the events that eventually engulf her.

In August 1944, several years after Kluger's eavesdropping, Grossman, who had volunteered for the Soviet army after Hitler's invasion of the Soviet Union in 1941 and who had been assigned the duty of war correspondent, arrived at the abandoned concentration camp at Treblinka. "The Hell of Treblinka" is one of the earliest depictions of the Holocaust, predating even Levi and De Benedetti's report. Halfway through, having described the chaos new victims would have experienced on arrival—separated from loved ones and possessions, shaved and otherwise physically humiliated, herded along a path lined by high fences toward an imposing brick building—Grossman tries to explain what would have happened next:

The door of the concrete chamber slammed shut. [...] Can we find within us the strength to imagine what the people in these chambers felt, what they experienced during their last minutes of life? All we know is that they cannot speak now. . . . Covered by a last clammy mortal sweat, packed so tight that their bones cracked and their crushed rib cages were barely able to breathe, they stood pressed against one another; they stood as if they were a single human being. Someone, perhaps some wise old man, makes the effort to say, "Patience now—this is the end." Someone shouts out some terrible curse. [...] With a superhuman effort a mother tries to make a little more space for her child: may her child's dying breaths be eased, however infinitesimally, by a last act of maternal care. [...] Heads spin. Throats choke. What are the pictures now passing before people's glassy dying eyes? Pictures of childhood? Of the happy days of peace? Of the last terrible journey?[...] Consciousness dims. It is the moment of the last agony. . . . No, what happened in that chamber cannot be imagined. The dead bodies stand there, gradually turning cold. (144–45, ellipses in original unless bracketed)

This passage exemplifies the ambivalence that seems to govern Holocaust literature. Even more than Kluger's voyeuristic attraction to the horrors of the Holocaust (which, after all, she would later experience directly), Grossman's text oscillates between a need to explain the central experience of the gas chamber and an opposing certainty that he cannot. The logic of the passage is one of attraction and repulsion. Note the proliferation of question marks—some are overtly genuine, as when he wonders about the objects of the victims' last thoughts. Even those that seem rhetorical, however, prove, on closer inspection, to be genuine as well. It is ultimately unclear whether one can "find the strength to imagine what the people in these chambers felt." On one hand, the passage is vivid, aiming to make readers feel present—seen most clearly in the use of physical and corporeal details: the clammy sweat, cracked bones, and crushed rib cages.

The passage even imagines how people might have acted and thought in those final moments. In its clearest attempt at seeking certainty (and thus intimacy with the dead), the passage switches from past to present tense. However, its attempts at immediacy fail. Even if the passage returns to present in the final sentence (suggesting an ongoing duration—these bodies are in some way still standing there), it has been forced to return to the past in its key statement: "No, what happened in that chamber cannot be imagined." Readers are left with only a statement of absence: "All we know is that they cannot speak now." The passage has tried to do that for them, but ultimately refuses the possibility.

One might argue that Kluger (at least before her deportation) and Grossman are witnesses to the event rather than direct participants in it. Also, one might posit that those who were there and returned—"real" participants—must have a different relation to expression. Surely they can straightforwardly avow aspects these other writers cannot. There are no such people, however. The proof that one was gassed at Auschwitz is that one was gassed at Auschwitz—a fact to which no one can testify, because, as Levi says, "no one ever returned to describe his own death" (*Drowned* 84). Thus, in some way, even survivors are not the true victims; even they have a mediated relation to the events of the Holocaust. Once again, Levi offers the most articulate and canonical expression of this difficulty:

I must repeat: we, the survivors, are not the true witnesses. . . . We survivors are not only an exiguous [small in number] but also an anomalous minority: we are those who by their prevarications or abilities or good luck did not touch bottom. Those who did so, those who saw the Gorgon, have not returned to tell about it or have returned mute, but they are the "Muslims,"[3] the submerged, the complete witnesses, the ones whose deposition would have a general significance. They are the rule, we are the exception. (*Drowned* 83–84)

Levi adds that survivors "speak in their stead, by proxy" (as he did in the case of Hurbinek). Elsewhere, he refines the metaphor, suggesting that to be a proxy is to be of a different order than the person in whose stead one claims to speak. For the Musselmans, which Levi typically refers to as "the drowned," do not have anything to speak about, no tale to tell: "All the musselmans who finished in the gas chambers have the same story, or more exactly, have no story: they followed the slope down to the bottom, like streams that run down to the sea" (*Survival* 90). The metaphor is disturbing. Is Levi implying that there is something natural, thus unavoidable, perhaps even right about their death? After all, streams cannot help but run to the sea. It seems, rather, that once they, for whatever reason, become "musselmans," only then is death inevitable. Levi is quick to suggest that although he opposes "the drowned" to "the saved" he does not understand those terms morally: "The 'saved' of the Lager [German for "camp"] were not the best, those predestined to do good, the bearers of a message . . . the worse survived, that is, the fittest; the best all died" (*Drowned* 82).

Levi tells readers that the dream of an authentic, direct, and immediate representation of the Holocaust is just that—a dream. As the examples of Kluger, Grossman, and Levi show, there is indeed something unknowable, something that always recedes from one's grasp, at the heart of any attempt to understand the Holocaust. Moreover, the impossibility of understanding should not be the central aspect of readers' understanding. One can recognize that something might not be possible (doing full justice to those who were murdered; seeking to be entirely commensurate and faithful to the sheer complexity and chaos of an overwhelming event) without saying that it is impossible. Readers can reflect on what it means to express what seems to be inexpressible and can accept that to bear witness is always to stand in the stead of a vanished other. Holocaust literature shows that language is necessarily metaphorical, necessarily about using one set of terms to talk about another (for which it is never exactly adequate) without abandoning language altogether. In short, readers can continue to value Holocaust literature as a set of stubborn experiments.

Notes

1. The Nazis were not the first to use concentration camps as places of internment. (That dubious distinction goes to the British during the Second Boer War in South Africa, 1899–1902.) As soon as they took power in 1933, however, they began to construct a system of work camps, primarily for political dissidents. These were forced labor camps in which, for example, prisoners quarried stone or performed other sorts of physically demanding labor. Although terrifying and destructive of human dignity and life, they were not extermination camps of the sort developed, beginning in 1941, specifically for mass murder. The first extermination camps were in German-occupied Poland and included Treblinka, Chelmno, and Sobibor. Later came camps that combined work and extermination parts, most notably Auschwitz. Auschwitz comprised three separate camps spread out over a wide area: Auschwitz I was a work camp and administration center; Auschwitz II, called Birkenau, or sometimes Auschwitz-Birkenau, was an extermination camp (almost no one who arrived here survived more than a few days); Auschwitz III, called Buna or Monowitz-Buna, was a work camp run by the chemical company IG Farben. The aim of the latter camp was to use forced labor to develop industrial products, such as synthetic rubber. Levi and Wiesel were both interned at Buna.

2. People have not always thought of the Holocaust as a Jewish tragedy. Indeed, Levi and De Benedetti's phrase "the annihilation of the European Jews" is one of the only references to Jews in the report, a fact that might seem surprising but that must be understood in light of the circumstances of the report's production, since the Soviet authorities who commissioned it were anxious to generalize, even universalize, the Nazis' victims, so as to present themselves as both the victims and heroic conquerors of fascism. (Millions of Russians died at the hands of the Germans.)

3. "Muslim" is a translation of the German *Musselman*, a term used in the camps to describe those who, through misfortune and constitution, quickly perished; elsewhere, Levi calls them "non-men who march and labour in silence" (*Survival* 90). No one knows from exactly where this term came. Some speculate that it refers to the spirit of submission that characterizes devout Muslims, especially fatalism in regards to death; in that case, the term would be ironic, since submission here was not to God but to harsh physical reality. The term refers to a caricature rather than a lived reality of Islam.

Works Cited

Agamben, Giorgio. *Remnants of Auschwitz: The Witness and the Archive.* Trans. Daniel Heller-Roazen. New York: Zone, 2002.

Albahari, David. *Götz and Meyer.* Trans. Ellen Elias-Bursac. 2004. New York: Harvest, 2006.

Amis, Martin. *Time's Arrow: Or the Nature of the Offense.* 1991. New York: Vintage, 1992.

Borowski, Tadeusz. *This Way for the Gas, Ladies and Gentlemen.* Trans. Barbara Vedder. 1967. New York: Penguin, 1976.

Clendinnen, Inga. *Reading the Holocaust.* 1999. Cambridge: Canto, 2007.

Frank, Anne. *The Diary of a Young Girl.* Eds. Otto H. Frank and Mirjam Pressler. Trans. Susan Massotty. 1995. New York: Anchor, 1996.

Franklin, Ruth. *A Thousand Darknesses: Lies and Truth in Holocaust Fiction.* New York: Oxford UP, 2011.

Grossman, Vasily. "The Hell of Treblinka." *The Road: Stories, Journalism, and Essays.* Ed. Robert Chandler. Trans. Robert Chandler, Elizabeth Chandler, and Olga Mukovnikova. New York: New York Review Books, 2010. 116–62.

Kertész, Imre. *Fatelessness.* Trans. Tim Wilkinson. New York: Vintage, 2004.

Kluger, Ruth. *Still Alive: A Holocaust Girlhood Remembered.* New York: Feminist P at CUNY, 2003.

LaCapra, Dominick. "Representing the Holocaust: Reflections on the Historians' Debate." *Probing the Limits of Representation: Nazism and the "Final Solution."* Ed. Saul Friedlander. Cambridge, MA: Harvard UP, 1992. 108–27.

Langer, Lawrence L. *The Holocaust and the Literary Imagination.* New Haven, CT: Yale UP, 1975.

Levi, Primo. *The Drowned and the Saved.* Trans. Raymond Rosenthal. 1988. New York: Vintage, 1989.

_____. *The Reawakening.* Trans. Stuart Woolf. New York: Touchstone, 1995.

_____. *Survival in Auschwitz: The Nazi Assault on Humanity.* Trans. Stuart Woolf. 1987. New York: Touchstone, 1996.

Levi, Primo, and Leonardo de Benedetti. *Auschwitz Report.* Trans. Judith Woolf. Ed. Robert S. C. Gordon. London: Verso, 2006.

Lipstadt, Deborah E. *The Eichmann Trial.* New York: Nextbook, 2011.

Spiegelman, Art. *Maus: A Survivor's Tale.* 2 vols. New York: Pantheon, 1986, 1991.

Wiesel, Elie. "The Holocaust as Literary Inspiration." *Dimensions of the Holocaust.* Evanston, IL: Northwestern UP, 1978.

_____. *Night.* Trans. Marion Wiesel. New York: Hill, 2006.

Young, James E. *Writing and Rewriting the Holocaust: Narrative and the Consequences of Interpretation.* Bloomington: Indiana UP, 1988.

RESOURCES

Additional Works on War

Graphic Novels
Palestine by Joe Sacco, 2002
In the Shadow of No Towers by Art Spiegelman, 2004
The Photographer by Emmanuel Guibert, Didier Lèfevre, and Frédéric Lemercier, 2009

Long Fiction
Le Morte d'Arthur by Sir Thomas Malory, 1485
The Spy: A Tale of the Neutral Ground by James Fenimore Cooper, 1821
First Love and Last Love by James Grant, 1863
One Man's Initiation—1917 by John Dos Passos, 1920
All Quiet on the Western Front by Erich Maria Remarque, 1929
For Whom the Bell Tolls by Ernest Hemingway, 1940
The Stalin Front: A Novel of World War II by Gert Ledig, 1955
The Hunters by James Salter, 1956
Fires on the Plain by Shohei Ooka, 1957
Catch-22 by Joseph Heller, 1961
The Things They Carried: A Work of Fiction by Tim O'Brien, 1990
The Sorrow of War: A Novel of North Vietnam by Bao Ninh, 1991
Ocean of Words: Army Stories by Ha Jin, 1996
S.: A Novel about the Balkans by Slavenka Drakulic, 1999
Absolute Friends by John Le Carré, 2003
The Reluctant Fundamentalist by Mohsin Hamid, 2008

Nonfiction
The Persian Expedition by Xenophon, c. 394–71 BCE
The Battle for Gaul by Julius Caesar, 52–51 BCE
The Art of War by Niccolò Machiavelli, 1521
Hospital Sketches by Louisa May Alcott, 1863
The River War: An Historical Account of the Reconquest of the Soudan by Winston Churchill, 1899
The Great Boer War by Sir Arthur Conan Doyle, 1900
Good-bye to All That: An Autobiography by Robert Graves, 1929
Hiroshima by John Hersey, 1946
The Face of War by Martha Gelhorn, 1988
The Book of War edited by John Keegan, 1999

The Eyes of Orion: Five Tank Lieutenants in the Persian Gulf War by Alex Vernon, 1999

In Times of War: An Anthology of War and Peace in Children's Literature edited by Carol Fox, Annemie Leysen, and Irene Koenders, 2000

The Mammoth Book of Sea Battles: Great Stories and Classic Tales from the Golden Age of Naval Warfare by Mike Ashley, 2001

Regarding the Pain of Others by Susan Sontag, 2003

Women on War: An International Anthology of Writings from Antiquity to the Present edited by Daniela Gioseffi, 2003

Veterans of War, Veterans of Peace by Maxine Hong Kingston, 2006

The Forever War by Dexter Filkins, 2008

Poetry

The Song of Roland, eleventh century

Dien Cai Dau by Yusef Komunyakaa, 1988

War Stories and Poems by Rudyard Kipling, 1990

No Rattling of Sabers: An Anthology of Israeli War Poetry edited by Esther Raizen, 1995

From Both Sides Now: The Poetry of the Vietnam War and Its Aftermath edited by Philip Mahony, 1998

Retrieving Bones: Stories and Poems of the Korean War edited by W. D. Ehrhart and Philip K. Jason, 1999

War Poems edited by John Hollander, 1999

American War Poetry: An Anthology edited by Lorrie Goldensohn, 2006

The Oxford Book of War Poetry edited by John Stallworthy, 2008

Short Fiction

War Stories and Poems by Rudyard Kipling, 1990

Retrieving Bones: Stories and Poems of the Korean War edited by W. D. Ehrhart and Philip K. Jason, 1999

The Vintage Book of War Fiction edited by Sebastian Faulks and Jörg Hensgen, 2002

Fighting the Future War: An Anthology of Science Fiction War Stories, 1914-1945 by Frederic Krome, 2011

Bibliography

Bates, Milton. *The Wars We Took to Vietnam: Cultural Conflicts and Storytelling.* Berkeley: U of California P, 1996.

Beidler, Philip. *The Good War's Greatest Hits.* Athens: U of Georgia P, 1998.

Bourke, Joanna. *An Intimate History of Killing: Face-to-Face Killing in Twentieth Century Warfare.* London: Granta, 1999.

Braudy, Leo. *From Chivalry to Terrorism: War and the Changing Nature of Masculinity.* New York: Knopf, 2003.

Bridges, Emma, Edith Hall, and P. J. Rhodes, eds. *Cultural Responses to the Persian Wars: Antiquity to the Third Millennium.* New York: Oxford UP, 2007.

Carlton, Charles. *Going to the Wars: The Experience of the British Civil Wars, 1638–1651.* New York: Routledge, 1992.

Chaliand, Gérard. *The Art of War in World History: From Antiquity to the Nuclear Age.* Berkeley: U of California P, 1994.

Cooper, Helen M., Adrienne Munich, and Susan Merrill Squier. *Arms and the Woman: War, Gender, and Literary Representation.* Chapel Hill: U of North Carolina P, 1989.

De Somogyi, Nick. *Shakespeare's Theatre of War.* Brookfield, VT: Ashgate, 1998.

Eberwein, Robert. *The War Film.* New Brunswick, NJ: Rutgers UP, 2005.

Eksteins, Modris. *Rites of Spring: The Great War and the Birth of the Modern Age.* New York: Mariner, 1989.

Fahs, Alice. *The Imagined Civil War: Popular Literature of the North and South, 1861–1865.* Chapel Hill: U of North Carolina P, 2001.

Forrest, Alan I. *Napoleon's Men: The Soldiers of the Revolution and Empire.* New York: Hambledon, 2002.

Fussell, Paul. *The Great War and Modern Memory.* New York: Oxford UP, 1975.

_____. *Wartime: Understanding and Behavior in the Second World War.* New York: Oxford UP, 1989.

Gill, Diana C. *How We Are Changed by War: A Study of Letters and Diaries from Colonial Conflicts to Operation Iraqi Freedom.* New York: Routledge, 2010.

Goldensohn, Lorrie. *Dismantling Glory: Twentieth-Century Soldier Poetry.* New York: Columbia UP, 2003.

Harari, Yuval Noah. *Renaissance Military Memoirs: War, History, and Identity, 1450–1600.* Rochester, NY: Boydell, 2004.

_____. *The Ultimate Experience: Battlefield Revelations and the Making of Modern War Culture, 1450–2000.* New York: Palgrave, 2008.

Haytock, Jennifer. *At Home, at War: Domesticity and World War I in American Literature.* Columbus: Ohio State UP, 2003.

Heberle, Mark, ed. *Thirty Years After: New Essays on Vietnam War Literature, Film, and Art.* Newcastle upon Tyne: Cambridge Scholars, 2009.

Hynes, Samuel. *The Soldiers' Tale: Bearing Witness to Modern War.* New York: Penguin, 1997.

Keegan, John. *The Face of Battle.* London: Cape, 1976.

Kendall, Tim. *Modern English War Poetry.* New York: Oxford UP, 2006.

Kotrüm, Hans-Henning, ed. *Transcultural Wars from the Middle Ages to the Twenty-First Century.* Berlin: Akademie, 2006.

Lande, Nathaniel. *Dispatches from the Front: A History of the American War Correspondent.* New York: Oxford UP, 1998.

Linder, Ann P. *Princes of the Trenches: Narrating the German Experience of the First World War.* Columbia, SC: Camden House, 1996.

Linderman, Gerald F. *Embattled Courage: The Experience of Combat in the American Civil War.* New York: Free, 1987.

Lynn, John A. *Battle: A History of Combat and Culture from Ancient Greece to Modern America.* Boulder, CO: Westview, 2003.

Lyon, Philippa. *Twentieth Century War Poetry: A Reader's Guide to Essential Criticism.* New York: Palgrave Macmillan, 2005.

MacKay, Marina. *Modernism and World War II.* New York: Cambridge UP, 2007.

MacKay, Marina, ed. *The Cambridge Companion to the Literature of World War II.* New York: Cambridge UP, 2009.

McLoughlin, Kate, ed. *The Cambridge Companion to War Writing.* New York: Cambridge UP, 2009.

McNeil, David. *The Grotesque Depiction of War and the Military in Eighteenth-Century English Fiction.* Newark: U of Delaware P, 1990.

Meredith, James H. *Understanding the Literature of World War I: A Student Casebook to Issues, Sources, and Historical Documents.* Westport, CT: Greenwood, 2004.

_____. *Understanding the Literature of World War II: A Student Casebook to Issues, Sources, and Historical Documents.* Westport, CT: Greenwood, 1999.

Norris, Margot. *Writing War in the Twentieth Century.* Charlottesville: U of Virginia P, 2000.

Norris, Stephen M. *A War of Images: Russian Popular Prints, Wartime Culture, and National Identity, 1812–1945.* Dekalb: Northern Illinois UP, 2006.

Paris, Michael. *Warrior Nation: Images of War in British Popular Culture, 1850–2000.* London: Reaktion, 2000.

Piette, Adam, and Mark Rawlinson, eds. *The Edinburgh Companion to Twentieth-Century British and American War Literature.* Edinburgh: Edinburgh UP, 2011.

Quinn, Patrick J., and Steven Trout, eds. *The Literature of the Great War Reconsidered: Beyond Modern Memory.* New York: Palgrave, 2001.

Sachsman, David B., S. Kittrell Rushing, and Ro Morris, eds. *Memory and Myth: The Civil War in Fiction and Film from* Uncle Tom's Cabin *to* Cold Mountain. West Lafayette, IN: Purdue UP, 2007.

Scarry, Elaine. *The Body in Pain: The Making and Unmaking of the World.* New York: Oxford UP, 1985.

Shaw, Philip. *Romantic Wars: Studies in Culture and Conflict, 1793–1822.* Burlington, VT: Ashgate, 2000.

Shepard, Ben. *War of Nerves: Soldiers and Psychiatrists in the Twentieth Century.* Cambridge, MA: Harvard UP, 2001.

Sherry, Vincent, ed. *The Cambridge Companion to the Literature of the First World War.* New York: Cambridge UP, 2005.

Stone, Albert E. *Literary Aftershocks: American Writers, Readers, and the Bomb.* New York: Twayne, 1994.

Suid, Lawrence H. *Guts and Glory: The Making of the American Military Image in Film.* Rev. and expanded ed. Lexington: UP of Kentucky, 2002.

Tritle, Lawrence. *From Melos to My Lai: War and Survival.* New York: Routledge, 2000.

Winn, James Anderson. *The Poetry of War.* New York: Cambridge UP, 2008.

About the Editor

Alex Vernon graduated from the US Military Academy at West Point in 1989 and served as a tank platoon leader in the Persian Gulf War of 1990–91. After earning a Ph.D. in 2001 from the University of North Carolina at Chapel Hill, he joined the faculty of Hendrix College, outside Little Rock, Arkansas, where he serves as an associate professor of English, the Humanities Area Chair, and the James and Emily Bost Odyssey Professor. He has written two war memoirs, *The Eyes of Orion: Five Tank Lieutenants in the Persian Gulf War* (1999) and *most succinctly bred* (2006), both of which are somewhat unusual. *The Eyes of Orion* is a five-author collaborative work and the winner of an Army Historical Foundation Distinguished Book Award; *most succinctly bred* is a war memoir with no war stories in it. Vernon is the author of two works of literary history and criticism—*Soldiers Once and Still: Ernest Hemingway, James Salter, and Tim O'Brien* (2004) and *Hemingway's Second War: Bearing Witness to the Spanish Civil War* (2011)—and a cultural study, *On Tarzan* (2008). He has also edited two scholarly collections: *Arms and the Self: War, the Military, and Autobiographical Writing* (2005) and, with Catherine Calloway, *Approaches to Teaching the Works of Tim O'Brien* (2010).

Contributors

Alex Vernon is associate professor of English, the Humanities Area Chair, and the James and Emily Bost Odyssey Professor at Hendrix College. He is the author of two war memoirs, *The Eyes of Orion: Five Tank Lieutenants in the Persian Gulf War* (1999) and *most succinctly bred* (2006); two works of literary history and criticism, *Soldiers Once and Still: Ernest Hemingway, James Salter, and Tim O'Brien* (2004) and *Hemingway's Second War: Bearning Witness to the Spanish Civil War* (2011); and a cultural study, *On Tarzan* (2008).

Will Hacker teaches courses in nineteenth-century British literature, romanticism, and literary theory at Hendrix College. He is interested in the intersection of literature, philosophy, and religion and the influence of the classics on British writing. His most recent project, "Fierce Miscreeds," studies the persistence of theodicy in writers from Godwin to Tennyson.

Mark A. Heberle, professor of English at the University of Hawai'i, is author of *A Trauma Artist: Tim O'Brien and the Fiction of Vietnam* (2001), editor of *Thirty Years After: New Essays on Vietnam War Literature, Film, and Art* (2009), and coeditor of *Infant Tongues: The Voice of the Child in Literature* (1994).

Doug Davis is associate professor of English at Gordon College in Barnesville, Georgia. He has published numerous essays on the narrative elements of American foreign policy and the Cold War's impact on science and literature. He has turned his attention to exploring the technological imagination of Cold War author Flannery O'Connor.

Ed Folsom is the editor of the *Walt Whitman Quarterly Review*, the codirector of the *Whitman Archive* (www.whitmanarchive.org), and the editor of the Whitman Series at the University of Iowa Press. The Carver Professor of English at the University of Iowa, he is the author or editor of numerous books and essays on Whitman and other American writers. He has completed a Guggenheim Fellowship, working on his biography of *Leaves of Grass*.

Philip Beidler is professor of English at the University of Alabama, where he has taught American literature since receiving his Ph.D. from the University of Virginia in 1974. His recent books are *American Wars, American Peace: Notes from a Son of the Empire* (2007) and *The Victory Album:Reflections on the Good Life after the Good War* (2010), a personal and social history of growing up in post–World War II America.

Tim Blackmore is professor of Media Studies at the University of Western Ontario, Canada. He teaches courses on war, media, and popular culture. His book *War X* (2005) lays out the connections between contemporary and future weapons. He writes about war, science fiction, graphic novels, film, and memory and is at work on a book about images and war.

Catherine Calloway, professor and director of graduate studies in English at Arkansas State University, has published numerous essays on Vietnam War literature and film. She is a regular contributor to *American Literary Scholarship, An Annual* and is the coeditor of *Approaches to Teaching the Works of Tim O'Brien* (2010).

Douglas A. Cunningham earned his Ph.D. in Film Studies from University of California, Berkeley, in 2009. He has published essays in *Screen, The Moving Image, Cineaction*, and *Critical Survey*. His edited essay collection, *The San Francisco of Alfred Hitchcock's Vertigo: Place, Pilgrimage, and Commemoration* (2012) was published by Scarecrow Press.

Pat C. Hoy II directs New York University's Expository Writing Program and has taught at the US Military Academy and Harvard. Author of numerous textbooks and essays, he was awarded the 2003 Cecil Woods Jr. Prize for Nonfiction from the Fellowship of Southern Writers. He has twice won NYU's Golden Dozen Award for excellence in teaching.

Tom McGuire is professor of English at the US Air Force Academy. An Irish Studies scholar and translator, he is also a poet and the poetry editor of *War, Literature, and the Arts*.

John Nelson is an academy professor in the Department of English and Philosophy at the US Military Academy, West Point, New York. He earned a doctorate in comparative literature from the University of Washington and has served on active duty in the US Army since 1983. He has deployed for Operations Urgent Fury (Grenada), Desert Storm (Saudi Arabia and Kuwait), Southern Watch (Kuwait), and Enduring Freedom (Afghanistan).

Robert C. Doyle is a professor of History at the Franciscan University of Steubenville. He served as an officer in the US Navy from 1967 to 1971, serving in South Vietnam in 1968 and 1970–71. In 1994, he published the first interdisciplinary study of the American captivity experience, *Voices from Captivity: Interpreting the American POW Narrative*, which was followed by *A Prisoner's Duty: Great Escapes in U.S. Military History* (1997) and *The Enemy in Our Hands* (1997).

Elisabeth Piedmont-Marton is an associate professor of English at Southwestern University, where she directs the writing center and teaches and writes about war and American literature and modern American poetry.

Lindsey Claire Smith is an assistant professor of English at Oklahoma State University, where she teaches English and American Studies courses in Native American and global indigenous literatures. She has published a monograph, *Indians, Environment, and Identity on the Borders of American Literature* (2008), and, with her colleague Paul Lai, an edited essay collection, *Alternative Contact: Indigeneity, Globalism, and American Studies* (2011). She is working on two additional book projects, one on Creek/Seminole filmmaker Sterlin Harjo and another on indigeneity and urban space.

Dorian Stuber is an assistant professor of English at Hendrix College, where he teaches twentieth-century and twenty-first-century British literature, literary theory, psychoanalysis, and film. He has published on D. H. Lawrence's *Women in Love* and Todd Haynes's film *Safe* and reviews academic books for *Choice*. His recent research examines the relationship between textual forms and life-forms; he is preparing a manuscript titled "Life Sentences: D. H. Lawrence's Living Language."

Index

Haldeman, Joe, 107
Hanoi Hilton, 231. *See also* captivity
    narratives; prisoners of war
HCUA. *See* House Committee on Un-
    American Activities
Heart of Darkness (Conrad), 9
Heinlein, Robert A., 62
"Hell of Treblinka, The" (Grossman),
    287. *See also* Treblinka
Hemingway, Ernest, 4
Henry V (*Henry V*), 40, 46
Henry V (Shakespeare), 37–51
    film versions of, 51
heroism, 163, 164, 167, 224, 237, 266
    Henry V and, 37
    Homer and, 19, 32
    illusion of, 187
    Virgil and, 25
Herr, Michael, 5
Hetherington, Tim, 154
Hiroshima (Hersey), 67
Hispanics, 90, 94, 269
Hitler, Adolf, 57. *See also* Nazis
Hoa Lo Prison. *See* Hanoi Hilton
Holocaust
    literature of, 275–91
    meaning of, 278, 279
    representations of, 284, 288
home front, depictions of, 77, 125, 203,
    205, 209, 267
Homer, 17–34
Horace, 22
Horror Trains, The (Pomykalski), 131
House Committee on Un-American
    Activities, 57, 58
Hundred Years' War, 44, 48
Hurbinek (*The Reawakening*), 276, 284
Hurt Locker, The (film), 8, 161
Hussein, Uday, 149
Hynes, Samuel, 160

IED. *See* improvised explosive device
*If I Die in a Combat Zone, Box Me Up
    and Ship Me Home* (O'Brien), 198,
    204–09
Iliad (Homer), 17–34, 181
    English translations of, 26, 28, 30
imperialism, 109, 122, 170, 184
improvised explosive device, 8
individuality, 116, 180
In Pharaoh's Army (Wolff), 162
International Security Assistance Force,
    145, 157
intertextuality, 5–13, 150, 210
invasion, 43, 51, 60
    Flannery O'Connor's use of, 62
    science fiction accounts of, 61
Invisible Man (Ellison), 58
Iraq
    invasion of Kuwait, 209
    soldiers of, 213
Iraq War
    civilians, 151
    depictions of, 8, 145, 149–53, 161
    women in, 137
ISAF. *See* International Security
    Assistance Force

Jackson, Andrew, 258, 262
Jacob's Room (Woolf), 162
*Jarhead: A Marine's Chronicle of
    the Gulf War and Other Battles*
    (Swofford), 11, 198, 209–14
Jarhead (film), 12
Jews, 276–87
journalism, 241–54
Junger, Sebastian, 154
jus ad bellum, 41
jus in bello, 41, 50
Just and Unjust Wars (Walzer), 41
just war theory, 41–52